Road Traffic Law

Road Traffic Law

Simon Cooper

MA LLB, Senior Lecturer, Salford Law School

and

Michael Orme

BA, Formerly Road Traffic Patrol Officer, Greater Manchester Police

OXFORD
UNIVERSITY PRESS

OXFORD
UNIVERSITY PRESS

Great Clarendon Street, Oxford OX2 6DP

Oxford University Press is a department of the University of Oxford.
It furthers the University's objective of excellence in research, scholarship,
and education by publishing worldwide in

Oxford New York

Auckland Cape Town Dar es Salaam Hong Kong Karachi
Kuala Lumpur Madrid Melbourne Mexico City Nairobi
New Delhi Shanghai Taipei Toronto

With offices in

Argentina Austria Brazil Chile Czech Republic France Greece
Guatemala Hungary Italy Japan Poland Portugal Singapore
South Korea Switzerland Thailand Turkey Ukraine Vietnam

Oxford is a registered trade mark of Oxford University Press
in the UK and in certain other countries

Published in the United States
by Oxford University Press Inc., New York

© Simon Cooper and Michael Orme 2006

British Library Cataloguing in Publication Data

Data available

Library of Congress Cataloging in Publication Data

Cooper, Simon, M.A., LL. B.
  Road traffic law / Simon Cooper and Michael Orme.
     p. cm.
  Includes index.
  ISBN-13: 978-0-19-929683-5 (alk. paper)
  1. Traffic regulations—Great Britain. 2. Traffic violations—Great
Britain. 3. Motor vehicles—Law and legislation—Great Britain. I.
Orme, Michael, B.A. II. Title.
  KD2617.C66 2006
  343.4109'46—dc22

                                                               2006028302

Typeset by Laserwords Private Limited, Chennai, India
Printed in Great Britain
on acid-free paper by
Ashford Colour Press Limited, Gosport, Hampshire

ISBN 0-19-929683-9   978-0-19-929683-5

10 9 8 7 6 5 4 3 2 1

Preface

We set out to write a practical guide for police officers in the hope that it would prove to be a useful working tool to those engaged in the daily business of enforcing traffic laws. The authors have practical front-line experience of traffic policing totalling some 35 years and we were both aware of the need to provide an accurate and yet manageable practical text for daily use. The complexity and technicality of road traffic law is second to none and producing an accurate text for non-lawyers has been challenging. We have not attempted to cover all areas that may arise in the career of a traffic patrol officer; such a task would be almost impossible. Instead, our aim was to produce a working and practical guide that addresses some of the more common problems and those situations that are encountered on a regular basis. We hope we have achieved our aim and that the book proves useful to those who read it, whatever their level of experience and service.

At the time of writing, the Road Safety Bill is still progressing through Parliament. If, as seems likely, it is enacted, it will amongst other things introduce new offences of causing death by careless driving and causing death by driving whilst disqualified, uninsured or unlicensed, as well as modifying several other areas of traffic law generally. Reference to the proposed new offences has been made in the text where appropriate on the assumption that the Bill will reach the statute books largely intact.

A heartfelt thank you is due to Chris Newman, formerly a Metropolitan police officer and now postgraduate research assistant in law at the University of Sunderland. Chris made very substantial contributions to several chapters and without his efforts publication would have been significantly delayed. Personal thanks are due to our respective partners, Linda and Sandra, and to the many others whose opinions and views we sought during preparation, especially PC 1640 Gemma Cooper of Northumbria Police who proofread and commented on several of the chapters. We have attempted to state the law as of 1 May 2006.

Simon Cooper
Michael Orme

Contents

Table of Cases

Table of Primary Legislation

Table of Secondary Legislation

EU Legislation

Definitions and Basic Concepts

The principal laws relating to road traffic are to be found in statutes enacted by Parliament. These statutes are designed so that driving is regulated in a way that attempts to improve the safety of all road users. In attempting to apply road traffic laws it is of fundamental importance to have a basic understanding of the key terms and concepts that are used to create the various offences. Reading and learning definitions can be monotonous but it is nonetheless necessary.

In the main, it is ss 185 to 192 of the Road Traffic Act 1988 (RTA 1988) that contain the definitions of many key terms that are encountered in road traffic law. The majority of substantive offences are also contained within this Act. This first chapter will provide an overview of the definitions and concepts which form the basis of the substantive law contained within the rest of this book.

The list of definitions and concepts provided is *not* exhaustive, nor is it intended to be. Words and phrases that are specific to a particular offence will be further defined and referred to within the necessary subject heading.

1.1 **Road**

A sensible first step in dealing with road traffic matters is to establish what the accepted meaning of 'road' is. The definition contained in the RTA 1988 is appropriate to the majority of offences where the word 'road' appears within legislation. Section 192 of the RTA 1988 provides that:

> (1) "road", in relation to England and Wales, means any highway and any other road to which the public has access, and includes bridges over which a road passes.

It is for the prosecution to prove that the road in question falls within the ambit of the Act. A road is held generally to include boundary grass verges and will also include any pavements (see *Worth v Brooks* [1959] Crim LR 885). If the boundary fences have been erected by an adjoining landowner and not the highway authority then any fences may not clearly establish the limits of the highway and the limits should be independently verified. There are a number of constituent elements within the definition of road which need further explanation.

1.1.1 **Highway**

A highway is anywhere that members of the public are afforded a right of way on foot, riding, accompanied by a beast of burden or with vehicles or cattle (see *Suffolk County Council v Mason* [1979] AC 705). Bridleways, footpaths and carriageways which are public are also 'highways'. A bridleway is a highway over which the public has a right of way on foot or horseback or when leading a horse.

Where any part of a vehicle is on a road, even where it is partly on some other private land, the vehicle is to be treated as being on a road for the purposes of all relevant road traffic legislation (see *Randall v Motor Insurers' Bureau* [1969] 1 All ER 21). A highway, unlike a road, does not cease to be such when it is temporarily closed off (see *McCrone v J & L Rigby (Wigan) Ltd* [1950] 50 LGR 115).

1.1.2 Access to the Public

In order to fall within the ambit of the definition in s 192(1), the road must be one to which 'the public have access'. In order to determine whether or not the public has access, a twofold test has developed. First, it is necessary to establish that the place concerned is a road and second, it must then be demonstrated that it is a road to which the general public have access and not just a section or special class of the public (see *Oxford v Austin* [1981] RTR 416; and *DPP v Vivier* [1991] RTR 205).

Whether or not the general public have access is a question of fact. Where a member of the public has to either overcome some form of physical barrier or act in defiance of a prohibition it is likely that this will be viewed as not falling within the terms of the definition (see *Harrison v Hill* [1932] JC 13; approved in *Cox v White* [1976] RTR 248).

The case law suggests that use of an area by members of a private club (eg a club car park limited to use by private members) will not be regarded as a road to which the public have access (see *Havell v DPP* (1993) unreported). Similarly a sign on a private road stating that 'Trespassers will be prosecuted' was held to be sufficient prohibition to members of the general public and thus the road did not fall within the definition (see *R v Beaumont* [1964] Crim LR 665). It may be that in certain circumstances, a road may be one to which the public have access, if it is used by the public as a short cut from one street to another (see *Bugge v Taylor* [1941] 1 KB 198).

Where 'Car Parks' are provided solely for the purpose of providing parking for vehicles, they will not be considered as roads (but they may be considered public places). Where there is any ambiguity, it should be noted that the House of Lords has stated that it would only be in exceptional circumstances that a car park would fall within the definition of a road (see *Clarke v Kato* [1998] 1 WLR 1647).

PRACTICAL POINT

Many offences may be committed by driving on a road *or other public place*. It follows that merely because the location does not meet the definition of road under the 1988 Act this does not necessarily mean that the offence will not be complete. If the relevant location is a public place (and many car parks that are not roads will still be public places—see 1.1.3) the offence may still be committed.

1.1.3 **Public Places**

The test for whether or not a place is 'public' is very similar to the test of whether a road is open to public access. A place is a 'public' place if those people who are admitted are members of the general public (not members of some special or particular class of the public) and admission is with the express or implied permission of the owner of the relevant land. The matter remains a question of fact to be judged on a case-by-case basis.

The following are examples of places that have been held to be 'public places':

- multi-storey car parks;
- school playground used by the public after school hours;
- pub car parks during licensing hours;
- pub car parks after licensing hours if, in fact, the public use the car park;
- a hospital car park.

1.2 **Motor Vehicles**

The next definitional issue centres on the different types of vehicle that can be used on a road. The definition of a motor vehicle is also set out in s 185 of the RTA 1988 which provides that:

> "Motor Vehicle" means a mechanically propelled vehicle intended or adapted for use on a road.

The definition contains two main elements—'mechanically propelled vehicle' and 'intended or adapted for use on a road'.

1.2.1 **Mechanically Propelled Vehicle**

It is not of much help to state that the term 'mechanically propelled vehicle' means a vehicle that can be propelled mechanically! Practically, the phrase covers both petrol and diesel powered vehicles and can also include steam and electrically driven vehicles. A vehicle will be mechanically propelled even if another form of non-mechanical propulsion is in operation at the material time (see *Floyd v Bush* [1953] 1 WLR 242 where a pedal cycle was fitted with a small, integrated engine).

Similarly, a vehicle will be mechanically propelled even where there is a breakdown in the vehicle's functions. A vehicle does not cease to be mechanically propelled unless there is no reasonable prospect of the vehicle ever being mobile again. It is for the prosecution to show that the vehicle is mechanically propelled and it is for the defence to prove that there is no reasonable prospect of the vehicle ever being made mobile again (see *Reader v Bunyard* [1987] RTR 406). A motor vehicle which is being towed still falls within the scope of the definitions in s 185 of the RTA 1988 (see *Cobb v Whorton* [1971] RTR 392).

1.2.2 **Intended or Adapted for Use on Roads**

This is an important qualification which limits the definition of motor vehicles under s 185 of the RTA 1988. The definition excludes mechanically propelled vehicles which are not intended or adapted for use on a road (eg go-karts). In order to discover whether or not a vehicle is intended or adapted for use on a road it is necessary to consider the vehicle's *general* construction. The test is an objective one. Would a reasonable person looking at the vehicle say that its *general* use could include potential road use? If the answer is 'yes', then it is intended or adapted for use on a road. The specific intention of the owner and particular use by a particular person is not generally relevant (see *Chief Constable of Avon & Somerset v Fleming* [1987] RTR 378).

Where a vehicle has been rebuilt and retains its underlying characteristics, then it will be deemed to continue to be intended for use on a road (see *Nichol v Leach* [1972] RTR 476 where the owner had rebuilt the vehicle to be used in off-road racing and never intended it to be used on the road).

It is possible that a vehicle intended for general road use may be substantially altered so as to exclude it from the definition under s 185 of the RTA 1988. If, however, the prosecution can produce evidence that such vehicles are still suitable for use on a road they may still be held to come within the ambit of s 185 (see *Daley v Hargreaves* [1961] 1 All ER 552).

PRACTICAL POINT

Occasionally, specific pieces of legislation provide different definitions of what constitutes a motor vehicle for the purpose of that legislation only. In most cases, definitions in other legislation are broader than the one contained in the 1988 Act.

For example, the Police Reform Act 2002, s 59 provides that for the purposes of this Act a motor vehicle is any mechanically propelled vehicle irrespective of whether or not it is intended or adapted for use on a road. Another example is provided by the Vehicles (Crime) Act 2001 which defines a motor vehicle as any vehicle whose function is or was to be used on a road as a mechanically propelled vehicle. If dealing with an incident or situation outside of the scope of the Road Traffic Act 1988 make sure that the 'motor vehicle' you are concerned with is actually covered by the relevant legislation.

1.2.3 **Motor Car and Heavy Motor Car**

Perhaps the most common and instantly recognizable group of motor vehicles used on a road is that of motor cars. Section 185 of the RTA 1988 provides:

(1) "motor car" means a mechanically propelled vehicle, not being a motor cycle or an invalid carriage, which is constructed itself to carry a load or passengers and the weight of which unladen—

(a) if it is constructed solely for the carriage of passengers and their effects, is adapted to carry not more than seven passengers exclusive of the driver and is fitted with tyres of such type as may be specified in regulations made by the Secretary of State, does not exceed 3050 kilograms,

(b) if it is constructed or adapted for use for the conveyance of goods or burden of any description, does not exceed 3050 kilograms, or 3500 kilograms if the vehicle carries a container or containers for holding for the purposes of its propulsion any fuel which is wholly gaseous at 17.5 degrees Celsius under a pressure of 1.013 bar or plant and materials for producing such fuel,

(c) does not exceed 2540 kilograms in a case not falling within sub-paragraph (a) or (b) above.

By virtue of s 185(1) a mechanically propelled vehicle, not being a motor cycle or an invalid carriage, which is constructed itself to carry a load or passengers and the weight of which unladen exceeds 2540 kilograms will be a 'heavy motor car'.

1.2.4 Invalid Carriage

Section 185(1) of the RTA 1988 also defines an 'invalid carriage'. The legislation provides that an 'invalid carriage' is a mechanically propelled vehicle the weight of which unladen does not exceed 254 kilograms and which is specially designed and constructed, and not merely adapted, for the use of a person suffering from some physical defect or disability and is used solely by such a person.

1.2.5 Small Vehicle

A 'small vehicle' (relevant for driver licensing purposes) is defined as a motor vehicle other than an invalid carriage, motor bicycle or moped, which is not constructed or adapted to carry more than nine persons including the driver and which has a maximum gross weight not exceeding 3.5 tonnes (s 108(1) of the RTA 1988).

1.2.6 Locomotives

A locomotive may be classified as either a 'light' locomotive or a 'heavy' locomotive. In either case, locomotive means a mechanically propelled vehicle which is not constructed itself to carry a load other than any of the excepted articles. If the unladen weight exceeds 11,690 kilograms it is a heavy locomotive. If the unladen weight is above 7,370 kilograms but less than 11,690 kilograms it is a light locomotive.

1.2.7 Motor Tractor

A motor tractor is defined as a mechanically propelled vehicle which is not constructed itself to carry a load, other than the excepted articles, and the weight of which unladen does not exceed 7,370 kilograms.

1.2.8 Recovery Vehicle

The Vehicle Excise and Registration Act 1994 defines a recovery vehicle as a vehicle which is constructed or permanently adapted primarily for any one or more of the purposes of lifting, towing and transporting a disabled vehicle (sch 1, para 5). It is essential that the vehicle is actually constructed or permanently adapted for the purpose. If the vehicle is used for multi-purposes not within the definition it is not a recovery vehicle.

1.3 Motor Cycles and Similar Vehicles

Although we all believe that we would easily be able to recognize a motor cycle when we see one, road traffic law has differing definitions (some rather convoluted) depending upon the context and situation. This is a good example of the complexity of road traffic law and which, try as one may, is difficult to simplify. The general definition is given at 1.3.1 below. The remaining definitions (see 1.3.2 and 1.3.3) are applicable to Pt III of the RTA 1988—ie driver licensing.

1.3.1 Motor Cycle

The general definition of 'motor cycle' can be found in s 185(1) of the RTA 1988 which defines a motor cycle as a mechanically propelled vehicle, not being an invalid carriage, with less than four wheels and the weight of which unladen does not exceed 410 kilograms. An example of a vehicle that falls within this definition is a 3-wheeled Robin Reliant, even though at first sight, most people would identify this as a motor car rather than motor cycle.

1.3.2 Motor Bicycle

A motor bicycle is a motor vehicle which (a) has two wheels; and (b) has a maximum design speed exceeding 45 kilometres per hour (kph) and, if powered by an internal combustion engine, has a cylinder capacity exceeding 50 cubic centimetres, and includes a combination of such a motor vehicle and a side car (s 108(1) of the RTA 1988).

1.3.3 **Moped**

A moped is a motor vehicle which has fewer than four wheels and (a) in the case of a vehicle first used before 1 August 1977, has a cylinder capacity not exceeding 50 cubic centimetres and is equipped with pedals by which the vehicle is capable of being propelled; and (b) in any other case, has a maximum design speed not exceeding 50 kph (30 mph approx) and, if propelled by an internal combustion engine, has a cylinder capacity not exceeding 50 cubic centimetres (s 108(1) of the RTA 1988).

PRACTICAL POINT

The important feature of a moped is the *design* speed and not the actual speed that might be achieved on a particular occasion. If, in fact, a moped actually exceeds its design speed of 50 kph, it nonetheless remains a moped for road traffic law purposes.

1.3.4 **Further Definitions of Motor Cycle**

Legislation also provides further definitions of motor cycle for certain purposes. These include the 'Learner Motor Bicycle' which is relevant for certain driver licensing restrictions and for provisional licence holders (see 6.5.1):

- A learner motor bicycle is one which is either (a) propelled by electric power; or (b) where the cylinder capacity does not exceed 125 cubic centimetres *and* the maximum power output does not exceed 11 kW (s 97(5)).

Also relevant for licensing restriction purposes is the distinction between a Large and Standard Motor Bicycle (see 6.5.1).

- A large motor bicycle is (a) in the case of a motor bicycle without a sidecar, a bicycle the engine of which has a maximum net power output exceeding 25 kW or has a power to weight ratio exceeding 0.16 kW per kilogram; or (b) with sidecar, having a power to weight ratio exceeding 0.16 kW per kilogram (reg 3 of the Motor Vehicles (Driving Licences) Regulations 1999).

If not within this definition, it is a standard motor bicycle!

PRACTICAL POINT

On most cycles will be a manufacturer's plate stating the machine type (ie standard/large/moped). This plate is usually located on the headstock of the cycle and can be seen by turning the handlebars.

1.4 **Goods Vehicles**

Goods vehicles are defined under s 192 of the RTA 1988. The legislation provides:

(1) "goods vehicle" means a motor vehicle constructed or adapted for use for the carriage of goods, or a trailer so constructed or adapted.

The term 'goods' has been held to include not only items for sale or delivery but also items such as tools of a particular trade (see *Clarke v Cherry* [1953] 1 WLR 268 where window cleaners' equipment was held to be goods). It does not include a permanent fixture on the vehicle (eg a generator) or any water or fuel used for the supply of power for propulsion of the vehicle. Goods vehicles are generally distinguished depending on their weight. (Large goods vehicles are dealt with later in Chapter 9).

1.4.1 **Medium-sized Goods Vehicles**

Medium-sized goods vehicles are defined under s 108(1) of the RTA 1988. A medium-sized goods vehicle is a motor vehicle which is constructed or adapted to carry or to haul goods and is not adapted to carry more than nine persons inclusive of the driver and the permissible maximum weight of which exceeds 3.5 but not 7.5 tonnes.

Where any medium-sized goods vehicle is drawing a trailer, the combined weight must still not exceed 7.5 tonnes and the weight of the trailer must not exceed 750 kg.

1.4.2 **Heavy Commercial Vehicle**

A heavy commercial vehicle (formerly referred to as a heavy goods vehicle) is defined under s 20 of the RTA 1988. The legislation provides:

(1) "heavy commercial vehicle" means any goods vehicle which has an operating weight exceeding 7.5 tonnes.

In this case, the operating weight is defined by s 20(2) as the maximum laden weight, or where a combination of a motor vehicle and a trailer, the aggregate weight of them both.

1.5 **Passenger Vehicles and Trailers**

1.5.1 **Passenger Vehicle**

The definition of a 'passenger vehicle' is to be found in the Road Vehicles (Construction and Use) Regulations 1986, SI 1986/1078. The legislation provides that 'passenger vehicles' are vehicles constructed solely for the carriage of passengers and their effects (reg 3(2)).

As a consequence, goods vehicles which have been adapted or which are intended to carry passengers do not fall within this definition. This is the case even if the vehicle has never been used to carry goods. According to reg 3(2) of the Road Vehicles (Construction and Use) Regulations 1986, where a passenger vehicle is constructed or adapted to carry more than eight but not more than sixteen passengers then it will be a 'mini bus'. Passenger vehicles which carry more than sixteen seated passengers will be a 'large bus' and large buses with a gross weight exceeding 7.5 tonnes and having a maximum speed exceeding 60 mph are 'coaches'.

1.5.2 **Trailers**

A trailer is defined as a vehicle drawn by a motor vehicle (s 185(1) of the RTA 1988). A vehicle may be both a motor vehicle and a trailer if, for example, one car is towing another.

1.6 **Other Basic Concepts**

Road traffic law is, of course, administered by the criminal courts. As a branch of criminal law, basic principles of criminal liability apply to road traffic offences just as they do to all other criminal offences. So, for example, there must be an *actus reus* and (if appropriate) *mens rea*. Defences such as automatism or duress of circumstances can be used to defend road traffic charges in just the same way that they can be used to defend any other criminal charges. Where relevant, defences are addressed in the appropriate subject heading (eg automatism is dealt with in the section on careless driving at 2.3.3 where it is particularly relevant) but general principles aside, there are a number of basic concepts that are directly relevant to road traffic law and these are addressed here.

1.6.1 **Drivers and Driving**

In most cases, who is the 'driver' of a particular vehicle will be perfectly obvious. It should be noted however, that the word 'driver' can extend to cover someone who is not actually sitting in the driver's seat and in full control of the vehicle. It may include, for example, a passenger who leans over to steer the vehicle while someone else sitting in the driver's seat operates the pedals (*Tyler v Whatmore* [1976] RTR 83). The Road Traffic Act 1988, s 192(1), also allows a 'steersman' to be treated as a 'driver'.

A person also remains the driver of the vehicle even though the journey has been temporarily halted by, for example, pulling into a lay-by or into a petrol station. Whether or not a driver is actually in the act of driving is a question of fact to be determined according to the circumstances of the case. Much will, of course, depend on the extent to which the said 'driver' had control over the vehicle, its speed and direction.

Practical Examples

(1) Pushing a car while steering has been held not to be 'driving' in England and Wales but has been held to be 'driving' in Scotland.
(2) Sitting astride a motor cycle and propelling it with the feet is 'driving'.
(3) Sitting astride a motor cycle and being pushed is 'driving'.
(4) Sitting in the driver's seat with the engine running was found to be 'driving'.
(5) Sitting in the driver's seat of a car being towed is 'driving' the car being towed.

1.6.2 Owners and Keepers

A person who owns a vehicle under a hire-purchase agreement does not, as a matter of strict civil law, own the vehicle. The legal owner is the hire-purchase company that provides the finance for the vehicle and who actually 'hire' the vehicle to the person in return for monthly payments. In a hire-purchase agreement, ownership does not actually pass until the end of the agreement and, usually, in return for a further nominal payment. Nonetheless, s 192 of the RTA 1988 provides that 'owner' for the purposes of the Road Traffic Acts means the person in 'possession' of the vehicle under a hire-purchase agreement. This obviously makes sense otherwise many offences and responsibilities the Act gives to 'owners' would be evaded by those who happen to be buying vehicles on hire-purchase.

A 'keeper' must, it seems, mean something other than owner. It would seem self-evident that a single person can (and often will) be owner, keeper and registered keeper of a vehicle, but this need not be so. If X owns a vehicle in law and lends it for a period of time to Y, then Y will, presumably, be the 'keeper' during the loan period, even though he may not be the registered keeper. The meaning of 'keeper' is becoming of more significance given the growing number of offences that can be committed by 'keepers', although most of these are restricted to offences committed by the 'registered keeper' (see the proposed new s 144A of the RTA 1988 of Keeping without Insurance—5.1.2 below).

1.6.3 Attempts

The law of attempts has had a long and chequered history in the criminal courts with numerous tests being devised in an effort to determine when a person is 'attempting' a particular activity. Numerous road traffic offences may be committed by drivers who are 'attempting' to drive and so recognizing what constitutes an 'attempt' to drive is important. At one end of the spectrum, it can be safely said that a person who sits in the driver's seat and puts the keys in the ignition starting the engine is 'attempting to drive', even though the vehicle has not yet been placed in gear. At the other end of the spectrum, approaching a car on foot and merely placing a hand on the door to open it does not amount to an attempt to drive. In between, fall those grey areas which require factual judgment on a case-by-case basis.

PRACTICAL POINT

As a general rule of thumb ask, 'Has this person gone as far as they possibly can without actually driving?' If the answer is 'Yes—the next step they will take is to actually drive' then, almost certainly, they have 'attempted'. If the answer is 'No—there are more stages to pass through before they actually drive' they have probably not yet reached the stage of 'attempting'.

Note also, that even if the relevant complete offence of 'driving' is factually impossible (perhaps because the vehicle is so defective that it cannot actually be driven) this is no bar to charging an offence of 'attempting' to drive. The general criminal law allows a person to be charged with and convicted of an offence of attempting that offence, even though it is factually impossible to commit it.

1.6.4 In Charge

Many road traffic offences may be committed by a person who is said to be 'in charge' of a vehicle. A person may be regarded as being 'in charge' of a vehicle (ie has some 'control' over it) if one of two things can be shown:

(1) If the defendant owns the vehicle *or* there is evidence that the defendant has recently driven the vehicle, the defendant is in charge of it unless he can demonstrate that there was no likelihood of 'control' being resumed during the relevant time.

(2) If the defendant is neither the owner, nor is there evidence of his having recently driven the vehicle, the prosecution must show the defendant has

voluntary 'control' of the vehicle or intends to have such 'control' in the immediate future.

PRACTICAL POINT

Establishing control or future intention to exercise control is a matter of evidence. Factors such as the location of the keys (were they in the defendant's possession?) and whether or not the defendant was trying to enter the vehicle are important indicators of control and intention to take control.

1.6.5 Use, Cause, Permit

An important feature of many road traffic offences is the concept of using, causing or permitting the prohibited activity. These concepts are especially prominent in construction and use offences.

Use

It may come as no surprise that a seemingly simple word like 'use' has acquired a varied and diverse meaning in road traffic law. There is certainly no one consistent meaning that can be applied to all situations. In general terms, a person who 'uses' a vehicle has some element of control or management over it, but this need not be control in the sense of driving it (eg an owner riding as a passenger still 'uses' the vehicle). An employer who instructs an employee to drive his (the employer's) vehicle on the employer's business is 'using' that vehicle just as the employee is using it by driving it. If, however, the driver is not an employee then the employer is not using the vehicle. A vehicle may even be 'used' without being driven. A motor vehicle 'uses' the road if it is merely stationary on the road and in this sense, there is no need to show the owner is operating or controlling it at all.

The aim or purpose of the vehicle's owner is not considered relevant in determining whether or not the vehicle was being 'used' at the relevant time. A vehicle may be available for 'use' even though the owner's purpose is not to drive it but to scrap or repair it.

Cause

A person 'causes' by making some form of contribution to the commission of the relevant offence. This will often take the form of an instruction (eg from an employer to an employee) or a positive authorization. It is not generally possible to 'cause' unless the defendant owner also has *knowledge* of the relevant circumstances (eg knowledge that the vehicle had defective tyres and then authorizes use in that condition).

Permit

The concept of 'permitting' requires that the defendant gives permission to do something. It may often overlap with 'causing' but lacks the necessary degree of authority or direction that 'cause' suggests. Permitting is a much more passive concept than causing. In general terms, it will be necessary to demonstrate that the person permitting had *knowledge* of the unlawful use of the vehicle (eg allowing a friend to use the vehicle knowing that it was overloaded).

Accidents, Dangerous and Careless Driving

The number of people killed or seriously injured on Britain's roads has seen a significant reduction in the past 40 years. In 1966, some 8,000 people were killed as a result of road traffic collisions. By 2000, the number killed had fallen to 3,409 and recent figures now suggest that the number of fatalities appears to have levelled out and that reductions are no longer being achieved. It is certainly a sobering thought that every single day of the year around 10 people lose their lives and a further 87 are seriously injured on our roads. It is, of course, entirely proper that every effort is made to further reduce the number of deaths and injuries, the vast majority of which are attributable to bad driving.

2.1 **Accidents**

The word 'accident' is commonly used to describe all types of road traffic collisions that occur. The word 'accident' itself also appears in several places in the legislation and, depending on the context in which it is used, can refer to both intended and unintended collisions. This section is concerned with those 'accidents' which are designated as 'reportable' and which impose obligations and duties upon those who are involved.

2.1.1 **Reportable Accidents**

What is a reportable accident? The definition can be found in s 170 of the Road Traffic Act 1988 (RTA 1988) which provides:

(1) This section applies in a case where, owing to the presence of a mechanically propelled vehicle on a road or other public place, an accident occurs by which—

(a) personal injury is caused to a person other than the driver of that mechanically propelled vehicle, or

(b) damage is caused—

(i) to a vehicle other than that mechanically propelled vehicle or a trailer drawn by that mechanically propelled vehicle, or

(ii) to an animal other than an animal in or on that mechanically propelled vehicle or a trailer drawn by that mechanically propelled vehicle, or

(iii) to any other property constructed on, fixed to, growing in or otherwise forming part of the land on which the road or place in question is situated or land adjacent to such land.

In *any* of the above circumstances the accident is a 'reportable' road traffic accident.

The accident is not reportable if injury is suffered *only* by the driver of the mechanically propelled vehicle, **or** damage is suffered *only* by the driver's vehicle, **or** damage is caused *only* to an animal carried in or on the driver's vehicle.

Reportable Accidents—Diagrammatic Form

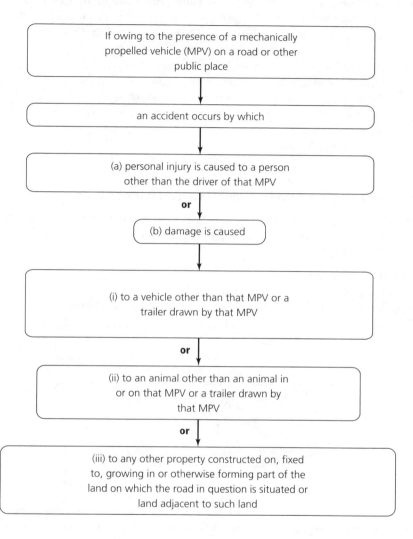

If owing to the presence of a mechanically propelled vehicle (MPV) on a road or other public place

an accident occurs by which

(a) personal injury is caused to a person other than the driver of that MPV

or

(b) damage is caused

(i) to a vehicle other than that MPV or a trailer drawn by that MPV

or

(ii) to an animal other than an animal in or on that MPV or a trailer drawn by that MPV

or

(iii) to any other property constructed on, fixed to, growing in or otherwise forming part of the land on which the road in question is situated or land adjacent to such land

Animal for these purposes means horse, cattle, ass, mule, sheep, goat or dog (s 170 (8) RTA 1988). It does *not* include cats or any other animal not specifically mentioned.

Practical Examples

(1) If a driver X collides with another vehicle driven by Y, causing injury to himself but no damage to the other vehicle or injury to Y, the accident is

not reportable. If in the same circumstances however, damage is caused to Y's vehicle, the accident *is* reportable. This is so even though Y may be completely uninjured and the only personal injury caused is to X. The requirements in (a) and (b) of s 170 are disjunctive and the accident is reportable if *either* is satisfied.

(2) There are occasions where motor cyclists or pedal cyclists fall from their vehicles causing injury to themselves or damage to their vehicles. In the absence of any damage to the road, land, other property or street furniture, then this would *not* be reportable. Note however, the local practice of some police forces may well dictate that a report for statistical purposes is taken.

2.1.2 Obligations on Drivers Involved in Reportable Accidents

The driver of any mechanically propelled vehicle involved in a reportable accident must **stop** and if so required by a person having reasonable grounds, the driver must give:

- his own name and address;
- the name and address of the owner of the vehicle; and
- the identification mark of the vehicle (s 170(2) of the RTA 1988).

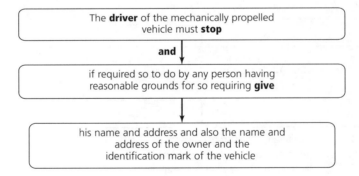

The **driver** of the mechanically propelled vehicle must **stop**

and

if required so to do by any person having reasonable grounds for so requiring **give**

his name and address and also the name and address of the owner and the identification mark of the vehicle

All three pieces of information must be given to the person so requiring; it is not sufficient to provide just one or two identifying features. Nor does fault matter. The duty to stop and report lies with any driver involved, regardless of responsibility.

PRACTICAL POINT

The 1988 Act imposes a requirement to stop *and* give details. It is not sufficient to simply stop without then providing the required information. If a driver stops and then fails to provide the required information then the driver has not stopped *and*

given the required information and is in breach of the section. Both elements are
required together.

2.1.3 Producing Insurance in Cases of Injury

In the case of a reportable accident involving personal injury not only has the
driver the responsibility of providing identification details, he must also produce a certificate of insurance or security. The certificate must be produced to
a constable or some other person who has reasonable grounds for so requiring
(s 170(5) of the RTA 1988).

If the driver cannot produce the required certificate at the time, then he must
report the accident and produce insurance to a police constable or at a police
station *as soon as practicable* or in any case within 24 hours of the occurrence of
the accident (s 170(6) of the RTA 1988 and see further at 2.1.6 below).

Practical Examples

A 'damage only' accident has occurred and the correct names and addresses
have been exchanged without any police involvement. Subsequently, one
of the drivers wishes to make an insurance claim against the other who
refuses to provide details of insurance. The police are contacted for assist-
ance. There is no obligation under s 170(5) or (6) as this was not an injury
accident and if all the requirements under s 170 have been complied with
then no offence of failing to stop and report has been committed. However, you should consider the obligation of an owner to provide insurance
details under s 154 of the RTA 1988 and an offence may be committed in
these circumstances (see further at 5.3.2).

2.1.4 Driver Must Know of the Accident

The requirement imposed by s 170 of the RTA 1988 applies only to a driver who
knows he has been involved in an accident (*Harding v Price* [1948] 1 All ER 283).
In most cases this will not be an issue of contention but may arise where, for
example, the driver of a large articulated vehicle has unknowingly collided with
a pedal cyclist causing injury and/or damage.

PRACTICAL POINT

(1) Once the prosecution have established that there has been damage or injury, it
is for the defendant who alleges a lack of knowledge to prove, on a balance of
probabilities, that he was unaware of the accident. If you are dealing with an

accident where this may become an issue, it would clearly assist the prosecutor if there is evidence to rebut any assertion a defendant may make suggesting unawareness. Try to obtain evidence that tends to show the defendant knew that an accident had occurred (eg stopping and looking at damage before driving off, or other witness statements that describe collision noise).

(2) If, following a road traffic collision, prosecution for other relevant driving offences is being considered, there is normally no need to issue a Notice of Intended Prosecution (see 3.1.2). Note however, if the circumstances are such that the offending driver may be unaware that a reportable accident has occurred you should issue a NIP, even if you yourself are in no doubt that there has actually been a reportable accident. For example, the trailer of an articulated lorry strikes and damages a parked car. You wish to prosecute for careless driving contrary to s 3 of the RTA 1988 and failing to stop/report contrary to s 170 of the RTA 1988. If the driver successfully persuades the court that he had no knowledge of the accident and is acquitted of the s 170 offence then, unless a NIP was issued, the court will not even be able to consider the driver's liability for the s 3 offence. In circumstances like this a NIP should always be issued.

2.1.5 **The Meaning of 'Stop'**

The driver must stop and remain at the scene for such time as would allow anyone who could reasonably have the right to ask for information to do so (*Lee v Knapp* [1966] 3 All ER 961). This responsibility cannot be delegated to another person (eg a passenger) or an employee or agent of the driver. There is, however, no obligation on the driver to take positive action to discover any other person who might have a right to require the necessary information. The driver does not, for example, have to make house-to-house enquiries in an effort to identify a person who could require his details but he must remain with his vehicle for a reasonable amount of time to allow others to make the relevant enquires from him (*Mutton v Bates (No 1)* [1984] RTR 56).

2.1.6 **Duty to Report to Police**

If the requirements of s 170 or s 170(5) of the RTA 1988 are not complied with then the driver must report the matter at a police station or to a police constable. This must be done as soon as is *reasonably practicable* and, *in any case*, within 24 hours of the occurrence of the accident (s 170(6) of the RTA 1988). It is for the court to determine what is reasonably practicable.

PRACTICAL POINT

The 24 hour time limit is an *overall* time limit. It does not permit the driver to take up to 24 hours to report the accident. The accident must be reported *as soon as reasonably practicable* and failure to do so is an offence (ie if it is reasonably practicable to report the accident after two hours then it must be reported at that time and not later). The report must be made in person to a police station or police constable. It is not sufficient to report the accident by telephone.

2.2 Dangerous Driving

This section will deal with the principal offences which involve poor standards of driving and which are likely to be encountered on a regular basis (ie dangerous driving and careless driving). (The Road Safety Bill 2005 proposes the introduction of a new offence of causing death by careless driving and this is dealt with at 2.3.2 below). Initially, consideration will be given to the more serious offence of dangerous driving.

2.2.1 The Meaning of 'Dangerous'

Driving may be dangerous either because of the poor quality of the defendant's driving or alternatively, because of the inherently poor condition of the defendant's vehicle.

Quality of driving

The statutory definition provides that driving is dangerous if:

(1) the way [the driver] drives falls far below what would be expected of a competent and careful driver; and
(2) it would be obvious to a competent and careful driver that driving in that way would be dangerous (s 2A(1) of the RTA 1988).

It follows that this is an objective test which focuses not on the state of mind of the driver but purely on the quality of the driving. It will be for the jury or magistrates to determine whether, in their view, the driving quality was sufficiently below that which would be expected of the competent and careful driver to be properly classified as dangerous. Dangerous means not only danger of injury to any person but also includes danger of serious damage to property (s 2A(3) of the RTA 1988). The factual variations of what might be considered dangerous are clearly enormous and there is little value in rehearsing numerous possible situations and speculating whether or not it might be considered as dangerous for the purposes of the Act. Much lies in the hands of the body deciding on the facts of the case. The Court of Appeal has ruled, however, that it is proper for a judge to withdraw from the jury a case where, on any reasonable point of view, the standard of driving is insufficiently below the statutory threshold. For example, in *R v Conteh* [2004] RTR 1, the defendant drove his car into an empty bus lane just before a pelican crossing. The lights were green in his favour and he intended to turn left just after the lights. A bus in the offside lane had stopped at the lights (even though they were green in his favour) to allow two pedestrians to cross. It was accepted that the defendant could not have seen the two pedestrians emerging from in front of the bus on his offside. One of the crossing pedestrians was killed even though the speed of the defendant's car was only about 20 mph. The Court of Appeal took the view that this quality of driving was insufficiently below the statutory threshold required for a conviction of dangerous driving and a conviction for the lesser offence of careless driving was substituted.

State of vehicle

Section 2A(2) of the RTA 1988 provides for an alternative method of establishing that the defendant's driving was dangerous. The section provides that 'A person is also to be regarded as driving dangerously ... if it would be obvious to a competent and careful driver that driving the vehicle in its current state would be dangerous'. It follows that the offence may be committed if the vehicle is in such a poor condition that it is 'obviously' dangerous to drive it. The defect or defects that render driving it dangerous should be apparent rather than latent or only discoverable on close and careful examination, otherwise they cannot be 'obvious'. However, s 2A(3) of the RTA 1988 further provides that in determining what is obvious, regard must also be given to any circumstances within the defendant's knowledge. It follows that a defendant who has particular knowledge of a serious and dangerous defect and who drives with that knowledge may be considered to be driving dangerously, even though the defect is not 'obvious' to other competent and careful motorists.

It has also been held by the courts that where it is the driver that is in a dangerous state (rather than the vehicle), this may also amount to dangerous driving. This would extend to drivers who drive knowing of serious medical conditions that render them likely to suffer diabetic attacks (*R v Marison* [1997] RTR 457) as well as those who drive knowing they are drunk (*R v Woodward* [1995] RTR 130).

2.2.2 **Causing Death by Dangerous Driving**

Section 1 of the RTA 1988 provides:

> A person who causes the death of another person by driving a mechanically propelled vehicle dangerously on a road or other public place is guilty of an offence.

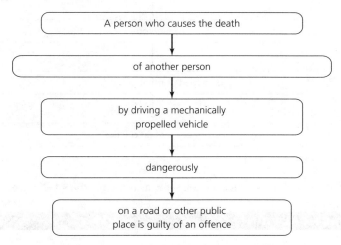

A person who causes the death

↓

of another person

↓

by driving a mechanically propelled vehicle

↓

dangerously

↓

on a road or other public place is guilty of an offence

2.2.3 **Elements of the Offence**

In order to convict the defendant of the offence it is necessary to establish that the dangerous driving of the defendant *caused* the death of another person, both in fact and in law. The meaning of causation in criminal law is extremely complex but causation will not, in most cases, be an issue. It is not necessary to prove that the defendant's driving was the *only* cause of death or even that it was a substantial cause of death, but it must be more than a very trivial cause. However, it will usually be clear that the defendant's driving has resulted in the victim's injuries from which the victim has died and medical evidence to that effect will be unequivocal. Note also that the defendant needs only to have been driving a mechanically propelled vehicle not the more narrowly defined motor vehicle (see 1.2.1). Mechanically propelled vehicles include vehicles not designed for use on roads, for example, dumper trucks solely used on building sites.

2.2.4 **Dangerous Driving**

Section 2 of the RTA 1988 provides:

> A person who drives a mechanically propelled vehicle dangerously on a road or other public place is guilty of an offence.

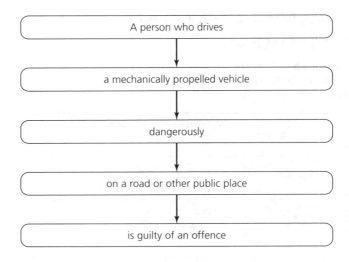

The elements of the offence are the same as those for the s 1 offence.

PRACTICAL POINT

This is an offence for which a Notice of Intended Prosecution (NIP) is required, except where a reportable accident has occurred. Remember, however, that if the circumstances are such that the driver may be unaware that he has been involved in a reportable accident, a NIP should always be issued.

2.3 Careless and Inconsiderate Driving

Section 3 of the RTA 1988 provides:

> If a person drives a mechanically propelled vehicle on a road or other public place without due care and attention, or without reasonable consideration for other persons using the road or public place, he is guilty of an offence.

PRACTICAL POINT

Note that s 3 creates two offences: (i) careless driving; and (ii) inconsiderate driving. Take care to ensure that any summons issued cites the correct offence.

2.3.1 Elements of the Offences

It is necessary to prove that the defendant has departed from the standard of driving that would be expected of a reasonable and competent driver in the circumstances. The question is purely objective and will be determined by the

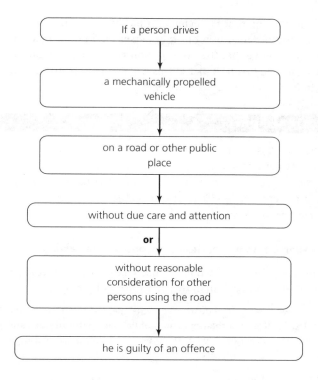

court. It is not necessary to consider the defendant's state of mind; awareness on the defendant's part that the driving is careless is irrelevant (but see the defence of automatism at 2.3.3 below). Similarly, it is not necessary to demonstrate that the defendant knew that his driving was careless. It is perfectly possible to convict a driver who has been careless even though he himself is not aware of that fact. In *Hampson v Powell* [1970] 1 All ER 929, the defendant lorry driver had struck a stationary parked vehicle and was convicted of careless driving even though he himself was unaware of the collision. His conviction for failing to report the accident was quashed because here, his lack of awareness was crucial (see 2.1.4 above).

The standard to be expected of drivers is constant and it is no defence to say that a driver did his level best if the driving actually departs from the standard to be expected. So, for example, a learner driver who drives at the best possible standard they can possibly attain given their limited experience still commits the offence if the standard is below that expected of the reasonable and competent driver (*McCrone v Riding* [1938] 1 All ER 157). Failure to observe the Highway Code may be an aide as to whether or not the defendant has actually been careless or inconsiderate but breaching the Code is, of itself, not conclusive of the issue.

25

If you are alleging that the defendant has driven without reasonable consideration for another road user or other person in a public place it seems that it is necessary to prove that the other person was actually inconvenienced (*Dilks v Bowman-Shaw* [1981] RTR 4) and this will certainly be the case once the Road Safety Bill is enacted (see 2.3.2 below).

PRACTICAL POINT

Careless driving is an offence for which a Notice of Intended Prosecution (NIP) is required, except where a reportable accident has occurred. Remember, however, that if the circumstances are such that the driver may be unaware that he has been involved in a reportable accident, a NIP should always be issued.

2.3.2 Causing Death by Careless or Inconsiderate Driving

The Road Safety Bill (expected to be enacted in late 2006) creates a new offence in the RTA 1988. A new s 2B in the RTA 1988 will provide:

> A person who causes the death of another person by driving a mechanically propelled vehicle on a road or other public place without due care and attention, or without reasonable consideration for other persons using the road or place, is guilty of an offence.

The elements of the offence involving cause of death and carelessness are the same as those discussed at 2.2.3 and 2.3.1 above. It should be noted, however, that when the change takes effect there will, for the first time, be a statutory definition of the meaning of carelessness. A new s 3ZA of the RTA 1988 will provide:

> (2) A person is to be regarded as driving without due care and attention if (and only if) the way he drives falls below what would be expected of a competent and careful driver.
> (3) In determining for the purposes of subsection (2) above what would be expected of a careful and competent driver in a particular case, regard shall be had not only to the circumstances of which he could be expected to be aware but also to any circumstances shown to have been within the knowledge of the accused.
> (4) A person is to be regarded as driving without reasonable consideration for other persons only if those persons are inconvenienced by his driving.

As can be seen, this is almost identical to the test for dangerous driving. As regards the standard of driving, the only differences between carelessness and dangerousness lies in the exclusion of the word 'far' from the definition of carelessness and exclusion of the requirement that the carelessness be 'obvious'. A driver drives dangerously if his driving falls *far below* the expected standard and is careless if his driving falls merely *below* the expected standard. This may, of course, lead to some interesting discussions on the difference between *below* and *far below* with different people taking different views. The benefit of flexibility which the test provides will doubtless come at the price of certainty. The test is entirely objective, focusing only on the standard of driving and, unlike dangerous driving, there is no necessity to show that the carelessness would have been 'obvious' to a competent and careful driver. In reality, the statutory formulation does not appear to significantly alter the test which is and has been applied by the courts under the existing law. The maximum penalty for this offence is five years imprisonment.

2.3.3 Automatism and Careless Driving

It is a basic requirement of all criminal liability that the defendant's conduct was 'voluntary'. Put very simply, this means the defendant must have been in conscious control of his bodily movements at the time of the conduct giving rise to the offence. If the defendant is in a state of automatism, he does not have conscious control or awareness of his bodily movements. If the state of automatism is not self-induced (ie the defendant has not been blameworthy in putting himself into this state), then it affords a complete defence to the vast majority of criminal offences.

If, for example, a person who is charged with careless driving adduces evidence that he suffered an unforeseeable seizure at the relevant time then this will act as a defence. If, however, the seizure was foreseeable (ie the defendant was aware of the condition and continued to drive) then the defence would not succeed because the courts have determined that the act of driving knowing of such conditions is of itself careless and may even be dangerous (*Watmore v Jenkins* [1962] 2 All ER 868). Other examples of states of automatism that have been accepted by the courts are unforeseeable epileptic fits, being rendered unconscious by a blow on the head and being attacked by a swarm of bees.

PRACTICAL POINT

If a driver claims medical conditions caused a state of automatism then consider making enquires with the DVLA to ascertain if the claimed condition has been declared. This may negate any defence and, in the event of non-declaration, may constitute an offence under s 94(3A) of the RTA 1988.

2.3.4 Mechanical Defect and Careless Driving

In some circumstances, a defendant can use a defence of mechanical defect. The defence is available if the driver, without fault, was deprived of control of his vehicle by a mechanical defect of which he did not know and which was not discoverable with the exercise of reasonable care. It would not, for example, be sufficient to say that the brakes have been poor for some time and they have now finally failed. Clearly, the defendant has knowledge of the defect which could, with reasonable care, have been avoided.

Similarly, if a vehicle fails an MOT test and the driver subsequently has an accident due to one of the defects recorded on the fail certificate, he could not use the defence of mechanical defect. In any case, once the defendant has introduced some evidence of a mechanical defect, the prosecution have the burden of disproving it. If you suspect such a defence may be raised then the vehicle should be examined by a qualified examiner (see further 5.7).

2.3.5 Emergency Vehicles and Careless Driving

There is no exemption from prosecution for careless driving provided for drivers of emergency vehicles. The drivers of emergency vehicles owe the same duty of care to other road users as other motorists and they will be judged according to the same standard (ie the standard expected of the competent and careful driver). Although drivers of vehicles being used to respond to emergencies have limited exemption from certain traffic regulations (eg speed/traffic lights) the use of sirens and blue lights confers no form of exemption from dangerous or careless driving offences. A driver convicted in such circumstances may, however, find that any penalty is reduced (*Wood v Richards* [1977] RTR 201).

2.3.6 Causing Death by Careless Driving Under the Influence of Drink or Drugs

Section 3A of the RTA 1988 provides:

> If a person causes the death of another person by driving a mechanically propelled vehicle on a road or other public place without due care and attention, or reasonable consideration for other persons using the road or place, and—
>
> (a) he is, at the time when he is driving, unfit to drive through drink or drugs, or
>
> (b) he has consumed so much alcohol that the proportion of it in his breath, blood or urine at that time exceeds the prescribed limit, or
>
> (c) he is, within 18 hours after that time, required to provide a specimen in pursuance of section 7 of this Act, but without reasonable excuse fails to provide it, he is guilty of an offence.

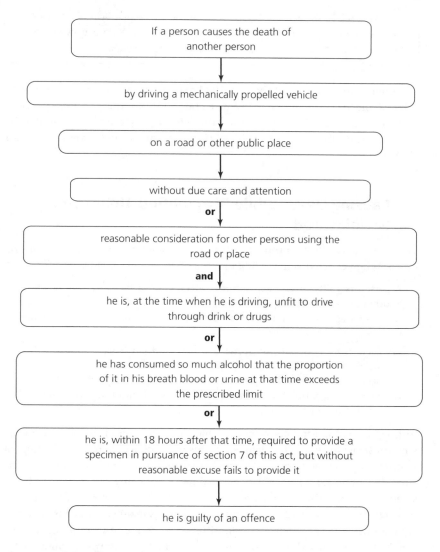

If a person causes the death of another person

↓

by driving a mechanically propelled vehicle

↓

on a road or other public place

↓

without due care and attention

or

reasonable consideration for other persons using the road or place

and

he is, at the time when he is driving, unfit to drive through drink or drugs

or

he has consumed so much alcohol that the proportion of it in his breath blood or urine at that time exceeds the prescribed limit

or

he is, within 18 hours after that time, required to provide a specimen in pursuance of section 7 of this act, but without reasonable excuse fails to provide it

↓

he is guilty of an offence

Elements of the offence

The elements of this offence that involve causing death and careless driving are the same as those discussed at 2.2.3 and 2.3.1 above.

PRACTICAL POINT

There is no requirement that there be a direct causal link between the impairment (ie the drink or drugs) and the quality of the driving, though obviously in most cases there will be such a link. Nevertheless, a driver who has consumed drink so as to be

> in excess of the limit and who then drives carelessly and kills is guilty even though the carelessness may not be attributable in any way to the drink.

The offence in s 3A(1)(a) of the RTA 1988 may be committed by a person who drives a 'mechanically propelled vehicle', but s 3A(3) of the RTA 1988 provides that in relation to s 3A(1)(b) and (c), the offence may only be committed by a person who drives a 'motor vehicle' (for meaning of 'motor vehicle' see 1.2 above).

2.4 Causing Death While Disqualified, Unlicensed or Uninsured

The Road Safety Bill also proposes a further new offence concerned with causing death. When enacted, a new s 3ZB in the RTA 1988 will provide:

> A person is guilty of an offence under this section if he causes the death of another person by driving a motor vehicle on a road and, at the time when he is driving, the circumstances are such that he is committing an offence under—
>
> (a) section 87(1) of this Act (driving otherwise than in accordance with a licence),
> (b) section 103(1)(b) of this Act (driving while disqualified), or
> (c) section 143 of this Act (using motor vehicle while uninsured or unsecured against third party risks).

Although there is general agreement that disqualified and unlicensed drivers who cause death should be included in this new offence there is, at the time of writing, an ongoing debate as to whether part (c) relating to uninsured drivers should be included. The element of the offence involving cause of death is the same as that discussed at 2.2.3 above. The new offence (referred to as 'illegal' driving) is concerned with those drivers who are disqualified, unlicensed or possibly uninsured. The offence is committed irrespective of whether or not the *standard* of driving exhibited on the occasion in question was a causal factor in the resulting death or injury. In other words, an unlicensed driver could be driving perfectly properly in terms of the quality of driving, be involved in a collision which results in death, and still be guilty of this offence.

Practical Example

An unlicensed driver is driving at 20 mph when a young child runs into his path. A collision is unavoidable (in the sense that no driver could do anything to avoid it) and the standard of driving is blameless. If the child

is killed the offence is complete, even thought the *quality* of the driving did
not contribute to the death.

The Government has justified this new offence by arguing that those who
take vehicles onto the road whilst disqualified, unlicensed or uninsured are
all culpable for creating risks beyond those presented by the general popula-
tion of drivers. Disqualified, unlicensed and uninsured drivers are or should,
it is said, appreciate that merely by taking a vehicle onto the road, creating an
unnecessary risk which, of itself, is careless of the safety of others. In the Government's view, the level of culpability exhibited at least equates with (and argu-
ably exceeds) the proposed new standard of carelessness, in that it is conduct
which falls below the standard to be expected of a competent driver. Certainly,
it is at least arguable that by consciously taking to the road whilst disqualified,
unlicensed or uninsured, a driver whose very presence then leads to death, irrespective of driving standards, is deserving of a more severe punishment based
on that higher level of culpability. The maximum penalty for this newly created
offence is two years imprisonment.

2.5 **Driver Improvement Scheme**

This scheme was introduced for less serious offences of careless driving and may
be considered as an alternative to prosecution. If it is adjudged that the driver
concerned would benefit from a short course of driver tuition rather than prosecution then it may be offered. The scheme is similar in principle to the Vehicle
Rectification Scheme (see further at 7.2 below) and gives drivers the opportun-
ity to improve upon or remove an identified problem. The present system of
driver licensing is such that once a driving test is passed, there is no procedure to monitor driving standards. This scheme enables a driver to be shown any
bad habits that may have been picked up over the years, and also the potential
consequences of poor driving. The course is entirely voluntary and this should
be emphasized when the offer is made. Courses are held at specific locations
and incur a fee which is payable by the driver. On successful completion of
the course the police are notified and the prosecution process is halted. In the
author's experience, there has generally been a positive feedback from drivers
who have attended the course.

PRACTICAL POINT

The correct procedure is to report the driver for the careless driving offence in the
usual way. They should not be offered the scheme at this point as a supervisor may
later decide that the circumstances warrant prosecution. If you have verbally offered
the scheme at the time of reporting the driver, it would be understandable if he later

---

> complained of unfair treatment having been led to believe the scheme was being offered. If asked by a driver it should be emphasized that no offer is yet being made and if it is to be offered he will receive notification in writing later.

2.6 **Questions and Answers**

Q1 An accident occurs and the only damage is to the offending driver's car. There are no apparent injuries to either party. Is this a reportable accident?

A1 On the face of it this would not be a reportable road traffic accident. You should be aware, however, that shock is classified as an injury and if someone other than the driver of the offending vehicle suffers any degree of shock caused by the accident then this would amount to an injury. In these circumstances, the accident would be reportable.

Q2 An articulated lorry has a minor collision with a parked car which causes slight damage to the car but none to the lorry. The lorry driver does not stop at the scene and does not report the accident to the police. The lorry driver is later traced but denies any knowledge of the incident. Are there any offences committed?

A2 In order to be convicted of failing to stop/report an accident under s 170 of the Road Traffic Act 1988, it would have to be shown that the lorry driver was aware he had been involved in an accident although the burden of proof is on the defendant to satisfy the court that, on the balance of probabilities, he did not know that an accident had occurred. An offence of careless driving may also have been committed and you should remember that a Notice of Intended Prosecution (NIP) is required in these circumstances (ie where there is doubt about the offender's knowledge that an accident has occurred). The obligation to send a NIP is only waived in accident cases if the driver must have known that an accident had occurred. If no verbal NIP is given at the time of the offence then a written NIP must be served within 14 days.

Q3 A motorist on a country lane loses control of his vehicle and leaves the road entering a field, causing damage to his vehicle. No damage or injury is caused to anyone else. The driver runs away from the incident and witnesses say the driver was bleeding from a head wound. What offences have been committed?

A3 As regards the accident, there appear to be no offences of failing to stop or reporting an accident under s 170 as no damage has been caused to anything but the driver's vehicle and the only injury was to the driver himself. It follows that there is no legal obligation to stop or report the accident. There may be other driving offences committed (eg careless driving) and this will depend on the evidence available. If there is evidence of careless driving then the need for a NIP would also have to be considered.

Q4 A 'damage only' accident occurs at which the driver also fails to stop. The police visit the registered keeper's house and ask the keeper to provide information as to who was driving the vehicle at the relevant time. The keeper refuses to reveal the identity of the driver. What should be done in these circumstances?

A4 A requirement under the provisions of s 172 of the Road Traffic Act 1988 can be made verbally at the time requiring the keeper to identify the driver of the vehicle. If the keeper fails or refuses to do so, then an offence is committed. Practically speaking, it may be more beneficial to make a written requirement. A written requirement can be produced in evidence and would make it much more difficult for the keeper to allege he was not required to provide the information.

Notices of Intended Prosecution and Driver Identification

3.1 **Notices of Intended Prosecution**

There are a number of offences (see below 3.1.1) that require a driver be specifically warned that consideration will be given to the question of whether or not to prosecute him for that offence. The notice is referred to as a Notice of Intended Prosecution (commonly abbreviated to NIP) and if the correct procedure is not followed then any prosecution that is instigated is likely to fail. The relevant law can be found in s 1(1) of the Road Traffic Offenders Act 1988 (RTOA 1988) which provides that:

(1) the defendant must have been warned of the possibility of prosecution at the time of the offence; **or**

(2) the defendant must have been served with a summons (or charged) within 14 days of the offence; **or**

(3) a notice setting out the particulars of the alleged offence, including the time and date it was allegedly committed, must have been sent to the driver (or rider if the offence is one involving a pedal cycle) or registered keeper within 14 days of commission.

It is only necessary for the prosecution to comply with any **one** of the above three requirements.

3.1.1 **The Offences**

The offences which attract the NIP procedure are listed in sch 1 to the RTOA 1988 and are:

- dangerous, careless or inconsiderate driving (see 2.2 and 2.3);
- failing to comply with traffic signs and directions (see 8.1);
- leaving a vehicle in a dangerous position (see 12.2);
- speeding offences under ss 16, 17(4), 88(7) and 89(1) of the Road Traffic Regulation Act 1984; and
- aiding and abetting any of the above offences.

Offences which are not listed above, even if similar in nature, do not require a NIP.

PRACTICAL POINT

If in doubt about whether or not the alleged offence requires a NIP then it makes sense to give it. You cannot prejudice a case by giving a NIP where none is actually required, but failing to give a NIP when it is required can prove fatal to a prosecution.

3.1 Notices of Intended Prosecution

3.1.2 Road Traffic Accidents/Fixed Penalties—An Exception

Although a NIP is required for dangerous, careless or inconsiderate driving, it is not required if, at the time of the alleged offence (whatever that offence may be) or immediately after, a road traffic accident occurs (see s 2(1) of the RTOA 1988).

PRACTICAL POINT

In most cases, it will be obvious to all concerned that a road accident has occurred. There may be occasions, however, where the defendant might be unaware that he has been involved in a road accident. For example, the driver of an articulated lorry may well have carried on driving completely oblivious to the fact that the rear of his trailer has struck another vehicle. Alertness to this possibility is important because the exception only applies where the defendant is **aware** that he has been involved in an accident. If there is **any** doubt about the defendant's awareness of his being involved in a road accident, then you should ensure that a NIP is still served.

You should also be aware that the requirement to serve a NIP does *not* apply in relation to an offence in respect of which a fixed penalty notice has been given or fixed (s 2(2) of the RTOA 1988).

3.1.3 Serving a NIP—Oral Warnings

It is perfectly acceptable for the officer who deals with the alleged offender to orally administer the NIP warning *at the time the offence was committed.*

PRACTICAL POINT

There is no prescribed formula of words for a NIP but the suggested wording is:

'You will be reported for consideration of the question of prosecuting you for (state the offence).'

Whether or not the NIP was orally delivered *at the time the offence was committed* is simply a matter of common sense. The courts have decided that the question is to be answered according to what is *reasonable* in the circumstances.

Perhaps of more significance in a practical context is the need to ensure that the recipient of a verbal NIP has understood what is happening. It is important that an officer who gives an oral NIP ensures the person receiving it fully understands its meaning. In other words, the officer should try to ensure that the warning is fully understood by the alleged offender because if the defendant can prove to the court that he did not understand or hear or appreciate the oral warning, then the warning will be treated as ineffective (see *Gibson v Dalton* [1980] RTR 410).

> **PRACTICAL POINT**
>
> If there is any doubt about whether or not a defendant has understood an oral NIP then it makes good sense to serve a NIP by post.

3.1.4 **Service of Written Notice or Summons**

The law will presume that a NIP has been properly served (see s 1(3) of the RTOA 1988) and the prosecution will not be obliged to routinely prove service as part of their case. It is, however, prudent to ensure that any defendant who might challenge service of the NIP can be defeated and prosecutors will, despite the concession in s 1(3), often choose to lead evidence of a NIP being properly served. A written NIP (or summons) can be served on any person by one of a number of methods. It may be:

- delivered personally;
- addressed to that person and left at his last known address; or
- sent by recorded delivery, registered post, or ordinary first-class post addressed to him at his last known address.

> **PRACTICAL POINTS**
>
> (1) If a NIP sent by post is returned as undelivered, or was for any other reason not received by the person, then provided it was sent by *registered* post or *recorded* delivery, service is still deemed to be effective (see s 1(2) of the RTOA 1988). If, however, the NIP was sent by ordinary first-class post, this presumption cannot be relied upon.
>
> (2) If the NIP actually arrives outside the 14 day time limit it will still be deemed to have been validly served if the prosecutor can show it was sent in such time that it could *reasonably* have been expected to have been received within 14 days. So, for example, if the NIP is posted by first-class post six days after the commission of the alleged offence it would be reasonable to suppose that it would arrive within the 14 day period. If, for some reason, it does not actually arrive until the fifteenth day, service is nonetheless still deemed valid. It would be different if the NIP was posted on the fourteenth day after commission of the alleged offence; service here would be ineffective. Note also, that the actual day of the alleged offence is excluded when calculating the fourteen day period.
>
> (3) To prove that the notice was sent it is important that whoever sent it completes a statement to this effect. This statement should be included in any prosecution file. If, subsequent to a requirement to identify the driver, several nominations

are made before the actual driver is identified, it is important that the *original NIP* and *statement of service* is included to prove, if necessary, that the time limit of fourteen days was complied with notwithstanding that it will not be in the defendant's name.

3.1.5 Failure to Comply with Serving a NIP

Failure to comply with the requirement to serve a NIP is not *always* a bar to conviction. If the prosecution can satisfy the court that neither the name and address of the accused nor the name and address of the registered keeper, if any, could have been ascertained *with reasonable diligence* in time *or* that the accused by his own conduct contributed to the failure, then the prosecution is not bound by the requirement (see s 2(3) of the RTOA 1988).

Practical Example

The DVLA supply the officer with the incorrect name and address of the registered keeper. Accordingly, the officer sends a NIP to the wrong person at the wrong address. The officer has shown due diligence by conducting normal and proper enquiries to trace the registered keeper. Failure to serve a NIP on the defendant will not, in these circumstances, be a bar to conviction (see *Haughton v Harrison* [1976] RTR 208).

3.1.6 Errors in a NIP

If the defendant is served with a NIP that contains an error, then it may still be effective. It will, however, be rendered ineffective if the error is one that is judged to prejudice the defendant. The type of error that will prejudice a defendant will be a matter for the judgment of the court and the test used, broadly speaking, will be to ask whether, due to the error, the defendant was disadvantaged in his ability to present a defence.

Some examples might be:

A simple error regarding the time of the alleged offence

This may not render the NIP ineffective so long as the defendant knows of the matter to which the NIP is referring (*Carr v Harrison* [1967] Crim LR 54). It would be different if the defendant used the road in question several times on the day of the alleged offence and was unable to tell which occasion of driving the NIP was referring to, as this would certainly prejudice his ability to present a defence.

The place of the offence

This must be identified with sufficient precision to enable the defendant to understand the offence being alleged and where it was committed. It would not be sufficient, for example, for the NIP to allege an offence of 'careless driving on the M60 motorway' without further identifying the location more precisely. Again, a defect of this nature clearly hampers the defendant's ability to defend himself.

Nature of the offence

An error in the precise nature of the offence is unlikely to affect the validity of the notice. A notice stating the offence as dangerous driving is good even though the offence prosecuted is careless driving.

Number plate errors

Number plate errors should not invalidate a NIP. The important point is that the defendant is not prejudiced in any defence he may wish to operate and that he is warned of an intention to prosecute. It follows that a simple error in the number plate is unlikely to affect the legality of a notice. In *Venn v Morgan* [1949] 2 All ER 562, the car's number was not given at all but the notice was still held to be valid. A notice that gives an incorrect car number must also be valid because, after all, the driver is still properly placed on notice that consideration is being given to his prosecution and he is not prejudiced in any defence he may wish to run. The number plate error is, in this sense, irrelevant.

3.2 Driver Identification—Road Traffic Act 1988, s 172

Where the driver of a vehicle is alleged to be guilty of an offence to which s 172 of the Road Traffic Act 1988 (RTA 1988) applies, the police have a power to require that certain information be given as to the identity of the driver of the vehicle at the relevant time. 'Driver of a vehicle' also includes 'rider of a cycle' and it follows that the provision also applies to riders of pedal cycles (s 172(10) of the RTA 1988). If the required information is not supplied then the person required to provide it commits an offence (s 172(3) of the RTA 1988). (Note also the very similar powers under s 46 of the Vehicle Excise and Registration Act 1994 for relevant excise offences—see further at 10.1.7).

Section 172 of the RTA 1988 might, at first sight, seem to be a relatively straightforward provision, but it has generated a disproportionate amount of case law as vehicle keepers have sought to evade the provision in a variety of ways. In order to ensure a successful outcome, it is crucial that the proper procedures are strictly observed.

3.2.1 **Offences to which Section 172 Applies**

The section applies to:

(1) any offence committed under the Road Traffic Act 1988 *unless* specifically excepted (see 3.2.2 below for the exceptions);
(2) any offence committed under ss 25, 26 or 27 of the Road Traffic Offenders Act 1988;
(3) any offence against any other enactment relating to the use of a vehicle on a road;
(4) an offence of manslaughter by the driver of a motor vehicle.

In practice, the most frequent use of s 172 will probably be in respect of speeding and traffic sign offences caught on camera or where an officer was unable to stop and deal with a vehicle driver at the time the alleged offence was committed.

3.2.2 **Exceptions**

There are a number of offences under the RTA 1988 which are specifically exempted from the s 172 provisions. For these offences there is no power to require information as to driver identity. The offences are:

- motoring events on public highways (s 13);
- wearing protective headgear (s 16);
- testing of goods vehicles (s 51(2));
- regulations for issue type approval certificates and related matters (s 61(4));
- obstructing an authorized vehicle examiner (s 67(9) and s 68(4));
- driving with uncorrected defective eyesight (s 96);
- licensing of drivers of large goods vehicles and passenger carrying vehicles (s 120);
- unlawful vehicle taking in Scotland (s 178).

3.2.3 **The Requirement Power**

The requirement to provide information as to driver identity is as follows:

(1) the person *keeping* the vehicle shall give such information as to the identity of the driver as he may be required to give by or on behalf of a chief officer of police; and
(2) *any other person* shall if required as stated above give any information which it is in his power to give and may lead to the identification of the driver (s 172 (2)(a) and (b)).

There is no obligation to make the requirement in writing (in other words an oral requirement will suffice) although, usually, it will be in written form (see below 3.2.4 for time periods and written requirements). The person **keeping** the vehicle includes a person who is keeper at the time the requirement is made

41

even if that person was not the keeper at the time the alleged offence was committed.

PRACTICAL POINTS

(1) A requirement to provide information under the s 172 power will usually be made in writing and sent to the vehicle keeper. Although the general requirement need not follow any particular form of wording, it is very important to ensure that the written notice does include the specific phrase '*by or on behalf of the chief officer of police*' as indicated by s 172(2)(a). If you fail to do so, the defendant may successfully submit that the written requirement was not made correctly and s/he was under no obligation to respond. You should also ensure that the notice includes a requirement that the person supplying the information *signs* the document (see Q1 below at 3.3 for the importance of this).

(2) In the event that the person required to provide the information does not respond and therefore commits an offence under s 172(3), it is important to ensure that any subsequent application for a summons correctly cites whether the requirement was made of the vehicle **keeper** under **s 172(2)(a)** or **any other person** under **s 172(2)(b)**, otherwise the summons may be judged defective.

3.2.4 Time Limits and Section 172

Unlike a Notice of Intended Prosecution there are, generally speaking, no formal time limits that apply to the requirement notices of s 172. The information required should, however, be provided by the person requested within a reasonable time. What constitutes a reasonable time will depend on the circumstances of the case. A written requirement to provide information may be sent by ordinary post.

PRACTICAL POINT

If a written requirement is sent by post then, in the event of a prosecution for non-compliance, the person who sent the requirement should complete a written witness statement to that effect. When preparing a statement to demonstrate posting of the NIP/s 172 notice it may be prudent to include the NIP/s 172 notice as an exhibit and give it a reference number, eg (PC/1). Some defence lawyers have tried to exclude the NIP/s 172 notice on the basis that it should be included as an exhibit and mentioned as such in the witness statement. Once it is shown as an exhibit, do not forget to include it on any exhibit list in the prosecution file.

Where the requirement for information is made in writing and served by post, then s 172(7)(a) states that the information should be provided within a period of 28 days, the time period beginning on the day that the notice is served. Subject to the defence provided in s 172(7)(b) (see below 3.2.5), failing to provide the required information within the 28 day period constitutes an offence.

Practical Example

A written requirement under s 172(2)(a) is sent by post to D, the registered keeper of a motor vehicle, and served on 1 August in respect of an alleged offence committed on 24 July. D must provide the information required on or before 28 August. If D fails to respond then the relevant offence (failing to comply with the requirement under s 172(3)) is committed on 29 August. It is crucial to ensure that any subsequent summons for the s 172(3) offence is correctly dated as being committed on 29 August (not 1 August—the date of service) as no offence under s 172(3) is committed until after the 28 day period has expired.

3.2.5 Defences

A person shall not be liable for the offence of failing to provide the required information as to driver identity under s 172(3) of the RTA 1988 if he can show that he did not know *and* could not have ascertained with reasonable diligence who the driver of the vehicle was (s 172(4) of the RTA 1988).

Practical Example

A defendant served with a s 172 notice and who does not respond may be prosecuted for non-compliance under s 172(3). Where a defendant asserts, in response to the summons, that he is not the keeper of the vehicle at the time of the alleged offence, the prosecution will be required to prove that the information which he has failed to give was information which was in his power to give and which may lead to identification of the driver. Where the defendant admits that he was the keeper, the prosecution need do no more than prove the failure to respond, leaving the defendant, if he wishes, to prove the defence under s 172(4). Where the defendant is silent the prosecution need do no more than prove the absence of any response (*Mohindra v DPP* [2005] RTR 7).

When a written requirement is sent by post, the person has 28 days from the date of service to provide the information (see above). It is a defence for the person required to provide the information to show that s/he gave the information as soon as reasonably practicable after the end of the 28 day period or that it had not been reasonably practicable for s/he to give it. Again, the burden of proving this defence lies with the person seeking to rely on it.

3.2.6 **Corporate Liability**

It will not be uncommon for the keeper of the vehicle to be a company and, of course, a company that fails to respond to a requirement under s 172(2) of the RTA 1988 commits the offence under s 172(3) and may be prosecuted. Serving the notice on the Company Secretary is deemed good service (s 172(8)). A company may be tempted to withhold the identity of an employee who was the driver of a vehicle when an offence was committed, preferring instead to face prosecution itself. The principal attraction is that as a company cannot hold a driving licence and cannot be punished with licence endorsement and penalty points, the offending employee manages to retain a clean licence. This might benefit the company who may rely on the employee's ability to drive. In an effort to minimize this danger, s 172(5) provides that where a body corporate is guilty of an offence under this section and the offence is proved to have been committed with the *consent or connivance of*, or to be *attributable to neglect* on the part of, a *director, manager, secretary* or *other similar officer* of the body corporate, or a person who was purporting to act in any such capacity, he, as well as the body corporate, is guilty of that offence and liable to be proceeded against and punished accordingly. In other words, a company officer who takes part in any decision to subject the company to prosecution rather than revealing the identity of the offending driver will themselves, as individuals, face prosecution for the offence under s 172(3) of the RTA 1988.

PRACTICAL POINT

A response made by a company to a requirement under s 172(2) may be that the company does not keep records of who drives which particular vehicle at any particular time and that the required information cannot therefore be supplied. In an ensuing prosecution, the company may argue the general defence that it did not know *and* could not have ascertained with reasonable diligence who the driver of the vehicle was (see s 172(4) above). Any such argument will fail unless the company can prove not only that it does not keep records but also that not keeping records was *reasonable* in the circumstances (s 172(6)). Given the advanced state of technology and the apparent ease which simple record keeping takes, it is difficult to imagine when not keeping a record would be deemed reasonable.

3.3 **Questions and Answers**

....

Q1 The vehicle keeper has responded to the s 172(2) requirement by completing the relevant forms in the notice and naming himself as the driver. He has not signed the form in space provided for the purpose, nor has he signed it anywhere else. Will this prevent a successful prosecution?

A1 In order to prove the offence then it is necessary to submit the keeper's response into evidence. Section 12 of the RTOA 1988 states that any written statement purportedly signed by the defendant may be admitted into evidence. It is vital that the forms are signed by the defendant in order to comply with s 12. There are numerous cases where defendants have returned unsigned forms and then relied on this requirement to evade conviction (see for example *Mawdsley and Yorke v CC of Cheshire Constabulary* [2004] 1 All ER 58). In order to avoid this regrettable situation occurring, simply ensure that the initial s 172 requirement contains an instruction that the information supplied must be in writing **and** signed by the person supplying it. If the forms are then returned unsigned, the person supplying the information may be treated as not supplying it and may be prosecuted under s 172(3) for non-compliance (see *Francis v DPP* [2004] EWHC 591).

....

Q2 The vehicle keeper has returned the s 172 forms uncompleted but with a separate letter identifying himself as the driver. The letter states that he will not complete the forms sent to him as this will be self-incrimination and infringe his human rights. He also states the letter cannot be used in evidence. He has admitted he is the driver. Can he be successfully prosecuted?

A2 It would seem that he can be prosecuted. There is no need for the information to be supplied on any official forms that the police might send with the s 172 notice. All that is required is that the relevant information be given in writing. If the letter is signed then this would seem to be sufficient to satisfy the requirement under s 12 of the RTOA 1988 as it is a statement in writing purportedly signed by the defendant. Any suggestion that the s 172 procedure conflicts with the defendant's human rights will not succeed (see *DPP v Wilson* [2002] RTR 6). The fact that the letter might state it cannot be used in evidence is meaningless.

....

Q3 The keeper has responded to a s 172 requirement by identifying the driver as a person who is resident overseas and outside the jurisdiction. I suspect this may be an attempt by the keeper to avoid identifying himself as being the driver at the relevant time.

A3 There is nothing to stop you from sending a s 172 notice to a person identified as the driver even though they reside outside the jurisdiction. In the event that the identified person responds and identifies himself as the driver then proceedings may, in a practical sense, become somewhat difficult. It is possible to issue a summons against a person resident in an EU country but this is something about which you will need to consult the CPS. If the reply from the identified person is that they were not in this country on the relevant date or have no knowledge of the keeper or vehicle (or some other similar denial), then you may wish to conduct a further investigation into the response initially supplied by the vehicle keeper. It is possible that you may be able to gather sufficient evidence to reveal an offence such as attempting to pervert the course of justice but, as with all investigations, it depends on the evidence you are able to gather. If the nominated driver simply fails to respond, then unless you can uncover evidence to suggest the information supplied by the keeper is false, there would seem to be no meaningful way forward. One possibility might be to require the keeper to produce insurance for the vehicle that covers the identified driver at the time the offence was committed.

....

Q4 The keeper responds to the s 172 requirement by identifying a person, X, as the driver. The nominated driver, X, is then sent a s 172 requirement but X responds denying that he was the driver. X also states he has no knowledge of who the driver was. I have spoken with X and he appears to be telling the truth and appears credible.

A4 This is not unlike Q3 above. The best course of action is to contact the keeper who was sent the original s 172 requirement. Ask for some evidence to support his assertion that the vehicle driver was in fact X. If the keeper cannot produce any evidence to confirm his assertion that X was the driver then you may consider prosecuting the keeper under s 172(3) for failing to furnish information and/or, if there is sufficient evidence, for attempting to pervert the course of justice. You can consider using X as a prosecution witness for this purpose.

....

Q5 The keeper has returned the s 172 requirement uncompleted. The keeper has asked for disclosure of all evidence suggesting his vehicle has been involved in the commission of an offence. He says he will furnish the information required by the s 172 notice but only after the disclosure he has asked for.

A5 The keeper has no right to any form of disclosure in these circumstances. You may choose to invite the keeper to view the evidence you have if you wish, but there is no necessity to do so. Indeed, as the keeper may not have been the driver at the relevant time, it may be prudent to reveal nothing about the circumstances of the alleged offence at this stage. If the keeper refuses to comply with the requirement then you should consider prosecuting for the offence under s 172(3).

....

Q6 The keeper has nominated X as the driver at the relevant time. X has nominated Y. Y has now nominated Z. I suspect the people involved are making nominations in an effort to pass the six month time limit on proceedings for the initial offence. What action can I take?

A6 In practice many police forces allow longer than the 28 day period for a keeper (or subsequent nominee) to respond to a s 172 requirement. In the face of multiple nominations, there is a risk that the six month time limitation in respect of the original offence may pass. In the absence of any evidence of the nominees and/or keeper conspiring to defeat the time period (and in practice obtaining such evidence would be difficult), you will be left with the option of reporting the relevant nominee for the offence under s 172(3), bearing in mind that this offence is committed 28 days after service of notice.

....

Q7 Do I need to give a caution when giving a verbal NIP?

A7 No you do not need to caution. PACE specifically caters for this situation. You must give a caution when you are going to ask questions of someone you suspect of committing an offence. A caution need not be given if you are merely informing someone that they may be prosecuted for an offence. Although administering a caution is not necessary, it will not prejudice matters if you do.

....

4

Driving with Drink or Drugs

This chapter will be concerned with the laws on driving while unfit through drink or drugs. This area of law can be extremely complex and technical, especially with regard to the procedures that need to be followed in the police station.

In the sections that follow, regard will be given to the principal offences and to the more common situations that are likely to be encountered by patrol officers on a routine basis. The detailed and more technical procedures to be followed at police stations are not dealt with in depth here, although an overview is given.

4.1 Unfitness to Drive

Section 4 of the Road Traffic Act 1988 (RTA 1988) provides that:

(1) A person who, when driving or attempting to drive a mechanically propelled vehicle on a road or other public place, is unfit to drive through drink or drugs is guilty of an offence.

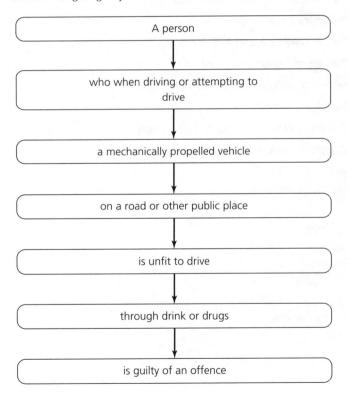

A person

who when driving or attempting to drive

a mechanically propelled vehicle

on a road or other public place

is unfit to drive

through drink or drugs

is guilty of an offence

(2) Without prejudice to subsection (1) above, a person who, when in charge of a mechanically propelled vehicle which is on a road or other public place, is unfit to drive through drink or drugs is guilty of an offence.

(3) A person shall be deemed not to have been in charge of a mechanically propelled vehicle if he proves that at the material time the circumstances were such that there was no likelihood of his driving it so long as he remained unfit to drive through drink or drugs.

An offence under s 4 of the RTA 1988 may be committed in any one of three separate ways. It may be committed by (1) *driving*, (2) *attempting to drive*, or (3) *being in charge* of, a *mechanically propelled vehicle*. (Offences under ss 5, 6 and 7 apply only to motor vehicles). The meanings of driving, attempting to drive, in charge and mechanically propelled vehicle are dealt with above at 1.6.1, 1.6.3, 1.6.4 and 1.2.1 respectively. The defence contained in s 4(3) of the RTA 1988 is considered at 4.3 below.

4.1.1 **Evidence of Unfitness to Drive**

A person is regarded as being unfit to drive if his ability to drive properly is for the time being impaired (s 4(5)). It is vital that the prosecution adduce evidence that the defendant's driving was impaired by drink or drugs but this need not be scientific or expert evidence. (It is, however, entirely acceptable to introduce as evidence of impairment, the results of any blood or urine analysis that may have been conducted.) It may be sufficient to show that the defendant was driving erratically for no obvious reason (eg swerving violently from side to side) provided that there is also evidence of the presence of alcohol or drugs. It is perfectly permissible to give evidence of the smell of drink on the defendant's breath, unsteadiness on the feet, glassy eyes, etc, and if available, appropriate medical evidence may be given as to the defendant's condition. The word 'drug' is defined in s 11 as including 'any intoxicant other than alcohol'. The meaning of 'drug' is clearly very extensive and would extend to many substances that affect the body beyond those clearly identifiable as 'drugs' in the sense that most people recognize (eg cannabis). Insulin, for example, would constitute a drug.

Medical evidence as to the extent of impairment is always useful and, it is suggested, should usually be sought although it may not, however, be essential. In one case, the Divisional Court upheld a conviction where the driver had been driving erratically, admitted cannabis use and blood analysis showed cannabis in the blood, together with the officers' testimony of slow and slurred speech (*Leetham v DPP* [1999] RTR 29).

4.1.2 **Power of Arrest**

The powers of entry and arrest formerly contained in ss 4(6)–(8) of the RTA 1988 have been repealed by the Serious Organised Crime and Police Act 2005. Accordingly, the power of arrest is the general power to arrest without warrant contained in s 24 of the Police and Criminal Evidence Act 1984 (PACE 1984). It follows that a constable must have reasonable grounds for believing that one of the arrest conditions in s 24(5) of the PACE is satisfied.

4.2 **Driving Over Prescribed Limit**

Section 5 of the RTA 1988 provides that:

   (1) If a person—
      (a) drives or attempts to drive a motor vehicle on a road or other public place . . . after consuming so much alcohol that the proportion of it in his breath, blood or urine exceeds the prescribed limit he is guilty of an offence, or
      (b) is in charge of a motor vehicle on a road or other public place, after consuming so much alcohol that the proportion of it in his breath, blood or urine exceeds the prescribed limit he is guilty of an offence.
   (2) It is a defence for a person charged with an offence under subsection 1 (b) above to prove that at the time he is alleged to have committed the offence the circumstances were such that there was no likelihood of his driving the vehicle whilst the proportion of alcohol in his breath, blood or urine remained likely to exceed the prescribed limit.
   (3) The court may, in determining whether there was such a likelihood [of his driving], disregard any injury to him and any damage to the vehicle.

Again, an offence under section 5 may be committed in any one of three separate ways. It may be committed by (1) *driving*, (2) *attempting to drive*, or (3) *being in charge* of a *motor vehicle*. (Offences under s 4 of the RTA 1988 apply to mechanically propelled vehicles). The meanings of driving, attempting to drive, in charge and motor vehicle are dealt with above at 1.6.1, 1.6.3, 1.6.4 and 1.2 respectively.

The courts have held that the word 'consuming' in s 5 is not restricted to just the oral consumption of alcohol. In one case, the Divisional Court held that magistrates were wrong to rule that introducing alcohol to the body by injection was not consumption (*DPP v Johnson* [1995] RTR 9). The 'prescribed limit' is presently 35 microgrammes of alcohol in 100 millilitres of breath, 80 milligrammes of alcohol in 100 millilitres of blood or 107 milligrammes of alcohol in 100 millilitres of urine (s 11(2) of the RTA 1988). These limits may, of course, be reviewed and changed by regulations.

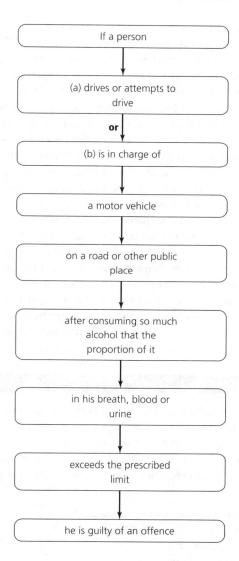

4.3 **Defence to 'In Charge' Offences**

4.3 **Defence to 'In Charge' Offences**

Sections 4(3) and 5(2) of the RTA 1988 provide a defence to the 'in charge' offences under ss 4 and 5. After some debate and uncertainty, the House of Lords has now held that the full legal burden of establishing the defence is on the defendant (*Sheldrake v DPP* [2004] UKHL 43). Accordingly, the defendant must satisfy the court, on a balance of probabilities, that there was no likelihood of his driving the relevant vehicle while unfit or over the prescribed limit, as the case may be. Many factual examples can be found in the law reports but perhaps a common one would be where the defendant is found in charge of a vehicle but is in such a drunken state he might be thought to be 'incapable' of driving. This argument has generally failed because although it might be accepted that the defendant is so drunk that there is no likelihood of his driving at the time of arrest, it is perfectly feasible that as the alcohol level decreases and he begins to recover capability, driving may follow (*Northfield v Pinder* [1968] 3 All ER 854).

The statute also provides that that in determining the question of likelihood of driving, any injury to the defendant or any damage to the vehicle *may* be ignored (ss 4(4) and 5(3)). It follows that, for example, a driver found 'in charge' following an accident which has rendered the vehicle incapable of being driven, may not escape conviction by arguing that the likelihood of his driving was now nil because of the damage. Note, however, the statute uses the word 'may' not 'must'. This gives the court discretion as to whether or not to ignore the injury or damage. No guidance is yet available as to when and how this discretion should be exercised but presumably the court will be influenced by the morality of the situation and in circumstances where the court takes the view that had it not been for the intervention of the damage or injury then the defendant would still have been driving, the damage or injury will be ignored.

PRACTICAL POINT

Whilst it is for the defence to prove that there was no likelihood that the defendant would drive whilst unfit through drink or drugs it makes good sense for the prosecution to prepare to rebut evidence the defence may lead.

Numerous points regarding the circumstances in which the defendant was found may, if appropriate, be made to rebut defence evidence. These might include the following:

(1) Location of vehicle keys (are they in the ignition?)
(2) Is the vehicle engine still warm indicating recent use?
(3) Does the vehicle actually start?
(4) Exact position of the defendant in the vehicle.
(5) Note the weather conditions. (Defendants have been known to say that the weather was so bad they could not walk home and they were merely sleeping in the vehicle until conditions improved.)
(6) Had the vehicle windscreen been cleared of any frost, ice or other obstruction thus indicating preparing to drive?

4.4 **Preliminary Testing**

In 2004, the Railways and Transport Safety Act 2003 replaced the existing legislation with a new regime of testing drivers for the presence of drink or drugs. There are now three types of preliminary test defined in the new provisions. These are a breath test, an impairment test and a drug test.

The RTA 1988 provides:

Preliminary breath test

6A (1)   A preliminary breath test is a procedure whereby the person to whom the test is administered provides a specimen of breath . . . , by means of a device of a type approved by the Secretary of State . . . .

6A (2)   A preliminary breath test administered in reliance on section 6(2) to (4) may be administered only at or near the place where the requirement to co-operate with the test is imposed.

Preliminary impairment test

6B (1)   A preliminary impairment test is a procedure whereby the constable administering the test—
 (a) observes the person to whom the test is administered in his performance of tasks specified by the constable, and
 (b) makes such other observations of the person's physical state as the constable thinks expedient.

6B (4)   A preliminary impairment test may be administered—
 (a) at or near the place where the requirement . . . . is imposed, or
 (b) if the constable who imposes the requirement thinks it expedient, at a police station specified by him.

Preliminary drug test

6C (1)   A preliminary drug test is a procedure by which a specimen of sweat or saliva is—
 (a) obtained, and
 (b) used for the purpose of obtaining, by means of a device of a type approved by the Secretary of State, an indication whether the person to whom the test is administered has a drug in his body.

6C (2)   A preliminary drug test may be administered—
 (a) at or near the place where the requirement . . . . is imposed, or
 (b) if the constable who imposes the requirement thinks it expedient, at a police station specified by him.

The power to administer the preliminary tests is contained in s 6 of the RTA 1988 which provides:

(1)   If any of subsections (2) to (5) applies a constable may require a person to co-operate with any one or more preliminary tests administered to the person by that constable or another constable.

(2) This subsection applies if a constable reasonably suspects that the person—

    (a) is driving, is attempting to drive or is in charge of a motor vehicle on a road or other public place, and

    (b) has alcohol or a drug in his body or is under the influence of a drug.

(3) This subsection applies if a constable reasonably suspects that the person—

    (a) has been driving, attempting to drive or in charge of a motor vehicle on a road or other public place while having alcohol or a drug in his body or while unfit to drive because of a drug, and

    (b) still has alcohol or a drug in his body or is still under the influence of a drug.

(4) This subsection applies if a constable reasonably suspects that the person—

    (a) is or has been driving, attempting to drive or in charge of a motor vehicle on a road or other public place, and

    (b) has committed a traffic offence while the vehicle was in motion.

(5) This subsection applies if—

    (a) an accident occurs owing to the presence of a motor vehicle on a road or other public place, and

    (b) a constable reasonably believes that the person was driving, attempting to drive or in charge of the vehicle at the time of the accident.

4.4.1 A Requirement to Cooperate

The requirement to cooperate with a preliminary test, broadly speaking, arises where the defendant commits (or has committed) a moving traffic offence, is (or has been) involved in an accident, or to any occasion where the defendant is reasonably suspected of having alcohol or drugs in his body while driving or attempting to drive or is in charge (or has been driving, attempting to drive or in charge).

A constable may require any such person as mentioned in ss 6(2)–(5) to cooperate with a preliminary test. Failing to cooperate with a preliminary test is an offence (s 6(6)) and 'fail' includes 'refuse' (s 11(2) of the RTA 1988).

4.4.2 Elements of the Test

A 'preliminary breath test' means a procedure using a device of a type approved by the Secretary of State (s 6A(1) of the RTA 1988). Numerous devices have been approved to date and the legitimacy of the device is unlikely to be an issue.

The officer who administers the test must be in uniform (s 6(7) of the RTA 1988) and this is a question of fact. Case law tells us that the object of this provision is to ensure that the tester is easily identifiable to the defendant as being a police officer. Accordingly, a police officer was held identifiable as such and 'in uniform' despite not wearing his cap or helmet (*Wallwork v Giles* [1969] 114 SJ 36) and even when wearing a civilian raincoat over the rest of his uniform (*Taylor v Baldwin* [1976] RTR 265).

There is no particular format of words to be used when requiring a person to take a breath test. The important point is simply that the words used must be understandable and convey that the request is a requirement.

The power to test arises on reasonable *suspicion* in ss 6(2)–(4) of the RTA 1988 (as opposed to reasonable *belief* in sub-s (5)). This is a question of fact to be determined on the circumstances of any particular case but note—there need not be any actual consumption of an intoxicant. The power in sub-ss (2)–(4) arises on reasonable suspicion, together with the relevant circumstance (ie traffic offence, accident, etc). A reasonable suspicion may arise not only from an officer's own individual observations and knowledge but also from information supplied to him by others. An example would be a radio message informing an officer that a vehicle was being driven erratically (*R v Evans* [1974] RTR 232).

A reasonable belief, as required for sub-s (5), requires a higher degree of certainty in the mind of the officer requiring the test. Again, this remains a question of fact to be decided on all the circumstances of the case.

A 'traffic offence' is defined as any offence under the RTA 1988, the Road Traffic Regulation Act 1984 or the Road Traffic Offenders Act 1988 (s 6(8)(b)). There are some exclusions (relating to driving instructors and fixed penalties) but these are unlikely to be of major practical significance. It is, however, crucial that the offence is committed while the vehicle is in motion.

4.4.3 Defence of Reasonable Excuse

If a person does not provide a preliminary test in the required manner then they cannot be convicted of the offence under s 6(6) of the RTA 1988 if they have a 'reasonable excuse' for failing to do so. The defendant has an evidential burden as to the existence of the reasonable excuse but, once some credible evidence of it has been introduced, it is for the prosecution to rebut the excuse beyond all reasonable doubt. In general terms, a 'reasonable excuse' must arise out of a physical or mental inability to provide the test or specimen (*R v Lennard* [1973] RTR 252).

The most obvious excuse that is likely to be encountered in practice is one based on medical grounds. Conditions like bronchitis or asthma may indeed amount to 'reasonable excuse' but the courts have been fairly consistent in stating that medical evidence of the existence of the condition will normally be required; rarely will the word of the defendant alone be sufficient to justify calling upon the prosecution to rebut it. There is a wealth of case law covering various factual situations that have been advanced as 'reasonable excuses'. These may be consulted in one of the more specialist works available or advice may be sought from the CPS, but to give just a couple of examples may be useful. An 'honest belief' on the defendant's part that he was not 'in charge' is not a reasonable excuse (*Williams v Osborne* [1975] RTR 181). If the defendant receives bad legal advice not to provide a specimen, this is incapable in law of amounting to a reasonable excuse (*Dickinson v DPP* [1989] Crim LR 741). If, however, there is medical evidence that the defendant has a phobia which leads him to refuse or fail to provide, that may amount to a reasonable excuse (*De Freitas v DPP* [1992] Crim LR 894).

4.4.4 Random Testing

There is not, as yet, any specific legal provision that sanctions the random testing of drivers. Nonetheless, it is perfectly legitimate to exercise the general power to stop vehicles given by s 163 of the RTA 1988. Once the vehicle has been stopped the officer may then, for the first time, form a reasonable suspicion that would then justify the administering of a preliminary test. There is a rather subtle distinction in randomly administering breath tests (which is not lawful) and randomly stopping vehicles and then, on forming a reasonable suspicion, administering a test (which is lawful).

4.5 Preliminary Test and Accidents

As previously mentioned, a constable may require cooperation with a preliminary test of any person who he reasonably believes was driving, attempting to drive or in charge of a motor vehicle at the time an accident occurred owing to that vehicle's presence on a road or other public place. Unlike the preceding provisions, the officer must have a reasonable *belief* that the person was driving, attempting to drive or in charge; reasonable *suspicion* alone is not sufficient.

PRACTICAL POINT

It has been held that mistaken use of the word 'suspect' in a statement rather than 'belief' will not invalidate a conviction where the evidence would still lead to the conclusion that the officer actually had a 'belief' (*Johnson v Whitehouse* [1984] RTR 38). Nonetheless, it would be prudent to ensure that all statements in connection with 'accidents' refer to 'belief' in the driver's identity rather than 'suspicion' of the driver's identity.

It is clear that the section requires there be an 'accident' rather than a suspicion there has been an accident. If there is no accident then there can be no lawful test under this provision (*Chief Constable of the West Midlands v Billingham* [1979] RTR 446). It follows that for there to be a lawful test there must, in fact, have been an accident owing to the presence of a vehicle on a road or other public place and the constable must have formed a reasonable belief that the defendant was driving, attempting to drive, or in charge of the vehicle at the relevant time.

PRACTICAL POINT

There is no need for the constable to suspect that drink has been consumed. If there has been an accident and the officer has the necessary belief in identity, then refusal to submit to the test is an offence.

The test following an accident may be administered 'at or near' where the requirement is made or, if the officer thinks fit, at a police station specified by the officer (s 6A(3) of the RTA 1988).

4.6 **Powers of Arrest and Entry**

The powers previously provided under s 4 of the RTA 1988 have now been repealed. The general arrest provisions under s 24 of the PACE 1984 may apply but there is a further specific power of entry and arrest provided by ss 6D and E of the RTA 1988.

4.6.1 **Power of Arrest**

The RTA 1988 provides:

6D (1) A constable may arrest a person without warrant if as a result of a preliminary breath test the constable reasonably suspects that the proportion of alcohol in the person's breath or blood exceeds the prescribed limit.

6D (2) A constable may arrest a person without warrant if—
   (a) the person fails to co-operate with a preliminary test . . . under section 6, and
   (b) the constable reasonably suspects that the person has alcohol or a drug in his body or is under the influence of a drug.

6D (3) A person may not be arrested under this section while at a hospital as a patient.

The power of arrest has two main provisions. A person may be arrested after providing a preliminary breath test under s 6A so long as the officer reasonably suspects that the proportion of alcohol in the breath or blood exceeds the prescribed limit. Reasonable suspicion will, of course, be provided by the test result reading positive. In all other cases of failing to cooperate with a s 6 requirement, the person may be arrested only if the constable has a reasonable suspicion that the person has a drug or alcohol in his body or is under the influence of a drug.

There is no power to arrest under this section for simply failing to cooperate without the additional reasonable suspicion.

4.6.2 Power of Entry

The RTA 1988 further provides:

> 6E (1)   A constable may enter any place (using reasonable force if necessary) for the purpose of—
>
> (a) imposing a requirement by virtue of s 6(5) following an accident in a case where the constable reasonably suspects that the accident involved injury of any person, or
>
> (b) arresting a person under section 6D following an accident in a case where the constable reasonably suspects that the accident involved injury of any person.

In order for this power of entry to apply it is essential that there has, in fact, been an accident which the constable reasonably suspects has involved injury to any person. It is not sufficient that the constable suspects there has been an accident—there must have been an accident. The power of entry may be exercised to impose a requirement, to arrest a person following a positive breath test, or to arrest for failing to cooperate so long as in this latter case the officer reasonably suspects the presence of alcohol or drugs or reasonably suspects the person is under the influence of a drug.

In *Fox v Gwent Chief Constable* [1985] RTR 337, it was held that where the constable was a trespasser and administered a breath test, the conviction for what would now be s 6(6) of failing or refusing a test should be quashed. The further conviction relating to the provision of specimens at the police station was, however, upheld. This leads to the rather curious situation that police officers who, in good faith, trespass on the defendant's own property are not entitled to require a breath test but should they do so and subsequently arrest the defendant for failing or refusing, notwithstanding that the arrest is unlawful, this will not invalidate any subsequent offences detected at the police station. It will however, prevent a conviction for any offence under s 6(6) of the RTA 1988.

4.7 Provision of Specimens for Analysis

A person may only be required to provide specimens of breath for analysis at a police station (s 7(2) of the RTA 1988). If one of five *exceptional* situations applies then it is possible to require blood or urine samples, but not otherwise. In all cases where blood or urine is exceptionally required, the defendant must be warned that failing to provide a specimen may render him liable to prosecution (s 7(7) of the RTA 1988). The five exceptional situations where blood or urine may be required at a police station are contained in s 7(3) of the Act and are:

(1) Where there is reasonable cause to believe that for medical reasons a breath specimen cannot or should not be provided (s 7(3)(a)).
(2) That at the relevant time the approved device is not available or it is not practicable to use it (s 7(3)(b)).
(3) That the approved device has been used but there is reasonable cause to believe it has not produced a reliable indication of the proportion of alcohol (s 7(3)(bb)).
(4) That as the result of a preliminary drug test, there is reasonable cause to believe that the person has a drug in his body (s 7(3)(bc)).
(5) That the suspected offence is one under ss 3A or 4 of this Act and the constable making the requirement has been advised by a medical practitioner that the condition of the person required to provide the specimen might be due to some drug (s 7(3)(c)).

Again, there is wide-ranging case law on these provisions, much of which is beyond the scope of this book and, should the need arise, a specialist reference work may be consulted or advice may be sought from the CPS. What follows is a brief overview of the relevant provisions.

4.7.1 Reasonable Cause to Believe (s 7(3)(a))

Whether or not a constable has reasonable cause to believe that the defendant cannot provide breath specimens for a medical reason is a decision that is entirely the officer's to make. There is no obligation to take medical advice (though it may be prudent to do so if it is available) and the officer may well choose to accept the word of the defendant; no one can reasonably expect the officer to be a medical expert. The draftsman chose to include a requirement for specific medical knowledge in other exceptional situations (see below) but presumably chose not to do so here for good reason. It must surely be sufficient if the officer reaches a decision based on the lay person's view of the circumstances. Note that the section requires the officer to have reasonable cause to *believe* that the specimen cannot be provided for medical reasons, not a *suspicion* that they cannot be provided. It has been held that this is an objective requirement. In other words, the subjective view of the officer himself is irrelevant. What matters is that there exists a reasonable cause for belief that the relevant specimen cannot or should not be provided rather than the personal view of the officer concerned (*Davis v DPP* [1988] RTR 156).

4.7.2 Device Not Available (s 7(3)(b))

A specimen of blood or urine may be required where the machine is unavailable because of a lack of reliability or cannot, for some other practicable reason, be used. A machine with unsatisfactory calibration would clearly meet this condition. If possible and practicable, the defendant may be taken for testing to another police station where a machine is available.

4.7.3 Cause to Believe Device has Produced an Unreliable Indication (s 7(3)(bb))

Some breath testing machines are able to automatically provide the operator with an indication of when the difference between the two breath specimens taken from the defendant exceeds a certain level. Generally speaking, an indication will be given to the operator when the difference between the readings exceeds 15 per cent. If the officer has reasonable cause to believe that the machine has not produced a reliable indication of the breath alcohol level then blood or urine specimens may be required. It would seem to follow that the greater the difference between the two breath readings, the more likely it is that there will be reasonable cause to believe the machine is not producing a reliable indication.

4.7.4 Drugs (s 7(3)(bc) and s 7(3)(c))

The condition in s 7(3)(bc) is self-evident. If a preliminary drugs test reveals the presence of a drug then a blood or urine specimen may be required. The condition in s 7(3)(c) requires that a medical practitioner advise the officer that the defendant's state may be due to the presence of a drug. This latter condition is also restricted to offences under ss 3A or 4. If a medical practitioner so advises then a specimen of blood or urine may be required.

4.7.5 Blood or Urine Specimens

In one of the exceptional situations where blood or urine is to be required (see above) then the choice of which specimen it is to be (ie blood or urine) is the officer's (s 7(4) of the RTA 1988). The only occasion when the officer's discretion may be overridden is where a medical practitioner or health care professional is of the opinion that for medical reasons blood cannot or should not be taken and should this be the case, then urine must be required (s 7(4A)). An important point that should be borne in mind is that, as with any discretion given by law, it has to be exercised *reasonably*. If a defendant advances *legitimate* reasons why blood should not be taken, those reasons should be considered when deciding on how the discretion is to be exercised. In *Joseph v DPP* [2003] EWCH 3078, the defendant explained to the officer that he was a Rastafarian and as a consequence could not give blood. The officer insisted that blood be provided even though there was no reason why urine could not be taken instead. The court held that the officer's choice was so unreasonable as to make it unlawful. It follows that consideration should be given to any reasons advanced by a defendant required to provide a blood specimen as to why this cannot or should not be done.

4.7.6 **Defendant's Right to Choose**

By virtue of s 8(2) of the RTA 1988, a defendant who has provided two specimens of breath for analysis, the lower of which contains no more than 50 micro-grammes of alcohol in 100 millilitres of breath, may require that it should be replaced by a specimen under s 7(4). If that specimen is subsequently provided then neither specimen of breath shall be used. If the specimen so provided then becomes evidentially unfit through no fault of the person providing it, the original machine readings may not be substituted (*Archbold v Jones* [1985] Crim LR 740).

It is *essential* to tell the person the reason why he is being given the option of providing a specimen under s 7(4), ie because the lower of the two breath specimens contained no more than 50 microgrammes. If the person elects to provide the further specimen, then as discussed above, the choice then becomes the officer's as to whether it is blood or urine.

4.7.7 **Specimens without Consent**

Section 7A(1) of the RTA 1988 empowers a police officer to request a medical practitioner to take a specimen of blood from a person irrespective of whether that person consents if:

(a) the person concerned is someone from whom the officer would be entitled under s 7 to require a specimen;

(b) it appears to the officer that the person concerned has been involved in an accident that constitutes or is comprised in the matter under investig-ation;

(c) it appears that the person concerned is or may be incapable of giving a valid consent to the taking of a specimen; and

(d) it appears that the person's incapacity is attributable to medical reasons.

The request may not be made to the medical practitioner who has clinical care of the person (s 7A(2)(a)). (See also hospital patients at 4.8 below.)

The section further provides that the specimen so obtained shall not be sub-ject to analysis unless the person from whom it was taken has subsequently been informed of its taking, has been required to give consent for its analysis, and has so consented (s 7A(4)). A warning that failure to consent may result in liability to prosecution must also be given (s 7A(5)). This provision is designed to allow blood to be taken from those who might otherwise escape convic-tion because, temporarily, they are unable to provide consent. The provision is clearly designed to catch those who are involved in road collisions and are incapacitated for a period of time and it relies on a later consent to analysis being provided by the person concerned.

It is an offence to fail, without reasonable excuse, to give permission for laboratory analysis of a specimen (s 7A(6)). The general meaning of 'reasonable excuse' is discussed at 4.4.3 but in the context of failing to give permission for an *already* taken sample to be analysed, the factual circumstances that might found a 'reasonable excuse' would appear to be severely limited.

4.8 Hospital Patients

Section 9 of the RTA 1988 provides that while a person is at a hospital as a patient he cannot be required to cooperate with a preliminary test or provide a specimen for a laboratory test, or have a specimen taken from him without consent, or be required to give permission for a specimen to be analysed, unless the medical practitioner in immediate charge of his case has been appropriately notified. The medical practitioner may object to any of the proposed courses of action, be they to take specimens or requirements (s 9(1), (1A)). The ground upon which the practitioner may object is that the proposed action would be prejudicial to the proper care and treatment of the patient. The procedure for requiring a specimen for analysis is similar to the procedure that occurs at a police station when requiring blood or urine. The constable shall decide whether the specimen shall be blood or urine but of course, if medical advice is given that blood should not be taken, then the specimen must be one of urine.

4.9 Failing to Provide Evidential Specimen

It is an offence for a person who, without reasonable excuse, fails to provide a specimen when required to do so (s 7(6) of the RTA 1988). 'Fail' includes refusal in the same way as it does with preliminary tests (see 4.4.1 above). The meaning of 'reasonable excuse' is dealt with at 4.4.3 above.

4.9.1 Consuming Alcohol or Drugs after the Offence

By virtue of s 15(2) of the Road Traffic Offenders Act 1988, it is assumed that the proportion of alcohol at the time of the offence is not less than that contained in the certificate of analysis. The section goes on to provide (in sub-s (3)) that this assumption will not apply if the defendant proves two things:

(1) that he had consumed alcohol after he had stopped driving, attempting to drive or be in charge, and before providing the specimen; *and*

(2) that had he not done so the proportion of alcohol would not have exceeded the prescribed limit, or impaired his driving ability.

The burden of proving both these issues lies on the defendant.

PRACTICAL POINT

This is commonly called the 'hip flask' defence. Although it is for the defence to prove that had the additional consumption of alcohol not taken place then the limit would not have been exceeded, it makes sense for the prosecution to be able to rebut any defence evidence on these issues. The most common situation where the defence is likely to be raised is where, following an accident, an offender is found at their home address and states that alcohol has just been taken to 'steady the nerves'. At the relevant address ensure that notes are made recording the defendant's claimed consumption, the amount involved and the number and location of any empty containers. Seize any containers and the contents (if any) that remain. The defendant's height, weight and build should be recorded and as soon as practicable, questions as to food and alcohol consumption during the previous 24 hours need to be put. This information can be used to calculate the rate that alcohol has left the body.

4.9.2 **Detention of Persons affected by Alcohol or Drugs**

Section 10 of the RTA 1988 provides for the detention of persons that have been required to provide specimens. The relevant provisions state:

(1) Subject to subsections (2) and (3) below, a person required to provide a specimen of breath, blood or urine may afterwards be detained at a police station until it appears to the constable that, were that person then driving or attempting to drive a mechanically propelled vehicle on a road, he would not be committing an offence under section 4 or 5 of this Act.

(2) A person shall not be detained in pursuance of this section if it appears to a constable that there is no likelihood of his driving or attempting to drive a mechanically propelled vehicle whilst his ability to drive properly is impaired or whilst the proportion of alcohol in his breath, blood or urine exceeds the prescribed limit.

(3) A constable must consult a medical practitioner on any question arising under this section whether a person's ability to drive properly is or might be impaired through drugs and must act on the medical practitioner's advice.

PRACTICAL POINT

The power contained in s 10 of the RTA 1988 to detain a person after they have provided samples should always be considered. There have been several cases where a person, still over the prescribed limit, has been released from police custody after giving samples but then driven and been involved in an accident. A person cannot be detained if there is no likelihood of them driving or attempting to drive whilst over the limit but this may be a difficult test to apply in practice. It is perfectly possible that a person may have access not only to the particular vehicle they were stopped in but they may also have access to other unknown vehicles. The custody officer may need to justify detention on each specific set of circumstances.

4.10 **Questions and Answers**

Q1 Can the police set up road blocks to test drivers for drink or drugs?

A1 Strictly, no. Nonetheless, the police have the power under s 163 of the RTA 1988 to stop any vehicle that is being driven on a road. Once a vehicle has been stopped, if the officer then has cause to suspect that the driver is under the influence of drink or drugs, he can exercise the power to test the driver accordingly.

Q2 An accident occurs and the two occupants of the vehicle run off. They are both found a short distance away, both smell of drink, but neither will state who the driver was. At this stage, there is no other evidence available to identify which one was the driver. Can both be breath tested?

A2 Yes, both occupants can be breath tested. If the tests are positive then both can be arrested. In order to carry out a test, an officer needs to have a reasonable belief that the person to be tested was driving, attempting to drive or in charge of the vehicle. The presence of such a belief in these circumstances is easily demonstrated.

Q3 A vehicle being driven erratically is stopped. The driver does not, apparently, speak any English. He smells strongly of drink and appears drunk. Even though he does not seem to understand any English can a breath test be required?

A3 A breath test can be required but there may be some practical difficulty if the driver does not cooperate and later uses the language barrier, as a reasonable excuse, to defend charges of failing to provide. In these circumstances, consider the offence under s 4 of unfitness through drink or drugs. The driver may be arrested for this offence and arrangements can then be made for an interpreter to be available at the police station.

....

Q4 A plain clothes officer is at the scene of an accident. He suspects one of the drivers has consumed alcohol and is in excess of the prescribed limit. Can he require a breath test?

A4 Yes, he can require the driver to submit to a breath test. However, the test itself must be conducted by an officer in uniform. Failure or refusal to take the test would still constitute an offence even though the officer who made the requirement was not in uniform.

....

5

Insurance and Vehicle Test Certificates

There is a whole raft of legislation and regulation designed to ensure that a driver of a motor vehicle is safe when driving on a public road. Legislation requires, for example, that drivers are properly licensed and that their vehicles are of acceptable mechanical quality. However, it is inevitable that these provisions will not eliminate all of the inherent dangers to the driver and risks to other road users. In recognition of these inherent dangers, there is a statutory requirement that the vast majority of road users are covered by an after the event insurance policy which *at least* provides security against third-party risks.

5.1 Requirement for Insurance

The relevant law can be found in s 143 of the Road Traffic Act 1988 (RTA 1988) which provides that:

(1) Subject to the provisions of this part of the Act—
   a) A person must not use a motor vehicle on a road or other public place unless there is in force in relation to the use of a motor vehicle by that person such a policy of insurance or such a security in respect of third party risks as complies with the requirements of this Part of this Act, and
   b) A person must not cause or permit any other person to use a motor vehicle on a road or other public place unless there is in force in relation to the use of the vehicle by that other person such a policy of insurance or such a security in respect of third party risks as complies with the requirements of this Part of the Act.

Section 144 of the RTA 1988 then details the occasions where there is no requirement to have a policy of insurance covering the use of a vehicle. These include, *inter alia,* crown vehicles that are being used as such and police vehicles. Also exempt is an off duty police officer using his own vehicle for a police purpose (see *Jones v Chief Constable of Bedfordshire* [1987] RTR 332).

5.1.1 The Offence—s 143

The offence of contravening the requirement for insurance is contained within s 143 of the RTA 1988 and states:

(2) If a person acts in contravention of subsection (1) above he is guilty of an offence.

This offence is wide-ranging and it covers the following situations:

- driving a motor vehicle on a road without valid insurance cover;
- driving a motor vehicle whilst not satisfying the conditions of use permitted by the insurance policy;
- using a motor vehicle for hire and reward—this is a specific condition of use that is usually excluded by most insurance policies;

- permitting a motor vehicle to be driven on a road without valid insurance cover.

PRACTICAL POINT

Many insurance companies have routinely included, as a term of the policy, the right for the policyholder to drive other motor vehicles which do not belong to the policyholder, provided the owner of the other vehicle gives permission. The cover provided is normally limited to third-party liability only. Increasingly, insurance companies are now excluding this cover from new policies and on renewal of existing policies. If a driver states that he is driving someone else's vehicle but using his own insurance, check carefully that the insurance certificate enables him to do so.

5.1.2 Keeping without Insurance—A New Offence

The Road Safety Bill, expected to become law in late 2006, contains a new offence relating to the keeping of an uninsured vehicle. Section 144A of the RTA 1988 will provide:

(1) If a motor vehicle registered under the Vehicle Excise and Registration Act 1994 does not meet the insurance requirements, the person in whose name the vehicle is registered is guilty of an offence.

A number of exceptions are then provided for and include:

- vehicles owned by a police authority or driven for police purposes by or under the direction of a constable;
- ambulances owned by and driven under the control of an NHS Trust;
- stolen vehicles;
- former keepers who have complied with requirements to notify they are no longer the keeper.

Any person claiming to fall within one of the listed exceptions has the burden of introducing some evidence of the exception fit to be considered by the court but once this is done, it is for the prosecution to prove beyond reasonable doubt that the exception does not apply (s 144A(9) of the RTA 1988).

5.1.3 'Using' a Motor Vehicle

As can be seen from the requirements of s 143 of the RTA 1988 above, a person will commit an offence if they 'use' a vehicle without a valid insurance policy. While 'to use' clearly refers to driving, the term is not exclusively restricted to driving a vehicle (see *Samuelson v National Insurance & Guarantee Corporation Ltd* [1986] 3 All ER 417).

Practical Examples

The following are examples of 'use' where, on a road or other public place:

(1) A vehicle is parked, immobilized and unattended.

(2) An employee drives a vehicle owned by his employer (the employer is held to be using the vehicle).

(3) The owner of a vehicle is sitting in the passenger seat and the vehicle is being driven by another person with permission.

(4) The owner of the vehicle expressly orders or authorizes the vehicle to be used.

There is an absolute prohibition (but see employees defence at 5.1.4 below) on using or causing or permitting the use of a vehicle on a road (see *Tapsell v Maslen* [1967] Crim LR 53). This means that the defendant cannot avoid prosecution by claiming to be unaware that the vehicle was uninsured. Similarly it is not important to show that the defendant owns the relevant vehicle, as proof of ownership is not an essential ingredient of the offence (see *Napthen v Place* [1970] RTR 248).

5.1.4 Defence

There is a defence to a charge of using a motor vehicle without insurance. This can also be found in s 143 of the RTA 1988, which provides:

(3) A person charged with using a motor vehicle in contravention of this section shall not be convicted if he proves—

(a) that the vehicle did not belong to him *and* was not in his possession under a contract of hire or of loan;

(b) that he was using the vehicle in the course of his employment; *and*

(c) that he neither knew nor had reason to believe that there was not in force in relation to the vehicle such a policy of insurance or security as is mentioned in subsection (1) above.

The scope of this narrow and exceptional provision is that it provides a defence for employees who use their employer's vehicle in the course of their employment. Each element of s 143(3) needs to be established by the defendant as it is he who has the burden of proof.

5.1.5 The Insurance Policy

For a policy of insurance to be valid under the terms of Pt IV of the RTA 1988, there are certain generic requirements that must be fulfilled. These are set out in s 145 of the RTA 1988. A valid policy must:

- be issued by an authorized insurer;
- cover third-party risk by insuring such persons or class of persons as may be specified in it in respect of any liability which may be incurred by them in respect of death or bodily injury to any person (excluding the driver) or damage to property caused by, or arising out of, the use of the vehicle on a road or other place in Great Britain;
- cover any liability for the payment of emergency treatment of persons injured;
- cover any liability incurred as a result of use within the Member States of the European Union, according to the law on compulsory insurance against civil liability in that state.

Section 145(4) details the exceptions to the requirements. This includes limiting the maximum amount of insurance cover to £250,000 in respect of damage caused to property. Property under the custody or control of the driver need not be included on a policy.

5.1.6 Scope of Policy

Where an insurance policy is restricted to a named individual then, as a general rule, only the named individual will be covered by that policy. However, many policies allow persons to drive with the permission of the policyholder providing such persons are not disqualified from driving and hold or have held a driving licence (see *Digby v General Accident Fire and Life Insurance Corporation* [1943] AC 12; and also *Rendlesham v Dunne* [1964] 1 Lloyd's Rep 1962). This will be acceptable to satisfy the requirements of s 145 of the RTA 1988. However, third-party insurance will only provide coverage to the policyholder if another authorized driver is driving (see 5.1 above).

PRACTICAL POINT

Insurance premiums for young inexperienced drivers are very high, reflecting the risk that insurance companies take when insuring such drivers. To reduce the amount of the premium, many parents insure the vehicle in their own name and have the young driver as a named driver on the policy. As the young driver holds a provisional licence, the insurance company often takes the view that as the named young driver is always accompanied by an experienced driver, then they are less of a risk and the premium is lowered accordingly. However, once the named driver passes the driving test and can drive alone, the insurance company will increase the premium to reflect the higher risk now that the young newly qualified driver may take to the road unaccompanied. When presented with a newly qualified driver using a parent's vehicle, you should check with the insurance company that the policyholder has declared the fact that the named driver has now passed the driving test and is not a provisional licence holder.

> Further, to avoid high premiums, many parents insure vehicles in their own names stating that they (the parent) are the principal user when, in reality, the principal user is the young driver. (Insurance companies routinely require a declaration as to who the principal driver will be.) Enquiries with the insurance company may reveal that the insurance is, in these circumstances, void. You may also consider the offence of making a false declaration to obtain insurance.

5.1.7 Insurance Certificates

Section 147(1) of the RTA 1988 provides that in order for a policy of insurance to have effect, the insurance company needs to provide the policyholder with a certificate in a prescribed format. This certificate should contain details of any conditions of which the policy is subject to. It should be noted that the certificate does not have to contain the registration mark of the vehicle. This means that at court the defendant has the burden of proving that the policy covers the use of the vehicle and this burden cannot always be discharged merely by producing the certificate at court. The defendant should be encouraged to attend court with all relevant insurance documentation (see *Leathley v Drummond* [1972] RTR 29; and also below—Inspection of Documents). If the terms are stated within both the certificate of insurance and the policy of insurance, then it has been held that terms of the policy will prevail (see *Biddle v Johnson* [1965] 2 Lloyd's Rep 121).

PRACTICAL POINT

As with stolen MOT certificates, there is a demand for stolen insurance documents to enable drivers that have been stopped to produce documents that will convince the police that they are correctly insured. The introduction of the insurance database makes it easier for patrol officers to check if a person is insured. If a person admits to the officer that no insurance is in force then matters are straightforward. If, however, the database does not record any insurance, the driver stating that the vehicle has just been acquired, the procedure of issuing an HO/RT 1 would be the norm. In the main, it is cover notes (see 5.1.8 below) stolen from insurance brokers that are most widely available, rather than actual insurance certificates that are issued by the insurance company. Cover notes are stolen in book form and generally handwritten by the thief or handler, relevant details being provided by the driver. They are rarely typed. If a handwritten cover note is presented which shows the broker being some distance away from where the driver lives, a telephone call to the relevant broker (or the relevant insurance company) will often reveal that the document is stolen.

5.1.8 **Cover Notes**

By virtue of s 161(1) of the RTA 1988 cover notes will be accepted as a valid policy of insurance providing they are in the prescribed form. This is of relevance because, clearly, the insurance policy must be shown to have been in force at the time of the journey and coverage is often required at short notice (see *Samuelson v National Insurance Ltd* [1986] 3 All ER 417).

5.2 **Terms and Conditions of Use**

The vast majority of insurance policies will prohibit certain uses or activities and limit the coverage of the policy to 'social, domestic or pleasure purposes'. This term covers a range of activities and has been held to include helping a friend move house (see *Lee v Poole* [1954] Crim LR 942). There is a whole raft of case law to suggest that courts look at the underlying *purpose* of the activity to decide whether the policyholder has strayed outside of the ambit of 'social, domestic or pleasure' (see for example *Seddon v Binions* [1978] RTR 163). However, it is also true to say that rather than having any general rule, the courts tend to scrutinize the facts of each individual case.

5.2.1 **Business Use**

Where insurance cover is obtained by business users, the policy will cover the vehicle being used by the employee in the course of the policyholder's business. This will be the case even where employees deviate from a predetermined route (see *Balance v Brown* [1955] Crim LR 384). As with the situations outlined above, this will be a matter of fact for the Court to determine in each case.

PRACTICAL POINTS

(1)   Not all small business users are aware of the need to upgrade their insurance policy to include business use. It may be helpful to check policies of the self-employed (eg window cleaners, landscape gardeners, builders) to ensure that their insurance coverage is valid.

(2)   Most general policies restrict use of the vehicle to journeys to and from the policyholder's *usual* place of employment. If the policyholder uses a privately owned vehicle at work (eg district nurses, social workers, police officers) then it is necessary to ensure that their insurance policy covers business use. Using a restricted policy for business use would be an offence under s 143(2).

5.2.2 **Hire or Reward**

Most insurance policies will specifically prohibit certain activities due to their inherent risk. Track racing and time trialling are examples of two such activities. A third and more widespread activity and one specifically prohibited by most insurance policies is the use of the vehicle for 'Hire or Reward'. Potentially this could include any journey where money is exchanged in return for a car journey. This may mean that a policy of insurance could be invalid if a friend offers some petrol money for a journey, or car sharing arrangements. In order to exclude such situations, s 150 of the RTA 1988 provides that if the arrangement meets the following conditions then it will not be considered 'Hire and Reward'. The conditions are that:

(1) the vehicle is not adapted to carry more than eight passengers and is not a motor cycle; and
(2) the money given over does not exceed the running costs of the vehicle. This includes wear and tear and can even include depreciation; and
(3) the arrangement for money to be paid for the journey occurred before the journey commenced.

5.3 **Inspection of Documents**

The provision which enables police officers to inspect insurance documentation for possible offences is s 165 of the RTA 1988. The law allows a driver, or someone who a constable believes to be committing a road traffic offence, to be required to produce certain driving documents. These documents will include the certificate of insurance or certificate of security. If these documents are not produced to a constable when required then an offence is committed under s 165(3). However, s 165(3) recognizes that many people do not carry these documents when driving and therefore a person will not be convicted if the documents are produced within seven days (or as soon as reasonably practicable) at a police station.

PRACTICAL POINT

There are instances where a vehicle owner is required to provide the police with the identity of drivers under ss 171 and 172 of the RTA 1988 (see Chapter 3). The owner may give details identifying a driver who is resident in another country. If a requirement to produce insurance is then made to the alleged driver in the other country and (as will be common) no response is received, the owner can be required under s 171 to provide such information as is necessary in order for the police to determine whether or not the vehicle was being driven without insurance. If the owner fails to give such information then he is guilty of an offence under s 171(2) of the RTA 1988.

Unlike the production provisions which apply to a driving licence, the insurance documents do not need to be produced in person. The HO/RT 1 itself requires the production of documents at a police station chosen by the person, not the police officer. The insurance documentation should be produced in such a way that the details can be recorded (see *Tremelling v Martin* [1971] RTR 196).

5.3.1 Returning Insurance Certificates

Section 147(4) of the RTA 1988 provides:

> When a certificate that has been delivered is cancelled by mutual consent or by virtue of any provision in the policy or security then the policy holder must within seven days surrender the certificate or security to the policy issuer or if the certificate has been lost or destroyed then a statutory declaration to that effect must be made.

If these conditions are not met then the policyholder commits an offence (s 147(5)).

5.3.2 Duty of Owner of Motor Vehicle to give Insurance Details

Section 154(1) of the RTA 1988 provides:

> A person against whom a claim is made in respect of any such liability required under section 145 of the Road Traffic Act 1988 must, on demand by or on behalf of the person making the claim—
> (a) state whether or not in respect of that liability—
>   (i) he was insured or had in force a security, or
>   (ii) he would have been so insured or would have had in force a security if the insurer or giver of the security had not avoided or cancelled the policy or security, and
> (b) if he was or would have been so insured,
>   (i) give such particulars as specified in the certificate or security, or
>   (ii) where no such certificate was delivered, give the registration mark or other identifying features of the vehicle, the number or other identifying particulars of the insurance policy, the name of the insurer and the period of insurance cover.

If a person fails to comply with the above conditions or wilfully makes a false statement in response to a demand then he is guilty of an offence (s 154(2)).

> **PRACTICAL POINT**
>
> This section is particularly useful when a 'damage only' accident has occurred and names and addresses have been exchanged without any police involvement. It would be common for one of the drivers to later make an insurance claim against the other. If the other fails to provide proper insurance details then the owner of that vehicle may commit an offence. If the police are contacted for assistance then you should, of course, check that all the legal requirements that arise following a road traffic accident have been complied with (see Chapter 2). You might then advise the owner of the vehicle refusing to provide details of the insurance cover of the obligations placed on him by s 154 and that failure to provide the required insurance details to the other driver may render him liable to prosecution under s 154(2) of the RTA 1988.

5.4 Seizure and Retention of Vehicles Driven without Licence or Insurance

A powerful new weapon has recently been added to the armoury available to police officers dealing with unlicensed and/or uninsured drivers. Section 165A of the RTA 1988 now provides that, subject to certain conditions, a vehicle that is being driven in contravention of s 143 (uninsured) or being driven in contravention of s 87(1) (otherwise than in accordance with a licence), may be seized and removed. A power of entry onto premises, except a private dwelling house, is given for the purpose of exercising the power of seizure.

5.4.1 The Conditions

Licensing

(1) a constable in uniform must make a s 164 requirement for the licence/counterpart to be produced; and

(2) the driver fails to produce the licence/counterpart; and

(3) the constable has reasonable grounds to believe the vehicle is or was being driven in contravention of s 87(1).

OR

Insurance

(1) a constable in uniform must make a s 165 requirement for the driver to produce evidence that the vehicle is not being driven in contravention of s 143; and

(2) the driver fails to produce such evidence; and

(3) the constable has reasonable grounds to believe the vehicle is or was being driven in contravention of s 143.

OR

Fails to stop

(1) a constable in uniform requires, under s 163, a person driving a motor vehicle to stop; and
(2) the person fails to stop, or fails to stop long enough for the constable to make lawful enquiries as thought appropriate; and
(3) the constable has reasonable grounds for believing the vehicle is being driven in contravention of s 87(1) or s 143.

The constable exercising the power of seizure must first warn the driver that he will seize the vehicle if the licence/counterpart is not produced, or evidence of insurance is not produced, unless it is impracticable in the circumstances to give such a warning (s 165A(6) of the RTA 1988). In the case of a seizure following a fail to stop, the seizure power may be exercised at any time within 24 hours beginning with the time at which the relevant condition is first satisfied (s 165A(7) of the RTA 1988).

Practical Example

D, who is driving a motor vehicle, is stopped by a uniformed police officer on traffic patrol duty. The officer suspects, on reasonable grounds, that D has no insurance. As the officer is speaking to D, D drives off at speed. The officer follows and sees that D has parked his vehicle on the driveway of a private house. The officer, who can see D inside the house, attempts to speak to him. D does not respond. The officer may now exercise the power to seize D's vehicle as all relevant conditions are satisfied. (Note—the definition of private dwelling house does *not* extend to any garage or land appurtenant to the dwelling—s 165A(9) of the RTA 1988).

5.4.2 **Retention**

Section 165B of the RTA 1988 enables the Secretary of State to make regulations governing the removal and retention of vehicles under s 165A. The regulations provide for the retention of seized vehicles and their release upon payment of the required fees. The present regulations can be found in Police (Retention and Disposal of Motor Vehicles) Regulations 2002 (as amended), SI 2002/3049 and SI 2005/2702.

5.5 **Vehicle Test Certificates**

All motor vehicles which were first registered more than three years before the time they are used on a road require a test certificate (s 47 of the RTA 1988). The requirement can be illustrated as follows:

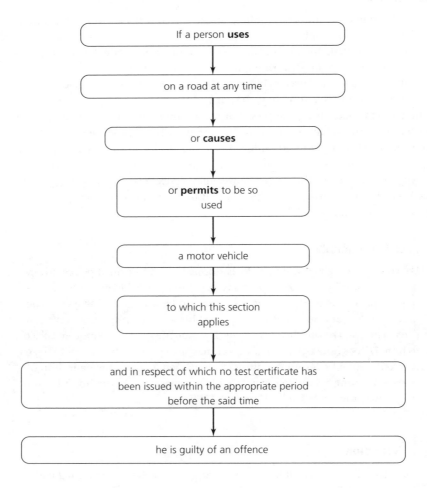

This section applies to all motor vehicles, including those manufactured abroad, that were first registered not less than three years before the date it is being used on a road. Until the three year threshold is reached no test certificate is required. Once the three year threshold has been reached, the vehicle must be tested and the certificate renewed annually. If a vehicle is used on a road, whether in Great Britain or elsewhere, before being registered with the DVLA then the three year period is calculated from the date of manufacture.

Practical Example

Vehicles are commonly used in the Channel Islands and then imported and registered with the DVLA. The V5 registration document will show two dates: (1) the date of manufacture; and (2) the date of first registration in the UK. The three year time period is calculated from the date of vehicle manufacture and not from date of first registration with the DVLA.

Although the vast majority of vehicles do not need a test certificate until three years has elapsed, there are some vehicles that require a test certificate after 12 months. These include:

- motor vehicles used for the carriage of passengers and with more than eight seats, excluding the driver's seat;
- taxis (These vehicles are licensed by local authorities and are tested at specific testing stations which include items that are not featured in a usual MOT test. Such licences are generally issued on a six monthly basis and the vehicles are tested at the same time.);
- ambulances;
- large goods vehicles.

PRACTICAL POINT

Testing stations are now introducing systems where the results of tests are electronically conveyed to the Department of Transport. In these cases a traditional paper MOT certificate is not issued. At present though, there are many stations that are not linked to the electronic database and so the paper MOT will remain for some time to come. Stolen MOT certificates will remain a common problem. It is not unusual for a thief to steal the station's embossing stamp along with the paper certificates. (Embossing stamps are restricted to designated geographical areas.) The same stolen stamp tends to be used irrespective of the geographical area the stolen certificates are ultimately passed on to. If a certificate is produced and the stamp indicates it is from another geographical area, it may be prudent to check when the person acquired the vehicle. It could be that they have acquired it since the certificate was issued or have moved address and nothing is suspicious. However, if the person owned the vehicle prior to the issue date shown on the certificate, then a telephone call to the MOT hotline, found on the reverse of the certificate, may prove fruitful.

5.5.1 Exemptions from the Normal Requirement of a Test Certificate

A number of exemptions exist that allow an untested vehicle to be used on a road. These include:

- Taking the vehicle to or from an approved testing station where a test is to be performed by prior arrangement.
- When a vehicle has failed a test, delivering it by prior arrangement or bringing it from the place where the relevant work is to be or has been carried out.
- When a vehicle has failed a test, taking it to a place where it is to be broken up by towing it.

PRACTICAL POINT

Although test certificates are generally valid for 12 months there is a facility to extend this period. If a vehicle is presented for test within a month of the expiry of the current certificate then, if the vehicle passes the test, the tester can write the expiry date of the new certificate as 12 months from the expiry date of the old certificate. To do this the tester must include the serial number of the preceding certificate that was presented to the tester before he issues the new certificate. For vehicles that are only just three years old, if they are presented up to a month before their third anniversary, then the tester can extend the certificate to 12 months from registration and include the V5 registration document number on the new certificate Using this procedure, a certificate can show a validity period of up to 13 months.

The introduction of a database in which all test results will be collated is likely to mean there will be less cause to require the production of paper test certificates at police stations by issue of form HO/RT 1. However, the power to do so is the same as the power to require production at a police station of a certificate of insurance (see 5.3 above).

5.6 Forgery of Documents

Section 173(1) of the RTA 1988 provides:

A person who, with intent to deceive—

(a) forges, alters, or uses a document or other thing to which this section applies, or

(b) lends to, or allows to be used by, any other person a document or other thing to which this section applies, or

(c) makes or has in his possession any document or other thing so closely resembling a document or other thing to which this section applies as to be calculated to deceive, is guilty of an offence.

The most common documents used in the commission of this offence are:

- driving licences;
- test certificates;

- insurance certificates;
- seat belt exemption certificates.

For a full list of documents see s 173(2).

5.7 **Vehicle Examiners and Testing of Vehicles**

Chief officers of police may authorize police constables to be authorized examiners of motor vehicles (including trailers) under the provisions of s 67(4) of the RTA 1988. Such officers are empowered to conduct roadside tests of vehicles in order to ensure they comply with construction and use requirements (eg brakes, steering, tyres, lights, noise and fume emissions) and that the vehicle's condition is such that its use would not involve a danger of injury to any person (s 67(1)). These officers are provided with a written authority which must be produced if required (s 67(5)).

The driver of the vehicle may ask for the test to be deferred (s 67(6)) and may specify a period of 7 days within the next 30 days. The police must then give two days notice of the day within that seven day period that they intend to carry out the test. If the driver does not specify a seven day period, the police must give seven days notice of their intention to carry out a test. The police are under no obligation to inform the driver that he may defer a test and where a driver requests that the test be deferred, an examiner can decline to defer in certain circumstances. These are:

(1) Where an accident has occurred and it appears to a constable that it is requisite that the test be carried out forthwith, he may require the test to be so carried out or, if he is not to test it himself, may require it to be taken away until such test has been carried out.
(2) If in the opinion of the constable the vehicle is apparently so defective that it ought not to be allowed to proceed without a test being carried out then he may require the test to be conducted forthwith.

5.7.1 **Testing Vehicles on Premises**

A further power to test vehicles is provided for by the Road Vehicles (Construction and Use) Regulations 1986, reg 74. Any vehicle on any premises may be inspected by a constable in uniform (not necessarily an authorized vehicle examiner) to ensure that the brakes, silencers, steering gear and tyres meet legal requirements. There are, however, conditions attached to this power:

- Authorization shall be produced if required to do so. (This would appear to refer only to authorized examiners as the regulation gives authority to any police constable in uniform.)

- The owner of the premises must consent. There is no power of entry onto premises to exercise the power of inspection.
- The owner of the vehicle must consent.
- If the owner of the vehicle does not consent then this can be overcome by serving a notice on him (either personally or left at his address) at least 48 hours before the proposed test. Alternatively, notice may be sent by recorded delivery at least 72 hours before the proposed test.
- The owner's consent is not required if the vehicle was involved in a reportable road traffic accident within the previous 48 hours.

5.7.2 Testing of Goods or Public Passenger Vehicles

Section 68(4) of the RTA 1988 provides that a constable in uniform may at any time require that the person in charge of a *stationary* goods or public passenger vehicle on a road to proceed with the vehicle to a suitable premises where it can be tested. The premises must not be more than five miles away from where the requirement was made. If a person refuses or neglects to comply with the request then he is guilty of an offence (s 68(5)).

PRACTICAL POINT

If an officer exercises his power to stop any vehicle on a road thereby rendering it stationary, he can then go on to require the vehicle to be driven to a testing station, so long as it is within five miles of where the vehicle was stopped.

5.8 Questions and Answers

Q1 A person that was disqualified does not apply for the return of the driving licence that he held prior to being disqualified. He buys a car and insures it. Will the insurance be invalid because he does not hold a current driving licence?

A1 The precise wording of insurance certificate should be examined but most insurance companies will provide valid cover so long as the policyholder holds or has held a driving licence. Subject to this, it follows that the driver would be insured.

Q2 A person is required to produce his insurance. He provides the policy schedule but not the certificate. Is this sufficient to prove that he was insured?

A2 No. Only a certificate is sufficient proof of insurance. The prosecution only need to prove that the vehicle was being used in circumstances that required it to be insured and once this is done, the burden of proving that valid insurance is held lies with the defendant.

Q3 A private motorist has a policy of insurance restricted to social, domestic or pleasure purposes. He shares a journey to work with a colleague who provides money for the journey. Has this now become a business transaction voiding the insurance?

A3 No, so long as certain conditions are met. In short, the vehicle shall not carry more than eight passengers, the price paid must be agreed before the start of the journey, and the price must not exceed the running costs of the journey.

6

Driver Licensing

There are a range of offences and regulations that are connected to driver licensing and documentation. A number of these stray into the area of criminal law and as such are outside the scope of this book. This chapter focuses on aspects of driver licensing from the issue of licences to those who commit licensing and related offences in road traffic law.

6.1 Obtaining a Licence

The relevant legislation governing driver licensing is largely contained in the Motor Vehicles (Driving Licences) Regulations 1999. These regulations are subject to constant revision and updates can be found by accessing the DVLA website. In addition to the 1999 Regulations, there are other pieces of legislation which comprise driver licensing, such as the Road Traffic Act 1988 (RTA 1988). Section 87 of the RTA 1988 requires that any person driving a motor vehicle on a road does so in accordance with a licence authorizing him to drive a motor vehicle of that class.

6.1.1 Classifications of Vehicles and Information Codes

The 1999 regulations provide details of the classifications by virtue of reg 4 and the details are contained in sch 2 to the regulations. Regulation 7 of the 1999 Regulations details the various categories of vehicle that a driver will be viewed as competent to drive. The categories of vehicle that the licence holder is authorized to drive will be shown on the licence and the counterpart. Details on relevant restrictions will appear in the information codes. The information codes will also detail any restrictions that have been imposed on the driver, for example the requirement to wear spectacles.

6.1.2 Driving Tests

The relevant law relating to driving tests can be found in s 89 and s 89A of the RTA 1988. This details the requirement that in order to obtain a licence the would-be driver needs to pass a prescribed driving test before being issued with a licence. The procedure and various provisions for the tests are contained in the 1999 Regulations. The test itself includes a two part theory test. For the practical driving element of the test, the candidate must prove their identity before taking the test. The offence of making false statements is found in s 174(1) of the RTA 1988 which provides that:

(1) A person who knowingly makes a false statement for the purpose of obtaining the grant of a licence under any part of this Act to himself or any other person is guilty of an offence.

There is no need under this provision to show that the making of the false statement actually resulted in the grant of a licence or any other gain.

The minimum age at which a person may take a driving test is governed by s 101 of the RTA 1988. The age will differ depending upon the type of vehicle. A person may start driving a moped or an invalid carriage at age 16. A person may start to ride a motor cycle, small vehicle or tractor at age 17, a medium-sized goods vehicle at age 18 and all other motor vehicles at age 21.

6.1.3 **Driving Licence and Counterpart**

The driving licence together with the photo card was introduced in its current form in 1998. The licences are colour-coded depending upon whether the licence is a full one or not. Provisional licences are green and full licences (even those subject to the different classifications mentioned above) are coloured pink. It is possible for a full licence to act as a provisional licence for other types of vehicles. Details of this will be provided on the licence itself. Prior to 1998, paper licences without any photographic identification were issued. The old style licences are still valid but it is intended that old style licences will be phased out over the course of the next few years as drivers renew their licences with the DVLA. Under reg 20 of the 1999 Regulations, it is an offence to fail to sign a driving licence in ink upon immediate receipt by the licence holder.

6.1.4 **Period of Validity**

To ensure that the photo card provides an accurate pictorial representation of the licence holder, it is renewable every 10 years. By virtue of s 99 of the RTA 1988, all full and most provisional licences are, in most circumstances, valid until the licence holder's seventieth birthday or for three years, whichever is the longer. On their seventieth birthday, the licence holder is able to renew their licence every three years. It is not ordinarily necessary for a person to submit to a medical examination on renewal at 70. The applicant will be asked to self-declare fitness but, so long as the applicant does so, there is no need to obtain independent evidence of fitness to drive (unless it is an LGV or PCV licence—see below). LGV and PCV licences last until the licence holder's forty-fifth birthday or for five years, whichever may be the longer. Following the licence holder's forty-fifth birthday, the licence can be renewed every five years or until the licence holder's sixty-sixth birthday, whichever is the shorter period of time. Following the sixty-sixth birthday, the licence needs to be renewed annually. To renew this type of licence the holder also has to submit to a medical examination, generally performed by a GP, and the result is then forwarded, with the application form to renew the licence, to the DVLA.

6.2 **Production of Licences**

The basic power for a police officer to demand the production of a driving licence is to be found under s 164 of the RTA 1988 which provides that:

(1) Any of the following persons—
    (a) a person driving a motor vehicle on a road,
    (b) a person whom a constable has reasonable cause to believe to have been the driver of a motor vehicle at a time when an accident occurred owing to its presence on a road,
    (c) a person whom a constable has reasonable cause to believe to have committed an offence in relation to the use of a motor vehicle on a road, or
    (d) a person
        (i) who supervises the holder of a provisional licence while the holder is driving a motor vehicle on a road, or
        (ii) whom a constable has reasonable cause to believe was supervising the holder of a provisional licence while driving, at a time when an accident occurred owing to the presence of the vehicle on a road or at a time when an offence is suspected of having been committed by the holder of the provisional licence in relation to the use of the vehicle on a road,

must, on being so required by a constable, produce his licence for examination, so as to enable the constable to ascertain the name and address of the holder of the licence, the date of issue, and the authority by which it was issued.

It should be noted that the requirement to produce the licence imposes a requirement to produce both the paper licence and the photo card. In order for the constable to check the name and address of the licence holder, the date of issue and the issuing authority, the driver must allow the constable a reasonable amount of time to check the licence. Merely showing the constable that the driver is in possession of a licence is not sufficient, nor is quickly flashing the licence at the constable (*Tremelling v Martin* [1971] RTR 196). Failure to comply with this provision is an offence under s 164(7) of the RTA 1988.

6.2.1 **Issuing Form HO/RT 1**

As with the production of other documents, there is provision within the legislation to deal with the commonplace occurrence of drivers not carrying their licence with them. It is possible, under these circumstances, for a police officer to issue a form HO/RT 1 which will require the driver to produce their driving licence at a police station of their choosing within seven days. Unlike the similar requirement under s 165 as regards insurance and MOT certificates, the licence must be produced in person by the relevant driver. The relevant legislation is found in s 164(7) of the RTA 1988 which provides:

(7) Subsection (6) above does not apply where a person required on any occasion under the preceding provisions of this section to produce a licence—

    (a) produces on that occasion a current receipt for the licence issued under section 56 of the Road Traffic Offenders Act 1988 and, if required to do so, produces the licence in person immediately on its return at a police station that was specified on that occasion, or

    (b) within seven days after that occasion produces such a receipt in person at a police station that was specified by him on that occasion and, if required to do so, produces the licence in person immediately on its return at that police station.

Section 164(8) provides that where a person is facing prosecution for the offence of failing to produce a licence it shall be a defence for him to show that within seven days after the production of his licence was required he produced it in person at a police station that was specified by him at the time its production was required. Failure to produce a licence and the requisite photo card as required by a constable is an offence under s 164(6) of the RTA 1988. Where a driver has surrendered his licence to a police officer in relation to the issue of a fixed penalty notice the driver is covered by the provision laid down in s 164(7)(a) of the RTA 1988.

6.2.2 Requirement to Provide Date of Birth

In addition to requiring production of the driving licence, s 164(2) of the RTA 1988 empowers a constable to require a driver to state his date of birth. Regulation 83 of the Motor Vehicles (Driving Licences) Regulations 1999 details the prescribed circumstances when this power can be exercised. These include:

- where the licence is not produced forthwith;
- when produced the constable has a suspicion that it was not issued to the relevant driver;
- the licence has been altered;
- the driver number has been altered removed or defaced.

This requirement can also be made where the person is supervising a learner driver and the constable has reason to suspect that the supervisor is less than 21 years of age.

6.3 Driving Otherwise than in Accordance with Licence

As stated above, s 87 of the RTA 1988 requires that any person driving a motor vehicle on a road does so in accordance with a licence authorizing him to drive a motor vehicle of that class. Accordingly, it is an offence for a driver to drive outside the terms of the licence of which he is a holder. Section 87 provides:

(1) It is an offence for a person to drive on a road a motor vehicle of any class if he is not the holder of a licence authorising him to drive a motor vehicle of that class.

(2) It is an offence for a person to cause or permit another person to drive on a road a motor vehicle of any class if that other person is not the holder of a licence authorising him to drive a motor vehicle of that class.

The offence covers two distinct situations. The first is when a person does not have a licence at all. The second is where a person causes or permits another who has a licence to drive outside of the relevant class authorized (for a discussion of 'causes' or 'permits' see the definitions in Chapter 1). The offence under s 87 of the RTA 1988 only requires the prosecution to prove that the relevant person was driving. Thereafter, the burden switches to the driver to show that the driving was done in accordance with a licence.

Section 88 of the RTA 1988 provides for a number of exceptions in relation to overseas drivers and those drivers who have been disqualified and are in the process of applying for another licence. Generally speaking, visitors from abroad together with new residents can drive using their own domestic driving licences for a period of up to 12 months. After this, they are then required to apply for a licence at the DVLA. Drivers from EU Member States (and some other countries that have an agreement with the UK) can apply to exchange their full domestic driving licence for an equivalent issued by the DVLA.

6.4 **Driving Whilst Disqualified**

There are a number of factors which combine to make driving while disqualified one of the more serious of the road traffic offences. The disqualified person is unlikely to have a certificate of insurance. Additionally, the disqualified driver is showing disregard for the criminal justice process by continuing to drive in spite of the court order prohibiting this.

The relevant legislation is contained within s 103 of the RTA 1988 which provides that:

(1) A person is guilty of an offence if, while disqualified for holding or obtaining a licence, he—
(a) obtains a licence, or
(b) drives a motor vehicle on a road.

By virtue of s 103(2) of the RTA 1988, a licence obtained by a person who is disqualified is of no effect and will not prevent a prosecution under s 103(1)(b). Driving whilst disqualified is an absolute offence and as such, it is no defence for the driver to claim ignorance or unawareness of the existence of the disqualification or that it was still in effect (see *Taylor v Kenyon* [1952] 2 All ER 726).

In order to establish the offence it is necessary for the prosecution to prove two distinct elements. First, the person is driving on a road and second that the person driving on the road was disqualified from driving. If the place where a person is driving is not on a road then the offence will not be complete. The best way of proving disqualification is by a certificate under s 73(4) of the Police and Criminal Evidence Act 1984. Courts will also accept the defendant's own confession that he was disqualified (providing the confession was obtained in interview and under caution). The court will also accept the evidence of someone who was present at court when the disqualification order was made (see *R v Derwentside Magistrates' Court, ex p Heaviside* [1996] RTR 384).

When the disqualification period is at an end, if the person wishes to drive, they must apply for another licence. Once the application has been correctly made to the DVLA, the driver becomes protected by virtue of s 88 of the RTA 1988. If the person drives before the correct application has been made, then he commits the offence under s 87 of the RTA 1988.

6.4.1 Disqualification until Passing Driving Test

Section 36 of the Road Traffic Offenders Act 1988 (RTOA 1988) gives the court a power to disqualify drivers and prevent them from holding a licence until they pass an 'appropriate' test. Section 36(5) of the RTOA 1988 defines an appropriate test as being either an extended test where a person has been convicted of an offence involving obligatory disqualification or disqualification under the totting-up procedure under s 35 of the RTOA 1988. For all other cases, the appropriate test will be a regular driving test as defined under s 89(3) of the RTA 1988. A person who is disqualified under this provision can apply for a provisional licence and drive under the terms of that licence according to s 37(3) of the RTOA 1988. This is because the purpose of the disqualification is to ensure that the driver establish competency to drive and not to remove the driver from the road.

6.5 **Learner Drivers**

Learner drivers must hold the appropriate provisional licence entitling them to drive. These licences generally last until the seventieth birthday of the holder and must be renewed at three yearly intervals thereafter except for those provisionally licensed for motor bicycles or mopeds which last for two years. A provisional licence holder must, when driving a vehicle for which he has provisional entitlement, be under the supervision of a qualified driver and must ensure that the appropriate 'L' plates are displayed (or 'D' in Wales). A person who drives unsupervised and/or without an 'L' plate displayed in the proper manner commits an offence under s 87 of the RTA 1988 (see 6.3 above).

6.5.1 **Motor Cycle Learner Drivers, Mopeds and Large Motor Bicycles**

Learner drivers of motor cycles are restricted to using learner motor cycles as defined (see 1.3) or, if first used before 1 January 1982, to cycles with a capacity that does not exceed 125 cubic centimetres (cc). A moped may not be driven on a road under a provisional licence unless the holder has passed an approved training course (Compulsory Basic Training—CBT) or is undergoing training. An unqualified passenger may not be carried on a moped or motor cycle (reg 16(6)), nor may the rider carry a passenger in any sidecar attached to the cycle. A person who is learning to drive a large motor bicycle (see 1.3) must hold a provisional licence authorizing the driving of motor bicycles (other than learner motor bicycles) and be at least 21 years of age. In addition, such learners must be in the presence and under the supervision of an appropriately qualified instructor who can communicate by radio. The rider must also wear fluorescent clothing.

Motor cycle and moped licence requirements—Summary

If a person holds a provisional motor cycle licence, then before they can ride that machine on a public road CBT must be completed. Once this has been completed, they will be given a certificate and can ride the machine on a road whilst displaying 'L' plates. This entitles the rider to ride on the road for a period of two years without taking any further test. To obtain a full licence entitlement, the rider must pass a motor cycle theory test and then pass a further practical test. If all three elements are successfully completed then a full licence can be applied for.

Light motor cycle licence (Group A1)

If the person takes and passes a test on a motor cycle between 75cc and 125cc, they can ride motor cycles up to 125cc with a power output of up to 11 kW.

Standard motor cycle licence (Group A)

If a person takes and passes a test on a motor cycle between 120cc and 125cc and capable of more than 100 kph then they will be entitled to a standard group A licence. The person is then restricted to motor cycles of up to 25 kW for two years. After the two year period has elapsed, that person can then ride any size of motor cycle.

Direct or accelerated access to larger motor cycles

This method allows riders over 21 years of age, or those who reach 21 before the end of the two year restricted period, to ride larger motor cycles. To obtain a licence to ride such motor cycles the rider must successfully complete a CBT course, pass a theory test if required and pass a practical test on a machine with a power output of at least 35 kW. When training and practising, riders can use larger motor cycles with 'L' plates on public roads, but must be accompanied by an approved instructor using another motor cycle and who is in radio contact. Subject to this, older riders may access larger machines more quickly.

6.5.2 Supervising Learner Drivers

A supervisor of a learner driver is expected to do whatever can be reasonably expected to prevent the learner from acting unskilfully or carelessly or in a manner likely to cause danger (*Rubie v Faulkner* [1940] 1 All ER 285). It is a question of fact whether or not the supervisor has fulfilled the requirements imposed on supervisors. A supervisor must be a properly qualified driver and the regulations define this generally as being a person who is 21 years of age or over, holds a relevant licence and has relevant driving experience. Relevant licence means a full licence and relevant experience means the licence has been held for a period of not less than three years. A supervisor who has a blood alcohol level in excess of the prescribed limit commits an offence under s 5(1)(b) of the RTA 1988 as he is in charge of the vehicle merely by supervising. Equally, a supervisor may be convicted of aiding and abetting a learner driver who is driving with excess alcohol.

6.5.3 Newly Qualified Drivers

The Road Traffic (New Drivers) Act 1995 provides that a driver who acquires six or more penalty points on his driving licence within two years of passing his test may have the licence revoked and be required to take another driving test.

6.6 Physical Fitness to Drive

As has already been mentioned, the nature of driving regulations is such that they are designed to ensure the safety of all road users and pedestrians. It is unsurprising that there is legislation that attempts to ensure that drivers have a sufficient level of eyesight and physical fitness so that they do not pose a danger to themselves or other road users. The relevant legislation is contained within s 92 of the RTA 1988 which requires, *inter alia*, that an application for a licence must include a declaration stating whether the applicant is suffering or has at any time suffered from any relevant disability.

6.6.1 Driving and Disability

Section 94(1) of the RTA 1988 imposes a duty upon drivers to inform the Secretary of State (in reality the DVLA) in writing of any relevant disability which was either not declared or has become more acute. Section 94(3) of the RTA 1988 creates the offence of failure to provide notification to the Secretary of State of a relevant disability as required by s 94(1). Section 94(3)A of the RTA 1988 further augments this offence by making it an offence to drive a motor vehicle before giving the notification required by s 94(1).

6.6.2 Eyesight Requirements

Section 96(1) of the RTA 1988 creates the offence of driving with uncorrected eyesight. It may be that the requirement to wear spectacles is detailed in the information codes. If a constable suspects that a person may be guilty of this offence then under s 96(2) of the RTA 1988, the constable may require that person to submit to an eyesight test. Failure to comply with this requirement is also an offence by virtue of s 96(3) of the RTA 1988. Details of the requirements and procedure of the test are contained within the Motor Vehicles (Driving Licences) Regulations 1999, SI 1999/2864. They are changed and updated on a regular basis and reference to the DVLA website is advised.

PRACTICAL POINT

A driver must be able to read a new style number plate (ie issued after 1 September 2001) from a distance of 20 metres *in good daylight*. If the plate is of the older style then the distance is 20.5 metres (approx 67 feet). Most police vehicles will have the new style number plate fitted so it is an easy matter to measure 20 metres and require a driver to submit to a test. Certainly it may be practical to include this simple test after minor RTCs but it *must* be conducted in good daylight. The officer must also have reason to suspect that a driver may have committed an offence. A general comment of 'I just didn't see him' may be sufficient to provide a suspicion.

6.7 Questions and Answers

Q1 A person that is disqualified from driving is found in the driving seat of a stationary car. Can he be successfully prosecuted for any offences?

A1 No offence is apparent in these circumstances. An offence is only committed when a disqualified driver actually drives a vehicle on a road. If it can be proved that the driver has merely stopped temporarily (ie has pulled into a lay-by) and the journey was to continue, then the person can still be regarded as 'driving' and the offence is committed. Note, however, that it is not sufficient to show that a disqualified driver was merely preparing to begin a journey as driver.

Q2 A person is disqualified for drink driving and receives a mandatory 12 month disqualification. The disqualification period expires. What steps with regard to licensing should be taken in order to lawfully drive on the road again?

A2 They should first apply for their licence to be returned to them; no reminder is sent by the DVLA. If the person drives without applying for a licence then the relevant offence committed is driving otherwise than in accordance with a licence under s 87 of the RTA 1988. Once the DVLA have received an application for a licence the person can lawfully drive on the road—it is not necessary to have physical possession of the licence before driving can begin again. It may, of course, be difficult to know or ascertain when the application is actually received by the DVLA. The prudent advice would be to not drive until there is certainty that the DVLA have received the application which, in most cases, will mean waiting for the licence to be received. (Obviously, valid insurance cover must also be obtained.)

....

Q3 A 16-year-old boy is stopped driving a motor car. As he could not and cannot apply for a licence due to age, is he disqualified from holding or obtaining a licence and therefore driving whilst disqualified?

A3 No he is not. There used to be an offence of driving whilst disqualified by reason of age but this is no longer the case. The offence committed here is one of driving under the age permitted for that class of vehicle and this constitutes driving otherwise than in accordance with a licence contrary to s 87 of the RTA 1988.

....

Q4 If new drivers accumulate six points on their licence are they disqualified?

A4 No they are not. If new drivers accumulate six penalty points on their driving licence during the first two years after passing the driving test the full licence is revoked by the DVLA and reverts to provisional status.

....

7

Construction and Use
and Vehicle Lighting

If a person takes a vehicle onto the road in a poor condition this poses a threat to other road users, either directly or indirectly. It may be that the specific circumstances give rise to a number of potential offences ranging from dangerous driving (as a result of the vehicle's condition—see 2.2) to a simple breach of the Construction and Use Regulations 1986. Construction and Use requirements can be found in the Road Vehicle (Construction and Use) Regulations 1986, SI 1986/1078. There are separate regulations dealing with vehicle lighting (see 7.4). The regulations deal, as the name suggests, with the construction of and equipment used by motor vehicles. They are detailed, sometimes very complex and, in situations that might be called 'non-routine', may need to be carefully studied. Failing to comply with the regulations is an offence (ss 41A, 41B and 42 of the Road Traffic Act 1988 (RTA 1988)) and a summons should indicate both the relevant section of the RTA 1988 and the particular regulation contravened. The offences are often expressed in terms of 'using', 'causing' or 'permitting', the meaning of which is dealt with at Chapter 1.

7.1 Type Approval Systems

In accordance with the European Community's common transport policy, the construction of motor vehicles will, in time, be controlled by type approval schemes based on uniformity of certain conditions throughout the Member States. A 'type approval' system will eventually replace Pt 1 of the regulations which presently deal with the way vehicles are built and equipped. Whether a vehicle is subject to an existing type approval will depend, generally speaking, on its date of manufacture or its date of first use. The present law is contained in ss 54–65 of the RTA 1988 which makes it an offence to use, cause or permit to be used, a vehicle subject to type approval on a road without a certificate of conformity (s 63(1)). If the need arises to determine whether or not a vehicle is subject to a type approval scheme the relevant regulations to be consulted are the Motor Vehicles (Type Approval) (Great Britain) Regulations 1984, SI 1984/981 and the Motor Vehicles (Type Approval for Goods Vehicles) (Great Britain) Regulations 1982, SI 1982/1271.

7.2 Vehicle Defect Rectification

Most offences contained in the Construction and Use Regulations may be dealt with under the Vehicle Defect Rectification Scheme. Generally speaking, offences arising from the use of taxis or large goods vehicles are excluded from the scheme. The scheme is voluntary and discretionary and does not have to be used by either the police or the motorist.

7.2.1 **Procedure**

The correct procedure is as follows. The reporting officer will identify a defect and deal with the alleged offender in the usual way, making notes as appropriate. Participation in the scheme can then be offered to the motorist and, if accepted, the relevant form listing the defects will be issued. The motorist may then have the identified defects remedied and should then present the vehicle at an approved vehicle testing station that will certify that the defects have been rectified. The testing station will charge a fee for this service. Alternatively, the vehicle may be scrapped and the vehicle dismantler may certify that scrapping has taken place. Again, a fee is payable to the dismantler. The certified form should then be sent to the police. In either case, the process has to be completed within 14 days. If these conditions have been met then no prosecution should follow in respect of the defects identified.

PRACTICAL POINT

Participation in the scheme does *not* authorize the motorist to continue driving for 14 days with the defect(s). If the motorist continues to drive the vehicle with the unrectified defect(s) within the 14 day period, the motorist can still be successfully prosecuted.

7.3 **Specific Construction and Use Regulation Offences**

There are numerous situations which the regulations extend to and cater for. The following represent some of the more common and important offences that are likely to be encountered on a more regular basis.

7.3.1 **Speedometers (regs 35 and 36)**

Speedometers must be fitted to all motor vehicles first used on or after 1 October 1937 except:

- agricultural motor vehicles not driven at more than 20 mph;
- invalid carriages;
- motor cycles first used before 1 April 1984 not exceeding 100cc;
- works trucks first used before 1 April 1984;
- certain other vehicles of low speed;
- other vehicles fitted with approved equipment indicating speed.

> **PRACTICAL POINT**
>
> Contrary to popular belief, there is no legal provision that permits a 10 per cent deviation in the accuracy of speedometers. Some police forces may operate a policy of non-prosecution of speeding offences where the excess speed is within a certain percentage of the relevant limit, but this is policy (usually ACPO policy) not law.

The speedometer must at all material times be maintained in good working order and free from any obstruction but it is a defence that:

(1) the defect occurred during the course of a journey; or
(2) at the time the defect was detected, steps had already been taken to have the defect remedied with all reasonable expedition.

> **PRACTICAL POINT**
>
> The burden of proving that the defect arose during the course of the journey will lie with the motorist. Similarly, a motorist who claims to be in the process of taking steps to have the defect rectified will need to produce some evidence to that effect to avoid conviction.

7.3.2 Brakes (regs 15–18 and sch 3)

The brakes that must be fitted to vehicles are detailed in reg 15 but in practice, reg 18 is likely to be the most important. Regulation 18 relates to maintenance contraventions. This widely drafted regulation covers all aspects of the braking system, including type approvals, approval marks and the need to ensure that brakes are maintained in good working order. The requirement to maintain brakes in good and efficient order is an absolute one (*Green v Burnett* [1954] 3 All ER 273). Accordingly, a defendant who claims to have done all that he possibly could to ensure proper maintenance will not have a defence if in fact the brakes are not working efficiently.

> **PRACTICAL POINT**
>
> It is not always necessary to call evidence from an authorized vehicle examiner in order to prove that brakes were not maintained in good and efficient working order. For example, in one case a constable (who was not an authorized examiner) testified that after obtaining the defendant's permission, he was able to push a vehicle forward with the handbrake fully applied. This evidence was found to be sufficient for conviction (*Stoneley v Richardson* [1973] RTR 229).

> Note, however, that the issue in *Stoneley* was straightforward. In complex cases, the more technical evidence of an authorized examiner may be required. All will depend on the facts of the case and the nature of the defect giving rise to the offence.

7.3.3 **Quitting (reg 107)**

Any person who leaves, or causes or permits to be left, a motor vehicle on a road unattended by a person duly licensed to drive it unless the engine has been stopped and the brake set commits an offence. An exception is provided for working fire engines, gas-driven vehicles, or vehicles being used for police or ambulance purposes.

PRACTICAL POINT

The offence is committed if *either* the engine is left running *or* the brake is not set (*Butterworth v Shorthouse* (1956) 120 JP Jo 97).

7.3.4 **Tyres (regs 24–27)**

Prosecutions for contravening the regulations in relation to tyres are now brought under s 41A of the RTA 1988, which provides that an offence is committed if a person contravenes or fails to comply with a construction and use requirement as to brakes, steering gear or tyres. The regulations, in reg 27(1), set out eight different types of defect which will constitute a breach. The eight circumstances are:

(a) the tyre is unsuitable having regard to the use to which the motor vehicle or trailer is being put ... ;

(b) the tyre is not so inflated as to make it fit for the use to which the motor vehicle or trailer is being put;

(c) the tyre has a cut in excess of 25 mm or 10% of the section width of the tyre, whichever is greater, measured in any direction on the outside of the tyre and deep enough to reach the ply or cord;

(d) the tyre has any lump, bulge or tear caused by separation or partial failure of its structure;

(e) the tyre has any of the ply or cord exposed;

(f) the base of any groove which showed in the original tread pattern of the tyre is not clearly visible;

(g) either—

   (i) the grooves of the tread pattern of the tyre do not have a depth of at least 1 mm throughout a continuous band measuring at least three-quarters of the breadth of the tread and round the entire outer circumference of the tyre; or

     (ii) if the grooves of the original tread pattern of the tyre did not extend beyond three-quarters of the breadth of the tread, any groove which showed in the original tread pattern does not have a depth of at least 1 mm; or

(h) the tyre is not maintained in such condition as to be fit for the use to which the vehicle or trailer is being put or has a defect which might in any way cause damage to the surface of the road or damage to persons on or in the vehicle or to other persons using the road.

In everyday policing situations, the most commonly encountered contraventions are likely to concern 'bald' tyres or tyres that do not meet the requirements of minimum tread depth (see (f) and (g) above).

PRACTICAL POINTS

(1) A 'bald' tyre is caught by (f) and means a patch of the tyre where the base of the original groove is no longer clearly visible. Any size of bald patch is contrary to the regulation even if it does not extend to a quarter of the breadth of the tread pattern.

(2) Where the tyre is not bald the regulations require the grooves of the tread pattern to have a depth of at least 1 mm throughout a continuous band measuring at least three-quarters of the breadth of the tread and round the entire circumference of the tyre. If, however, the vehicle is a passenger motor car for not more than eight passengers in addition to the driver, a goods vehicle under 3,500 kg or a light trailer, the minimum depth of tread must be 1.6 mm. This will obviously apply to the vast majority of domestic cars on the road.

Regulation 27(4) contains a number of exemptions to the requirements imposed by reg 27(1)(a)—(g). In practice, the most likely to be encountered are:

- agricultural motor vehicles driven at not more than 20 mph;
- agricultural trailers;
- vehicles that have broken down and which are being drawn by a motor vehicle at not more than 20 mph.

The following table may be a useful reference:

Type tread depths

Passenger motor cars other than cars constructed or adapted to carry more than eight passengers and light trailers	Minimum 1.6 mm in continuous band over at least three-quarters of breadth and around the entire circumference of tyre
Goods vehicles *not* exceeding 3,500 kg maximum gross weight	Minimum 1.6 mm in continuous band over at least three-quarters of breadth and around the entire circumference of tyre
All other applicable vehicles	Minimum 1 mm in continuous band over at least three-quarters of breadth and around the entire circumference of tyre

---

PRACTICAL POINT

To examine tyre treads and pressures accurately a tyre depth and/or pressure gauge should be used. In either case it may be necessary to demonstrate the accuracy of these devices to a court. Your local trading standards authority may test such equipment for you and issue a certificate to show accuracy. Remember that tyre pressures increase when the tyre is hot (eg during use). This is an important point to bear in mind as the recommended pressures supplied by manufacturers are based on the tyre being cold.

Tyre markings

The sidewall of a tyre contains information that can prove useful. As an example, a tyre may typically be marked: **255/55 R 16 100 Y**. The first number, **255**, indicates the tyre width in millimetres. The second number, **55**, indicates the aspect ratio between the height and width of the tyre. The letter **R** indicates the tyre type (ie radial). The next number, **16**, indicates the diameter of the tyre rim in inches. The final number and letter, **100 Y**, indicate the tyre load capacity and maximum speed at load capacity. The following table gives maximum sustainable speeds for tyres under normal use:

Recommended tyre speed ratings

Symbol	Approx max speed (mph)
J	62
K	68
L	75
M	81
N	87
P	93
Q	99
R	106
S	112
T	118
H	130
V	149
W	168
Y	186

PRACTICAL POINT

Manufacturers commonly fit 'space saver' tyres as spares. Tyres of this type have much reduced speed capabilities. If a vehicle is fitted with this sort of tyre and is travelling at high speed then the offence of unsuitable use can be considered and recording the information on the tyre sidewall will be essential evidence.

7.3.5 Reversing (reg 106)

No person shall drive, or cause or permit to be driven, a motor vehicle backwards on a road further than may be requisite for the safety or reasonable convenience of the occupants of the vehicle or other traffic, unless it is a road roller or is engaged in the construction or maintenance or repair of the road.

7.3.6 **Mobile Phones (reg 110)**

Although a contravention of the Construction and Use Regulations, mobile phones are dealt with at 12.5. (See also 7.3.13 below.)

7.3.7 **Weight Offences (s 41B of the RTA 1988)**

Breaches of any requirements relating to weight for goods and passenger vehicles are dealt with by s 41B of the RTA 1988. The section provides that a person who contravenes or fails to comply with a construction and use requirement as to any description of weight applicable to (a) a goods vehicle or a motor vehicle or trailer adapted to carry more than eight passengers; or (b) uses on a road such vehicle which does not comply with such requirement, or causes or permits a vehicle to be so used commits an offence. It is a defence to prove either (a) that the vehicle was proceeding to or from a weighbridge; or (b) that where the excess weight does not exceed 5 per cent, that the limit was not exceeded at the time of loading and no further additions have been made to the load since that time.

PRACTICAL POINT

Only constables authorized by chief officers of police on behalf of the Highways Authority have the power to require a person in charge of a motor vehicle or trailer to have the vehicle weighed and they must produce their authority **before** making the requirement. If, however, the authority is not shown but the vehicle is found to be overweight the offence is still committed. Failure to produce the authority is not a defence (*Wurzal v Reader Brothers* [1974] RTR 383).

7.3.8 **Dangerous Use or Condition (reg 100)**

Regulation 100(1) provides that vehicles and trailers should be maintained and used so as not to cause danger to anyone on the vehicle or trailer or to another road user. The regulation, broadly speaking, caters for three situations:

- that motor vehicles/trailers and all parts and accessories thereof shall at all times be in such condition that no danger is caused or is likely to be caused to any person on the vehicle or on the road;
- that the number of passengers carried by the vehicle/trailer and the manner in which they are carried, must not cause danger to any person on the vehicle or on the road;
- that the weight, distribution, packing and adjustment of the load of the vehicle/trailer shall be such that no danger is caused or is likely to be caused to any person on the vehicle or on the road.

(Remember also the potential, if appropriate, to proceed for the offence of dangerous driving arising from a vehicle's state or condition—see 2.2.)

Regulation 100(2) requires that loads carried by vehicles should be secure and in such a position that neither danger nor nuisance is caused to persons or property by reason of the load or any part thereof falling or being blown from the vehicle.

Regulation 100(3) provides that no vehicle/trailer shall be used for any purpose for which it is so unsuitable as to cause or be likely to cause danger or nuisance to any person in or on the vehicle or on a road.

PRACTICAL POINT

A common example of an insecure load is a large goods vehicle using ropes instead of chains or strapping. The rope proves to be too weak, snaps and the load spills onto the highway. It is no defence for a driver in such circumstances to state that the load was secured with ropes at the outset of the journey. The test is whether or not the load itself was secure. If the ropes have snapped and the load has spilled then clearly it was not secure.

7.3.9 Maintenance of Glass (reg 30)

This regulation provides that all the glass or transparent material shall be maintained so as not to obscure the vision of the driver on the road.

PRACTICAL POINT

This includes *all* glass, side and rear, not just the windscreen. It is important that any visual impairment should obscure the driver's view of the road for an offence to be complete. This offence may be considered for those motorists who do not sufficiently clear their glass on frosty days.

7.3.10 Windscreen Wipers and Washers (reg 34)

This regulation provides that every vehicle fitted with a windscreen shall, unless the driver can see to the front without looking through the windscreen, be fitted with one or more efficient automatic windscreen wipers capable of clearing the screen so the driver can see the road in front on both sides of the vehicle. All vehicles required to be fitted with windscreen wipers must also have a windscreen washer capable of clearing mud or similar deposit.

PRACTICAL POINT

The regulation as to maintenance applies only to those wipers and washers that must be fitted to the windscreen. It follows that the regulation does not apply to rear windscreen washers and wipers.

7.3.11 **Mascots (reg 53)**

No mascot, emblem or other ornamental object shall be carried by a motor vehicle first used on or after 1 October 1937 in any position where it is likely to strike any person with whom the vehicle may collide unless the mascot is not liable to cause injury.

PRACTICAL POINT

Mascots carried on cars like Rolls Royce are spring-loaded. If the vehicle strikes a person the mascot moves and is not liable to cause injury. Spring-loaded mascots of this type are therefore beyond the scope of this regulation.

7.3.12 **Emission of Smoke etc (regs 61 and 61A)**

Every vehicle shall be constructed and maintained so as not to emit any avoidable smoke or visible vapour. No person shall use, cause or permit the use of a motor vehicle from which smoke, visible vapour .... or oily substance is emitted if it causes, or may cause, damage to any property or injury or danger to any person who is, or may be, on the road.

PRACTICAL POINT

This regulation can be used for vehicles that spill oil or diesel on the road surface *if* it can be shown that danger is likely (eg the spillage causes a skidding risk). If confronted with a vehicle that is emitting smoke, it would not be sufficient to merely state that the vehicle was emitting smoke; it would be necessary to demonstrate the potential for danger (ie that the smoke was so severe that the visibility of other drivers was impaired—thus demonstrating the danger element).

7.3.13 **Position to have Proper View or Control (reg 104)**

No person shall drive or cause or permit any other person to drive a motor vehicle on a road if he is in such a position that he cannot have proper control of the vehicle or have a full view of the road ahead. At some point, most road traffic patrol officers will encounter circumstances which give rise to this offence, some of which are likely to cause severe embarrassment to the offender!

The Road Safety Bill proposes to insert a new s 41D into the RTA 1988 as follows:

A person who contravenes or fails to comply with a construction and use requirement—

(a) as to not driving a motor vehicle in a position which does not give proper control or a full view of the road and traffic ahead, or not causing or permitting the driving of a motor vehicle by another person in such a position, or

(b) as to not driving or supervising the driving of a motor vehicle while using a hand-held mobile telephone or other hand-held interactive communication device, or not causing or permitting the driving of a motor vehicle by another person using such a telephone or other device, is guilty of an offence.

In effect, the offence of not being in proper control or using mobile phones while driving enters *primary* legislation for the first time. The offences under s 41D will attract compulsory endorsement and discretionary disqualification.

7.3.14 Opening of Doors (reg 105)

No person shall open, cause or permit to be opened any door of a vehicle on a road so as to injure or endanger any person.

PRACTICAL POINT

The offence is complete when any person is endangered. Actual injury is not necessary. So, for example, opening a car door and causing a pedal cyclist to swerve would constitute the offence even if the cyclist is not harmed or injured in any way.

7.3.15 Exhaust Systems and Silencers (reg 54)

Every vehicle propelled by an internal combustion engine shall be fitted with an exhaust system including a silencer and the exhaust gases from the engine shall not escape into the atmosphere without passing through the silencer. Every exhaust system and silencer shall be maintained in good and efficient working order and shall not be altered so as to increase the noise made by the escape of exhaust gases.

7.3.16 Audible Warning Instruments (reg 37)

Every motor vehicle which has a maximum speed of more than 20 mph shall be fitted with a horn, not being a reversing alarm or a two-tone horn. This does not apply to an agricultural motor vehicle, unless it is being driven at more than 20 mph.

The sound emitted by any horn, other than a reversing alarm or a two-tone horn, fitted to a wheeled vehicle first used on or after 1 August 1973, shall be continuous, uniform and not strident. Horns may not be sounded between 22.30 hours and 07.00 hours or whilst stationary.

Generally, no motor vehicle shall be fitted with a bell, gong, siren or two-tone horn but a bell, gong or siren may be fitted to prevent theft or attempted theft of the vehicle or its contents and also to a bus to summons help for the driver, conductor or an inspector. If the device is fitted to prevent theft and the vehicle was first used on or after 1 October 1982 another device must be fitted so as to stop the bell, gong or siren after it has sounded continuously for more than five minutes. Every such device shall be maintained in good working order. As an exception to the general rule, the following vehicles may fit a bell, gong, siren or two-tone horn:

- if used for fire brigade, ambulance or police purposes;
- if used by a body formed primarily for the purposes of fire salvage and used for those or similar purposes;
- if used by the Forestry Commission or local authority for fighting fires;
- bomb disposal vehicles;
- blood transfusion service vehicles;
- coast guard vehicles;
- mine rescue vehicles;
- Royal Air Force mountain rescue service vehicles;
- Royal National Lifeboat Institute vehicles used for the purposes of launching lifeboats.

7.4 **Lighting**

The law relating to lighting is contained in the Road Vehicles Lighting Regulations 1989, SI 1989/1796, made under s 41 of the RTA 1988 except for cycles which are made under s 81 of the RTA 1988. As with Construction and Use Regulations, the law relating to lighting is often complex and detailed. This section will deal only with the broader principles and those offences and situations that are likely to be encountered on a more regular basis. In complex and difficult cases, reference should be made to the full regulations (see also Appendix 2).

7.4.1 **Scope**

The regulations deal with the fitting of lights, the maintenance of lights and the use of lights. The principal lights referred to are:

(1) headlamps;
(2) front and rear position lights (formerly known as side lights);
(3) stop lamps;
(4) reversing lamps;
(5) fog lamps;
(6) rear registration plate lamps;
(7) other non-obligatory lamps.

7.4.2 **Offences**

A person who causes or permits a vehicle to be used in breach of the 1989 Regulations commits an offence under s 42(b) of the RTA 1988.

7.4.3 **Fitting of Lamps**

The fitting of lamps and reflectors is governed by Pt II of the 1989 Regulations. It is an offence to use, cause or permit to be used on a road a vehicle specified in sch 1 that is not properly fitted with lamps and/or reflectors.

7.4.4 **Headlamps — General Requirements**

All vehicles must have two headlamps fitted except solo motor bicycles and certain other old three-wheeler motor vehicles. Pairs of headlamps must be properly matched and coloured white or yellow. All headlamps must be kept lit during the hours of darkness or during seriously reduced visibility (see 7.4.6 below).

> **PRACTICAL POINT**
>
> If the road is restricted for the purpose of s 81 of the RTRA 1984 (ie 30 mph) and street lamps are actually illuminated, then there is no requirement for headlamps to be used during the hours of darkness. Position lamps (or sidelights) are sufficient in these circumstances.

7.4.5 **Parked Vehicles**

Generally speaking, passenger vehicles constructed or adapted to carry not more than eight passengers, smaller goods vehicles, invalid carriages and motor cycles, that are parked, are not required to display lamps provided that the road is subject to a 30 mph speed limit or less. The vehicle must be parked so that its nearside is close to, and parallel with, the carriageway. In a one-way street then the vehicle may be parked on the right-hand side, again parallel with and close to the carriageway. The exemption from lighting for these parked vehicles also

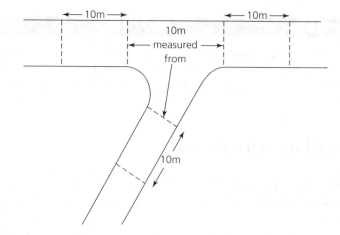

applies only if no part of the vehicle is within 10m of a junction measured from the point at which the kerb edge becomes straight (see diagram above).

7.4.6 Seriously Reduced Visibility

Headlamps must be displayed in conditions of seriously reduced visibility. Whether or not visibility is seriously reduced is a question of fact to be determined according to the circumstances. The phrase is not specifically defined in the regulations or elsewhere but would seem to include fog, heavy rain and snow. Nothing in the regulations confines the phrase to weather conditions and it could, for example, include driving through a dark tunnel.

PRACTICAL POINT

The crux of the offence is that visibility must be seriously reduced and any statement must make reference to the serious reduction in visibility. Take note of all the surrounding circumstances such as traffic flow and reduced speeds, all of which can help illustrate how visibility was seriously impaired.

7.4.7 Fog Lamps

Almost all vehicles first used on or after 1 April 1980 must have at least one rear fog lamp. Vehicles fitted with front fog lamps must ensure they comply with sch 6 as to fitting. It is an offence to use a front or rear fog lamp on a road other than in conditions of seriously reduced visibility (reg 27).

113

PRACTICAL POINT

Many drivers seem to routinely display fog lamps during the hours of darkness as though they were a fashion accessory, oblivious to the annoyance and potential danger this causes to other road users. This constitutes an offence under reg 27.

7.5 **Questions and Answers**

Q1 A vehicle has failed the MOT test and the owner is driving it to a scrapyard to be broken up. Is the vehicle exempt from the need to have a current MOT test certificate?

A1 No. The vehicle may be towed to a scrapyard without an MOT certificate but it may not be driven.

Q2 A person buys a vehicle from a car auction and later finds it has defects that make it unfit for use on a road. Has the auction house committed an offence of supplying an unroadworthy vehicle?

A2 Probably not. There is a statutory defence that if the supplier of the vehicle has reasonable cause to believe that the vehicle will not be used on the road in such a condition then the offence is not committed. Auction houses will commonly be able to bring themselves within the scope of this defence because their conditions of sale usually provide that all vehicles are sold on the understanding that they will not be used on the road in an unroadworthy condition.

Q3 A vehicle has different size tyres fitted to its wheels. Is there any offence committed in these circumstances?

A3 Not necessarily. It is not always an offence to have a different size tyres fitted. It is an offence to have differently constructed tyres (eg cross-ply or radial) on the same axle but some vehicles are manufactured with larger tyres at the rear than the front. Commonly, manufacturers fit 'space saver' tyres as spares and these can be used quite lawfully with those normal tyres fitted to the other wheels. These spare tyres have restrictions as to maximum permitted speeds and if they are used at speeds in excess of those imposed then an offence of unsuitable use can be considered.

If there is a large difference in the size of tyres fitted on the same axle then take advice from the vehicle manufacturer as to how this will affect the handling of the vehicle. If appropriate, consider the offence of unsuitable use but it may well be necessary to obtain expert evidence to proceed with a successful prosecution.

Traffic Signs and Pedestrian Crossings

Directions and instructions (mandatory and/or advisory) may be communicated to road users by signs or signals placed on or near the road. In many circumstances, failing to comply with mandatory directions given by a traffic sign or signal will constitute an offence. Similarly, directions and instructions may also be given to drivers by a police constable (or traffic officer—see further 8.2 below) who is engaged in the regulation of traffic, and failing to comply with a direction may also constitute an offence. Selected provisions that deal with road crossings and street playgrounds are also included in this chapter.

8.1 **Traffic Signs**

A traffic sign is any object or device (whether fixed or portable) for conveying—to traffic on roads—warnings, information, requirements, restrictions or prohibitions of any description (s 64 of the Road Traffic Regulation Act 1984 (RTRA 1984)). Traffic signs must be specified in regulations made by Ministers or authorized by the Secretary of State. The current regulations are the Traffic Signs Regulations and General Directions 2002, SI 2002/3113 and, amongst other things, they provide for signs to be of a certain colour, size and type. A sign may only be placed on or near a road by an authorized person, the principal one being the local traffic authority, but in cases of emergency or temporary obstruction, a constable (or other person authorized by the chief officer of police) may also place a sign on or near a road and this will have legal effect for a maximum of seven days (s 67 of the RTRA 1984). All traffic signs will be presumed to be in conformity with the regulations and lawfully placed unless the contrary is proved (s 36(3) of the Road Traffic Act 1988 (RTA 1988)).

8.1.1 **Temporary Traffic Signs**

A person who is in charge of or who accompanies an emergency or breakdown vehicle which is temporarily obstructing a road is authorized to place a 'Keep Right' sign to warn vehicular traffic of the obstruction caused by the vehicle (reg 15(1) of the Traffic Signs (Temporary Obstructions) Regulations 1997). A driver who fails to comply with the 'Keep Right' sign will commit an offence under s 36 of the RTA 1988 (see 8.1.2 below). The regulations also permit the placing of cones, triangles, warning lamps, delineators and traffic pyramids for the purpose of warning traffic of a temporary obstruction in the road (other than one caused by roadworks). Such signs shall convey to vehicular traffic a warning of a temporary obstruction (reg 4(5–7)).

8.1.2 **Traffic Sign Offences**

The principal offence is failing to comply with a traffic sign contrary to s 36 of the RTA 1988 and this will, in practice, be the offence that you are most likely to deal with. Remember that a Notice of Intended Prosecution (NIP) is required for this offence (see Chapter 3). The s 36 offence applies only to those signs that are listed in reg 10 of the 2002 Regulations and, if in doubt, consult the regulations to make sure the sign you are concerned with is listed. Some of the more commonly encountered signs listed in reg 10 are:

Stop sign

This common sign with a red background is mandatory and must always be obeyed. The word 'STOP' must also be painted on the road surface together with a solid transverse line. Regulation 16 provides that all vehicles must stop before crossing the line or, where the line is not visible, before entering the major road that the sign is protecting. Although it may seem somewhat unnecessary to make the point, the word STOP means the vehicle must be brought to a complete standstill. Attempts by drivers to argue that they have complied with the spirit of the sign by reducing their speed to a crawl without completely stopping have failed (see *Tolhurst v Webster* [1936] 3 All ER 1020).

Give way sign

The road surface will be marked with a triangle and broken transverse lines at the junction. The regulations provide that no vehicle shall cross the transverse line nearer to the major road at the side of which that line is placed, or if that line is not clearly visible, enter that major road, so as to be likely to endanger the driver of or any passenger in any other vehicle or to cause that driver to change the speed or course of his vehicle in order to avoid an accident. It is not necessary for the vehicle to be brought to a complete standstill.

Directional signs

These signs, with a blue background and white arrow, are commonly found at roundabouts. It is important to ensure that the driver alleged not to have complied with this direction sign was within that area of the road to which the sign applies. In one case, a driver did a U-turn in the road 60 feet before reaching a roundabout with a 'Keep Left' sign. The court concluded that no offence under s 36 had been committed because the driver had not entered the area in which the sign became effective (*Brazier v Alabaster* [1962] Crim LR 173).

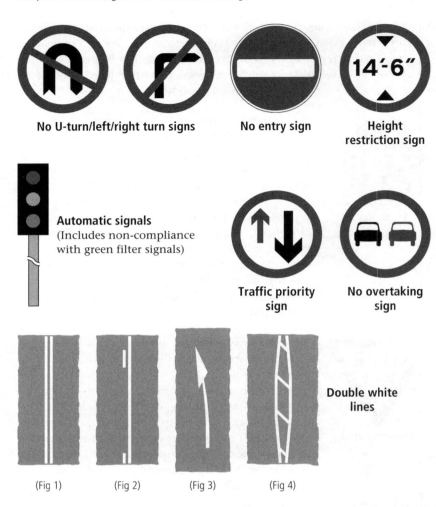

No U-turn/left/right turn signs

No entry sign

Height restriction sign

Automatic signals
(Includes non-compliance with green filter signals)

Traffic priority sign

No overtaking sign

Double white lines

(Fig 1)   (Fig 2)   (Fig 3)   (Fig 4)

The white lines found on roads will be regarded as traffic signs if they indicate a warning, prohibition, restriction or requirement (s 64 of the RTRA 1984). In order to be a lawfully placed sign, a warning arrow must appear on the road at the beginning of a double white line system (see Fig 3 above).

Single white lines

A single broken white line is not a traffic sign and no offence is committed under s 36 if a driver crosses over it (*Evans v Cross* [1938] 1 KB 694).

Double white lines

Regulation 26 of the Traffic Signs Regulations and General Directions 2002 provides that where there is a *system* of continuous (ie unbroken) white lines then:

(i)   no vehicle shall stop on any length of road along which the marking has been placed; and

(ii) no vehicle shall cross a continuous white line that is, when viewed from the direction of travel, on the left of a broken line or of another continuous line.

Non-compliance with a double white line system is an offence and should be prosecuted under s 36 of the RTA 1988.

PRACTICAL POINT

It is *not* necessary for there to be two solid continuous white lines in order to be classed as a white line system. It is a double white line system whenever there are two white lines in the centre of the road *either* one of which is continuous (see Fig 2 above). Consequently, a driver who stops his vehicle on that side of the road which has the continuous solid white line will commit an offence under s 36 of the RTA 1988, even though the second white line is broken.

If there are two continuous white lines that contain hatch markings (as shown in Fig 4 above), then crossing the continuous line and entering the hatch markings also constitutes an offence under s 36.

Exceptions to white line systems

It will not be an offence to stop a vehicle in a continuous white line system if using a lay-by, the vehicle is being used for police, fire or ambulance purposes, the driver is required to stop to comply with the law, or to avoid an accident or he cannot proceed because of circumstances outside his control, to comply with a direction of a constable or traffic warden, or where the road has more than one traffic lane in each direction. It is not an offence to cross a continuous white line if doing so in order to turn right, to pass a stationary vehicle, to avoid an accident, to pass a maintenance vehicle travelling at less than 10 mph, to pass a horse being ridden or led at similar slow speed, to comply with a direction from a constable or traffic warden, or in other circumstances that are outside the driver's control.

8.1.3 **Automatic Traffic Signals**

It is an offence under s 36 of the RTA 1988 to fail to comply with the direction given by an automatic traffic signal (ie traffic lights). The vehicle in question should not proceed beyond the white stop line on the road surface or, if the line is not visible, beyond the post on which the primary signal is mounted. This requirement applies whenever the light is showing red or red together with amber. It also applies whenever the light is showing amber alone unless the vehicle was so close to the light that it cannot be safely stopped without crossing the stop line (reg 36 of the Traffic Signs Regulations and General Directions 2002).

PRACTICAL POINT

The signal will be contravened if *any part* of the vehicle crosses the stop line or, if the line is not visible, travels beyond the post on which the signal is mounted. So if, for example, the vehicle comes to rest with its front part over the stop line and its rear part behind the stop line, the signal has not been complied with. It may be unlikely that a driver would be prosecuted in circumstances like this where the offence is more 'technical' and where the driver has complied with the 'spirit' of the regulations but prosecution may be appropriate if, for example, a pedestrian has been inconvenienced or endangered. If appropriate, consideration may also be given to prosecuting for a more serious offence such as driving without due care and attention.

8.1.4 Other Traffic Signs—s 91 of the Road Traffic Offenders Act 1988

Where the traffic sign is not one listed in reg 10 or other Act, then the offence should be prosecuted under s 91 of the Road Traffic Offenders Act 1988 (RTOA 1988). This would include authorized signs made by Order or Regulation (other than reg 10).

PRACTICAL POINT

Drivers of police vehicles (along with the other emergency services) are permitted by reg 36 to treat a red traffic light as a 'Give Way' sign if observing the red light would hinder the purpose for which the vehicle is being used. In other words, in response to a genuine emergency, they may cross red lights provided it is safe to do so. The exemption applies only to the s 36 offence and does not absolve emergency vehicle drivers from the need to drive with due care and attention. Non-compliance with a red traffic light may be used as evidence of careless or dangerous driving, even in an emergency situation.

8.2 Directing and Stopping Traffic

8.2.1 Power to Direct Traffic

Section 35 of the RTA 1988 contains two offences relating to police powers to issue traffic directions to drivers of vehicles. Section 35(1) states that where a constable or traffic officer (see further 8.2.2 below) is for the time being engaged in the regulation of traffic on a road, anyone driving or propelling a vehicle who neglects or refuses to stop the vehicle or to make it proceed in, or keep to, a particular lane of traffic, when directed to do so by a constable in the execution of his duty commits an offence.

PRACTICAL POINT

The constable must be acting both 'in the execution of his duty' and 'engaged in the regulation of traffic' for the offence to be complete. A constable will be acting in the execution of his duty if he is protecting life and property arising from the danger of unregulated traffic (*Hoffman* v *Thomas* [1974] 1 WLR 374). It would, for example, clearly extend to controlling traffic at the scene of a road accident or where automatic traffic signals have failed. It does not extend, however, to directing traffic for the purposes of a survey or census (but see s 35(2)).

Section 35(2) states that where a traffic survey of any description is being carried out on or in the vicinity of a road, and a constable or traffic officer gives to a person driving or propelling a vehicle a direction (i) to stop the vehicle, (ii) to make it proceed in, or keep to, a particular line of traffic, or (iii) to proceed to a particular point on or near the road on which the vehicle is being driven or propelled, for the purposes of the survey the person is guilty of an offence if he neglects or refuses to comply with the direction.

PRACTICAL POINT

No one can be compelled to actually provide information for survey purposes and so a driver who complies with the direction in s 35(2) but who then refuses to take part in the survey commits no offence. Similarly, the power in s 35(2) should not be exercised so as to cause any unreasonable delay to anyone who indicates they do not wish to take part in the survey.

8.2.2 **Non-Police Traffic Officers**

Section 35 applies not only to directions given by constables but also to directions given by traffic officers. A traffic officer in this context is not a police officer engaged on traffic duties but a person appointed by the traffic authority under the powers contained in the Traffic Management Act 2004 (TMA 2004). Non-police traffic officers have been given limited powers to stop and direct traffic and the TMA 2004 also aims to enable some basic traffic management functions (currently carried out by the police) in future to be carried out by traffic officers. Traffic officers, in carrying out their functions, must comply with any direction given to them by a constable (s 4 of the TMA 2004).

8.2.3 **Power to Stop Vehicles**

A general power to stop traffic is provided in s 163(1) and (2) of the RTA 1988. These sections state that a person driving a mechanically propelled vehicle on a road, or riding a cycle on a road, must stop the mechanically propelled vehicle or cycle when required to do so by a constable in uniform or traffic officer. Any person who fails to comply with the requirement commits an offence (s 163(3)).

8.2.4 **Directing Pedestrians**

Any pedestrian who proceeds along the carriageway and who fails to stop when directed to do so by a constable or traffic officer engaged in vehicular traffic regulation commits an offence (s 37 of the RTA 1988). As with the s 35 offence, the constable must be acting in the execution of his duty (see 8.2.1 above). A constable may require a person committing an offence under s 37 to give his name and address and failing to do so is an offence (s 169 of the RTA 1988).

8.3 **Pedestrian Crossings**

The relevant law that deals with pedestrian crossings is the Zebra, Pelican and Puffin Pedestrian Crossings Regulations and General Directions 1997 (as amended). Toucan (combined cycle and pedestrian crossings) and other crossings are dealt with by the Traffic Signs Regulations 2002.

8.3.1 **Zebra Crossings**

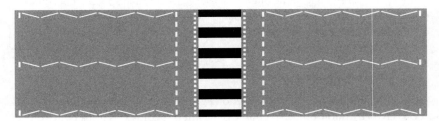

The crossing must conform to the specifications in sch 1 of the Regulations. As the diagram above shows, the crossing must be shown by black and white stripes and there will usually be two lines of studs across the road, although the provision of studs is no longer essential. At each side of the crossing there will be a flashing yellow globe, usually mounted on a black and white post. There will be a system of white zigzag markings on the approach to the crossing, ending in a 'give way' line.

> **PRACTICAL POINT**
>
> If the illuminated globe or globes of the crossing fail or they (or the posts) suffer from any other imperfection or disfigurement, this will not enable a driver to successfully argue that the crossing is no longer properly indicated (see sch 1, Pt 1.4 of the 1997 Regs and below).

8.3.2 Pelican Crossings

A pelican crossing is, in effect, a set of pedestrian controlled traffic lights. As with zebra crossings, there will be a controlled area with zigzag markings on the approach. The light signals will follow the normal sequence of green, amber, red. After the red signal, the lights will flash amber to indicate that pedestrians still have precedence.

> **PRACTICAL POINT**
>
> A zebra crossing has a 'give way' line protecting the limits of the crossing. A pelican crossing (as well as puffin and toucan crossings) has a 'stop line' indicating the crossing limits. If the signal is showing red and a vehicle partly crosses the stop line before coming to a halt then it has failed to comply with the signal (see 8.1.3 above).

8.3.3 Puffin Crossings

A puffin crossing differs from a pelican crossing in several respects but most notably, the crossing has detectors which will extend the time available for pedestrians to cross the road and a further set of detectors will cancel the demand for the crossing if the pedestrian moves away from the crossing area. The traffic lights follow a normal sequence; there is no flashing amber stage. Zigzag markings are laid on both the approach to and the exit of the crossing.

8.3.4 Toucan Crossings

A toucan crossing is provided for both cyclists and pedestrians and is usually associated with a cycleway. A green cycle indicator is provided alongside the green man. The toucan crossing also has detectors which will extend the time available for pedestrians and cyclists to cross the road and a further set of detectors will cancel the demand for the crossing if the pedestrian or cyclist moves away from the crossing area. Zigzag markings are laid on both the approaches and the exits to the crossing.

8.3.5 **Offences**

The Secretary of State is authorized by s 25 of the RTRA 1984 to make regulations regarding pedestrian crossings and it is an offence to contravene the regulations (s 25(5)).

PRACTICAL POINT

There can be confusion as to what is meant by the 'controlled' area of a crossing and the 'limits' of a crossing. It is important to understand the difference between the two terms as some offences are committed in 'limits' and some in 'controlled' areas. The 'controlled' area of any crossing means the whole of the crossing from the beginning to the end of the zigzag markings. In the case of a zebra crossing, the 'limits' of the crossing means that part of the crossing *within* the innermost lines of studs or if there are no studs present, the black and white stripes marked on the road surface. In the case of a light controlled crossing, the 'limits' are that part of the crossing within the stud markings (ie that part of the crossing intended for use by the pedestrian to cross from one side of the road to the other).

Stopping within crossing limits

It is an offence to stop within the crossing limits unless the driver is prevented from proceeding by circumstances beyond his control or he must stop to avoid injury or damage to persons or property (reg 18).

Pedestrian remaining on crossing

It is an offence for a pedestrian to remain on the carriageway within the crossing limits for longer than is reasonably necessary to cross (reg 19).

Stopping within controlled area

The driver of a vehicle shall not cause the vehicle or any part of it to stop in a controlled area (reg 20(1)). Pedal cycles are not vehicles for this purpose (reg 20(2)). Regulations 21 and 22 provide exceptions for stopping:

(1) when giving precedence to pedestrians on the crossing;
(2) in circumstances beyond the driver's control or to avoid injury or damage to persons or property;
(3) where the vehicle is being used for police, fire or ambulance purposes;
(4) for so long as is necessary to enable the vehicle to be used for the purposes of building, demolition or excavation, removing traffic obstructions, roadworks or maintenance of utilities (eg gas, electricity), but only if, in each case, the vehicle cannot achieve its purpose without stopping in the controlled area;

(5) where the vehicle is a PSV on a local service, carrying passengers at separate fares, and is picking up or setting down passengers;

(6) when making a left or right turn.

Failing to comply with red signals

It is an offence to fail to comply with the red signal displayed at a pedestrian controlled crossing (reg 23). An exemption is provided for vehicles being used for police, fire or ambulance purposes in terms similar to those discussed at 8.1.4 above. No NIP is required for this offence.

Overtaking within controlled area

It is an offence to overtake any moving motor vehicle on the approach to a crossing within the controlled area (ie within the zigzag markings) or overtake a stationary vehicle in the controlled area that has stopped *either* to allow pedestrians to cross or at a red signal (reg 24).

PRACTICAL POINT

The overtaking offence can only be committed on the *approach* to the crossing, so overtaking a vehicle that has already entered the limits of the crossing or on the exit side of the crossing is not an offence. Overtaking means allowing any part of that vehicle (the overtaking vehicle) to pass ahead of the other vehicle (the overtaken vehicle). It is *not* necessary for the overtaking vehicle to completely pass the overtaken vehicle. So, for example, if two cars approach a zebra crossing along side each other with the nearside vehicle being closer to the crossing than the offside vehicle, the driver of the car on the offside cannot allow any part of his vehicle to move ahead of the foremost part of the vehicle that is on the nearside.

Failing to give precedence to pedestrians at zebra crossing

It is an offence to fail to give precedence to a pedestrian at a zebra crossing not controlled by a constable or traffic warden, provided the pedestrian is within the crossing limits, and is on the carriageway before the vehicle has entered the crossing limits (reg 25(1)). Where there is a central reservation or other similar refuge, with a zebra crossing on either side, then each side shall be treated as a separate crossing (reg 25(2)).

Failing to give precedence to pedestrians at pelican crossing

It is an offence when the lights at a pelican crossing are showing flashing amber to fail to give precedence to a pedestrian, provided the pedestrian is within the crossing limits, and is on the carriageway before the vehicle has entered the crossing limits (reg 26). A person travelling solely on foot is clearly a pedestrian, but whether the courts will be prepared to interpret the natural meaning of that word to include, for example, people pushing bicycles or propelling scooters by foot, remains to be seen. In earlier legislation, the regulations referred to 'foot passengers' rather than 'pedestrians' and the courts held that a person who was walking on two feet and pushing a bicycle was a foot passenger but had that person been using it as a scooter with one foot on a pedal then they would not be a foot passenger (*Crank v Brooks* [1980] RTR 441). This might suggest that a similar interpretation will be adopted when the word pedestrian falls to be interpreted in the new legislation, but the matter remains arguable and uncertain. The offences in regs 25 and 26 impose a duty upon a driver to give precedence to any pedestrian crossing within the limits of the crossing. This duty includes approaching and driving at a speed so as to enable him or her to stop the vehicle should a pedestrian step out into his or her path (*Hughes v Hall* [1960] 1 WLR 733). The duty appears therefore to be strict and liability absolute. However, the general defence known as 'automatism' is still available. In other words (and put simply), the driver must be in conscious control of the vehicle and if something occurs which, through no fault of his own, takes that control away, then he will not be guilty of the offence. An example would be where the driver has a seizure, like an epileptic fit, or is propelled forward because he is struck from behind by another vehicle (see *Burns v Bidder* [1967] 2 QB 227).

8.4 School Crossings

A school crossing patrol can, in certain circumstances, require the driver of a vehicle to stop and remain stationary. The person in charge of the crossing patrol (affectionately known as the 'lollipop' man or woman) must be wearing an approved uniform and exhibiting the prescribed sign to require drivers to stop.

School Crossing

The driver must, when the sign is exhibited, stop in a manner that does not impede the person crossing (s 28(2)(a)) and must remain stationary for so long as the sign is exhibited (s 28(2)(b)). Failure to do either is an offence (s 28(3) of the RTRA 1984). As with traffic signs generally, once it is proved that a sign was exhibited it will be presumed that the sign was of the proper type as required by the regulations (s 28(5)(a) of the RTRA 1984). Similarly, once it is proved that a school crossing patrol was wearing a uniform, the uniform will be presumed to be of the approved type (s 28(5)(b) of the RTRA 1984). Consequently, a driver who wishes to challenge the legitimacy of the sign or the uniform bears the burden of proof on that issue. There is no longer any restriction on the operating times of a school crossing patrol nor is there any requirement that children must be crossing for the section to be effective.

PRACTICAL POINT

The most common situation an officer is likely to encounter is receiving a complaint from a crossing patrol that a motorist has failed to stop. If the alleged offender is traced and denies the incident then, practically speaking, the CPS is unlikely to take proceedings in the absence of any other supporting evidence. One avenue that might be considered is to obtain a supporting statement from any witnesses; presumably the crossing patrol was acting to allow pedestrians to cross. It may be possible to identify who those pedestrians were and then obtain the necessary further evidence.

8.5 **Questions and Answers**

....

Q1 If the white stop line at automatic traffic signals has worn away could a driver argue that he has not committed an offence if he fails to stop at the signal?

A1 If the stop line is not visible then the regulations clearly state that drivers must not allow any part of their vehicle to proceed beyond the post on which the primary signal is mounted. The primary signal is the one nearest to the vehicle from the perspective of the traffic flow. In most cases, the primary signal will be the one mounted on the nearside of the road as the driver approaches. This rule applies to ordinary automatic traffic signals and crossings controlled by automatic signals.

....

Q2 What if a traffic sign is damaged or defective in some way—say a red signal at traffic lights is not working properly for instance. Can a driver still be prosecuted for failing to comply with a traffic sign that is defective?

A2 If you are considering prosecuting a driver under s 36 of the RTA 1988 then, as mentioned at 8.1 above, the law presumes the sign has been properly placed and conforms to the regulations. If, however, a sign is damaged or defective in some way, then a driver may argue that as the sign does not conform to the regulations then no offence has been committed. The burden of proving that the sign does not conform to the regulations falls upon the driver. The courts have ruled that even though a sign may still be clearly recognizable, if it does not actually conform to the specifications set out in the regulations then it is of no legal effect (*Davies v Heatley* [1971] RTR 145). It would, of course, still be possible to consider alternative offences (eg driving without due care and attention) in appropriate circumstances.

....

Q3 How does a central reservation affect pedestrian crossings?

A3 If it is a zebra crossing, then a central reservation always turns the crossing into two separate and independent crossings. If it is a pelican (or other light controlled) crossing, then this is treated as one single crossing unless they are staggered in some way. In other words, if the two pelicans are *not* in a straight line straddling the central reservation they should be treated as two separate crossings. If they are in a straight line on either side of the central reservation, then they should be treated as one single crossing.

....

Q4 It is not uncommon to find faded zigzag lines at crossings or broken beacons at zebra crossings. Could a driver argue that this means he cannot be properly convicted of a relevant offence—say overtaking within the controlled area?

A4 The 1997 regulations make provision for this type of situation. As far as zebra crossings are concerned, then a failure or defect in the beacons will not stop the crossing from being treated as properly signed and indicated (see 8.3.1 above). A driver could not successfully defend a charge of, for example, failing to give precedence to a pedestrian on the basis that one of the beacons was not illuminated. Where the other road markings are discoloured or displaced then it becomes a matter of judgment, the regulation providing that so long as the 'general appearance' of the markings remains intact, then the zebra crossing is still properly indicated. As regards other crossings (pelicans, puffins, etc) then the position is similar. The regulations provide that if studs or road markings are discoloured, temporarily removed or displaced, the crossing remains properly signed unless the general appearance is 'materially impaired'. It will be for a court to determine whether any alleged defect has impacted sufficiently so as to materially impair the appearance of the crossing as a whole. If you notice any defect on a crossing, it would be good practice to make a record of it and perhaps, if possible, photograph it. If there is no defect with the crossing then again, it makes good sense to briefly include in your evidence the fact that that the crossing was checked and all markings etc were clearly visible.

....

Operators Licences, Driver Hours and Tachographs

This chapter will look at the law relating to operator's licences, drivers' hours and tachographs (see 1.4 and 1.5 for relevant definitions of goods and passenger vehicles). The two areas most commonly encountered by officers are likely to be concerned with operators' licences and drivers' hours. Driver hours are one of the most complex of all topics in road traffic law and it is neither desirable nor possible in a work of this type to cover all conceivable situations that might arise. The aim of this section is to summarize the principal issues most likely to be encountered by officers on patrol. In more complex cases specialist advice should be sought.

9.1 Goods Vehicle Operator's Licences

9.1.1 General Requirements

An operator's licence is generally required when goods vehicles carry goods in connection with a trade or business. The licence is issued by the traffic commissioners. The relevant requirement can be found in s 2 of the Goods Vehicles (Licensing of Operators) Act 1995 (GV(LO)A 1995) which provides:

> (1) ... no person shall use a goods vehicle on a road for the carriage of goods—
>   (a) for hire or reward, or
>   (b) for or in connection with any trade or business carried on by him, except under a licence issued under this Act; and in this Act such a licence is referred to as an 'operator's licence'.

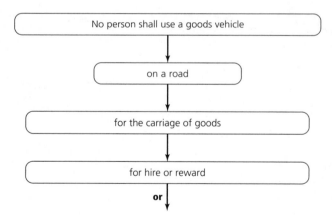

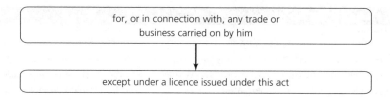

The licence issued may extend to vehicles or trailers in the licence holder's possession. It may contain conditions, prohibitions and/or restrictions relating to various aspects of the operation (eg weight restrictions).

9.1.2 **Exemptions**

Numerous vehicles are exempted from the need to have an operator's licence. The principal exemptions are:

- Small goods vehicles with a plated weight of 3.5 tonnes or less or, if the vehicle does not have a plated weight, an unladen weight of 1,525 kg or less.
- Goods vehicles used for international carriage of goods by a haulier established in a Member State other than the United Kingdom and not established in the United Kingdom.
- Goods vehicles used for international carriage by a haulier established in Northern Ireland and not established in Great Britain.
- Vehicles specified in regulation 33 of the Goods Vehicles (Licensing of Operators) Regulations 1995, SI 1995/2869.

Schedule 3 of the 1995 Regulations provides a long list of vehicle exemptions. The principal exemptions that may be encountered are:

- vehicles used for police, fire brigade or ambulance purposes;
- vehicles used for fire fighting or rescue operations at mines;
- vehicles used by or under control of Her Majesty's United Kingdom forces;
- a road roller and any trailer drawn by it;
- an electrically propelled vehicle;
- a showman's goods vehicle and any trailer drawn thereby;
- a steam propelled vehicle;
- a recovery vehicle;
- a vehicle which is being used for snow clearing, or for the distribution of grit, salt or other materials on frosted, icebound or snow covered roads or for going to or from the place where it is to be used for the said purpose or for any other purpose directly connected with those purposes;
- a trailer not constructed primarily for the carriage of goods but which is being used incidentally for that purpose in connection with the construction, maintenance or repair of roads.

> **PRACTICAL POINT**
>
> Manufacturers recognize that there is a market for vehicles that are exempt from operators' licences and commonly aim to produce small goods vehicles with an unladen weight of 1,525 kg or less. As mentioned above, these smaller goods vehicles do not need to be plated. (An example would be certain Ford Transit box vans.) As these vehicles are not plated, this may lead to some practical difficulty in establishing weight. A quick and practical method of discovering the weight of the vehicle is to examine the Vehicle Excise Licence. The Excise Licence will show the vehicle's weight and thus it can be determined whether or not an operator's licence is required.

9.1.3 Types of Operators' Licence

The GV(LO)A 1995 provides for two types of operators' licence. These are the standard GV(LO)A 1995 licence and the restricted licence. The standard licence allows the operator to use the vehicle for hire or reward **or** in connection with the holder's trade or business. The licence can be issued for international use and/or national use. The restricted operators' licence restricts the holder to the carriage of goods only in connection with his trade or business. It cannot be used for the carriage of goods for hire or reward.

9.1.4 Offences

It is an offence to use a vehicle without an operator's licence (s 2 of the GV(LO)A 1995). It is necessary to prove that the vehicle concerned was carrying goods at the relevant time.

> **PRACTICAL POINT**
>
> It is necessary to show that any goods carried were for hire or reward **or** for use in connection with the person's trade or business. A legitimate inference may be drawn from the type of goods being carried. So if, for example, the vehicle has goods that can be associated with a person's trade (eg a trolley on a furniture removal van), this is good evidence that any goods carried are in connection with the person's trade or business.

It is also an offence under s 22 of the GV(LO)A 1995 for any person to contravene any condition attached to a licence of which he is the holder (eg goods not to exceed a certain weight). Routinely, one condition attached to all licences, is an obligation to report to the traffic commissioners, any change of circumstances which come to the notice of a transport manager within 28 days.

PRACTICAL POINT

Complaints are often received about large goods vehicles being parked overnight in residential areas to the annoyance of local residents. One method of dealing with such complaints is as follows.

An operator's licence has to specify the location of the operating centre. The 1995 Act defines the operating centre as *'the base or centre at which the vehicle is normally kept'*. If it can be shown that the vehicle is not *normally* kept at the specified centre (ie because it is being parked in a residential area away from the operator's base), then the company's transport manager should be informed that this may be in breach of the licence. Hopefully, the conduct will cease but if not, evidence of the circumstances should be collected and a report sent to the traffic commissioners for their consideration.

It is also an offence for a person, with intent to deceive, to forge or alter an operator's licence. Similarly, it is an offence to lend or allow a licence to be used by another, or make or possess any document or other thing so closely resembling a licence, plate, mark or other thing by which a vehicle is to be identified as being authorized to be used under an operator's licence so as to be calculated to deceive (s 38). This offence would, therefore, extend to forged, altered or illegally manufactured identity discs (see further 9.1.6 below).

9.1.5 **Other Powers**

The following additional powers are given to police officers:

- An officer or police constable may require production of an operator's licence by the holder within days at an operating centre or (if the requirement is made by a constable) at a police station nominated by the licence holder (reg 26).
- An officer or police constable may, at any reasonable time, enter premises of an applicant for, or holder of, an operator's licence and inspect any facilities for maintaining vehicles in a fit and serviceable condition. It is an offence to obstruct the officer or constable exercising these powers (s 40).
- If an officer or police constable has reason to believe that (a) a document or article carried on or by the driver of a vehicle, or (b) a document produced to him under this Act, is a document or article in relation to which an offence under s 38 or s 39 relates, the officer or constable may seize the document or article (s 41).

9.1.6 **Identity Discs**

Holders of operators' licences normally use more than one vehicle. The traffic commissioners must be notified of each vehicle that the holder intends to operate under the licence and for each of these vehicles, the holder will be provided with an 'identity disc'. The identity disc is colour-coded to show the type of operator's licence under which it has been issued. The colour codes are:

- blue for a standard (national) licence;
- green for a standard (international) licence;
- orange for a restricted licence.

The licence holder shall cause the identity disc, appropriate to the vehicle, to be fixed to, and exhibited in a legible condition on that vehicle in a waterproof container. The disc should be fixed to the nearside of the windscreen near to the lower edge or, in the case of a vehicle without a windscreen, it should be exhibited in a conspicuous position on the front or nearside of the vehicle (reg 23). Only the traffic commissioners (or persons authorized on their behalf), can write on, or make any other alteration to, the disc.

9.1.7 Temporary Addition of a Motor Vehicle

The operator's licence will specify which vehicles are allowed to be used under its terms. There may be occasions, however, where the operator may wish to use another vehicle not specified in the licence. Where a specified vehicle has been rendered unfit for service, or withdrawn from service for overhaul or repair, the licence holder can inform the traffic commissioners of his desire to have a variation in the licence specifying an alternative vehicle to replace the specified vehicle. Any vehicle used on a temporary basis will not, of course, have an identity disc.

9.2 Driver Hours—Community Rules

The topic of driver hours, as mentioned at the outset, is extremely complex. Hours may be restricted and controlled depending upon a number of factors such as, for example, the type of vehicle and the type of journey. The interrelationship between domestic law and European law further complicates this topic. The following summarizes some of the principal points likely to be encountered on a more frequent basis but in any case of doubt, specialist advice should be sought.

9.2.1 Drivers' Hours—General

The appropriate law to be complied with depends on the type of vehicle and the nature of the work associated with the journey. There are two principal pieces of legislation. These are:

- Community rules contained in Council Regulations (EEC) 3820/85 and 3821/85; or
- Domestic rules contained in the Transport Act 1968.

The rules govern maximum driving hours and rest periods and the Community rules were implemented in an effort to harmonize laws throughout the European Union. This regulation applies to:

(1) all goods vehicles that exceed 3.5 tonnes permissible maximum weight; and
(2) all passenger vehicles which in construction and equipment are suitable for carrying more than nine persons including the driver.

9.2.2 When Will the Rules Apply?

Generally speaking, the Community rules apply to:

(1) all journeys made in vehicles used for the carriage of passengers or goods within the EC; and
(2) to journeys to, from or through non-EU countries if that country has entered into an agreement to comply with the rules; although
(3) certain UK-only journeys made by certain vehicles are exempt from the Community rules. The UK exempted journey/vehicle *may*, however, need to comply with the domestic rules.

PRACTICAL POINT

The starting point should always be to assume the Community rules apply unless there is reason to conclude otherwise. The most frequent reason for not applying the Community rules will be because the vehicle falls within an exempt category (see 9.2.3 below).

9.2.3 Exempted Vehicles

A long list of exempted vehicles appears in Article 4 of the Community Regulations and also in the Community Drivers' Hours and Recording Equipment Regulations 1986. The following are just *some* examples of exempted vehicles taken from the regulations so, in any case of doubt, the full list in the relevant regulation should be consulted.

Exempted by Article 4

- vehicles used for the carriage of passengers on a scheduled service where the route covered by the service in question does not exceed 50 kilometres;
- vehicles with a maximum authorized speed not exceeding 30 kilometres per hour;
- vehicles used by or under the control of the armed services, civil defence, fire service and forces responsible for maintaining public order;
- vehicles used in connection with sewerage, flood protection, water, gas and electricity services, highways maintenance and control, refuse collection and

disposal, telephone services, carriage of postal articles, radio and television broadcasting and the detection of radio or television transmitters or receivers;

- vehicles used in emergencies or rescue operations;
- specialized vehicles used for medical purposes;
- vehicles transporting circus and funfair equipment;
- specialized breakdown vehicles;
- vehicles undergoing road tests for technical development, repair or maintenance purposes, and new or rebuilt vehicles which have not yet been put into service;
- vehicles used for non-commercial carriage of personal goods;
- vehicles used for milk collection from farms and the return to farms of milk containers or milk products intended for animal feed.

Exempted by the 1986 Regulations

- vehicles carrying animal carcasses not intended for human consumption;
- vehicles carrying live animals for slaughter between market and slaughterhouse or between farm and market;
- vehicles not exceeding a weight of 7.5 tonnes carrying materials for the drivers use within a 50 kilometre radius of the vehicle base;
- vehicles used for driver instruction so long as no goods for hire or reward are carried.

9.2.4 Community Rules for Non-Exempt Vehicles

Driver hours

The permitted driver's hours under Community rules are generally as follows:

(1) maximum period of continuous driving without break—4.5 hours;
(2) maximum daily driving hours—9 hours (but can be 10 hours twice a week);
(3) maximum driving period in any one week—56 hours;
(4) maximum driving period in any one fortnight—90 hours.

Rest breaks

(1) at least 45 minutes break after maximum permitted period of continuous driving unless the driver is beginning a daily or weekly rest period;
(2) the 45 minute break can be replaced by breaks of at least 15 minutes taken during the maximum continuous driving period as long as they total the 45 minutes required to be taken after the maximum driving period (ie 3 × 15 minutes during the 4.5 hours is permissible).

PRACTICAL POINT

Breaks are in addition to daily rest periods (see below). The driver of the vehicle may not perform any other work during a rest break although 'waiting time' (eg at a train or bus station) is not 'work' for this purpose.

Daily rest periods

(1) drivers must have daily rest period of at least 11 consecutive hours in any 24 hour period;

(2) the daily rest period can be reduced to at least 9 consecutive hours not more than three times a week if an equivalent period is given before the end of the following week.

Weekly rest periods

(1) a weekly rest period of 45 hours must be taken after no more than six daily driving periods;

(2) a weekly rest period may be postponed until the end of the sixth day provided that the total driving is no more than six daily periods.

PRACTICAL POINT

(1) A week for the purposes of the regulations commences at midnight on a Sunday.

(2) A driver may deviate from the above provisions in order to reach a suitable stopping point, provided always that road safety is not jeopardized and it is necessary to ensure the safety of the vehicle, its load or the safety of persons (Art 2).

9.3 **Driver Hours—Domestic Rules**

If a vehicle journey is subject to the Community rules then the domestic rules do not apply but if the Community rules do not apply then consideration must be given to the domestic rules.

9.3.1 **Type of Vehicle**

The domestic rules are made applicable according to the vehicle type. Part VI of the Transport Act 1968, s 95 (as amended), applies the rules to the following types of vehicle:

(1) Public service vehicles;

(2) Motor vehicles (other than public service vehicles) constructed or adapted to carry more than 12 passengers;

(3) Goods vehicles—defined as

(a) Heavy locomotives, light locomotives, motor tractors and any motor vehicle so constructed that a trailer may by partial superimposition be attached to the vehicle in such a manner as to cause a substantial part of the weight of the trailer to be borne by the vehicle (eg articulated vehicles) or

(b) Other goods vehicles constructed or adapted to carry goods other than the effects of passengers;

(4) Vehicles in the public service of the Crown (but not police, fire, navy, military or air force vehicles).

9.3.2 Driver Hours—Domestic Rules

Driver hours

The permitted driver's hours under domestic rules are generally as follows:

(1) maximum period of continuous driving without break—5.5 hours;

(2) maximum daily driving hours—10 hours;

(3) maximum daily working hours—11 hours;

(4) maximum working period in any one week—60 hours.

The daily working hours may be extended to 12.5 hours if within that period the driver is not working for an amount of time equivalent to or greater than the amount of time by which the 11 hour maximum is exceeded.

Rest breaks

(1) at least 30 minutes break after maximum permitted period of continuous driving unless the break is taken within that period;

(2) at least 11 hours rest each day;

(3) at least 24 hours rest each week;

9.3.3 Modifications to Domestic Rules

If a driver spends all or the greater part of a working day driving passenger vehicles then the basic rules at 9.3.2 above have been modified by the Drivers' Hours (Passenger and Goods Vehicles) (Modifications) Order 1971. The daily driving hours and continuous driving period remain at 10 hours and 5.5 hours respectively. After the continuous driving period of 5.5 hours, a break of at least 30 minutes must be taken and refreshment must be obtainable. A further 15 minute break must be taken within any 8.5 hour period, making the total driving time no more than 7.75 hours after which a further minimum break of 30 minutes must be taken. The total working day must not exceed 16 hours (including other work and rest periods).

9.4 **Tachographs**

Drivers are obliged under both Community rules and domestic rules to keep accurate records of their journeys. The Community rules regarding the fitting and use of tachographs apply to all those vehicles in s 97 of the Transport Act 1968 (see 9.3.1 above). If the vehicle is exempted by the Community rules (see 9.2.3 above) then a tachograph need not be fitted or used. In practice, the overwhelming majority of situations will require records to be kept in the form of a tachograph and, for this reason, only tachograph records (rather than other paper records) are dealt with here.

9.4.1 **Nature, Fitting and Use of Tachographs**

All EU vehicles to which the Community rules on drivers' hours apply must be fitted with a tachograph unless exempted. Tachographs may only be fitted and repaired by fitters or workshops approved for the purpose. A tachograph must be capable of recording certain activities. The activities capable of being recorded include:

- distance travelled;
- speed;
- driving time;
- other periods of work or of availability;
- breaks from work and daily rest periods;
- opening of the case containing the record sheet;
- interruptions in the electrical supply (except illumination) to the distance and speed sensor.

Where there are two drivers, the equipment must be capable of recording simultaneously but distinctly and on two separate sheets, the driving time, other periods of work, breaks from work and daily rest periods. Tachograph charts record the speed of the vehicle and the time. The record can be used as evidence in a speeding prosecution by either the prosecution or the defence. It may also be used in other cases (eg dangerous or careless driving). The time recorded on the tachograph must be the time which agrees with the official time in the country of registration and so time differences for foreign vehicles must be taken into account.

PRACTICAL POINT

Drivers of vehicles fitted with tachographs may seek to use the charts to prove that at the time of an alleged speeding offence they were travelling at a different speed than that alleged. The time on the tachograph is set by the driver who should, of course, ensure that it is accurate. The time on any automatic speed detection device is set by the operator who should also ensure it is accurate. Any discrepancy between the time settings on both devices, no matter how small, would result in the tacho-graph chart showing a different recorded speed for the relevant time. This seriously undermines the reliability of the tachograph chart should a speeding allegation be defended in this way.

Fitted tachographs must be inspected and re-calibrated every six years or after a repair. The driver and the employer are both obligated to ensure the tachograph is in proper working order.

9.4.2 **Chart Use**

General points

Article 15 of the Regulations provides that drivers shall use the record sheets every day on which they are driving. Records must start from the moment they take charge of the vehicle and charts must not be withdrawn before the end of the daily working period unless withdrawal is otherwise authorized. No record sheet shall be used to cover a period longer than that for which it is intended. (Most charts are designed to cover a 24 hour period and as such if they are left in the machine for more than 24 hours the machine will begin to overwrite the previous recordings.)

Return of charts to employer

A driver or driver's mate must return any record sheet which relates to him, to his employer within 21 days of completing it (s 97A). (For offences see below.) If he has two or more employers he must notify each employer of the name and address of the other.

Entries to be made by driver on tachograph chart

The driver (and driver's mate if appropriate) has to enter on each chart used the following information:

(1) on beginning to use the sheet, his surname and first name;
(2) the date and place where the use of the sheet begins and the date and place where such use ends;
(3) the registration number of each vehicle to which he is assigned;

(4) the odometer reading at the start of the first journey recorded on the sheet and the odometer reading at the end of the last journey recorded on the sheet (and this will be in kilometres). In the event of a change of vehicle during the working day, he must enter the odometer reading of the vehicle to which he was assigned and the vehicle to which he is to be assigned;

(5) the time of any change of vehicle.

Charts to be retained and produced by drivers

Drivers and mates, when requested by an authorized officer, must produce charts for the current week and, in any case, for the last day of the previous week on which he drove. A week commences at midnight Sunday. (For offences see below.)

> **PRACTICAL POINT**
>
> When a tachograph head is opened to remove the chart for inspection, the fact that it has been opened is recorded on the chart. The driver may well have to account for this to his employer and/or others. As an authorized officer, if you remove a chart for inspection, you should sign it in an empty part of the chart so as not to interfere with any recordings. This will then verify that the machine was opened for the chart to be inspected by an authorized officer.

Dirty or damaged charts

Article 15 further provides that record sheets shall be adequately protected from becoming damaged or dirty and drivers shall not use a record sheet that is damaged or dirty. If a sheet that bears recordings becomes damaged, then the driver shall attach the damaged sheet to the spare sheet used to replace it. (For offences see below.)

Issue and retention of charts by employers

Employers shall issue sufficient charts of an approved type for use in the equipment installed in the vehicle. When deciding how many charts to issue, the employer should bear in mind that they may become damaged or be taken by authorized officers. The employer shall keep the charts in good order for a period of at least 12 months after their use. The employer must give copies of the charts to drivers on request. Note that the driver is entitled to a copy, not the original, which should always be retained by the employer. (For offences see below.)

Inspection of charts

By virtue of s 99(1) of the Transport Act 1968, an officer may, on production if so required of his authority, require any person to produce, and permit him to inspect and copy:

- any book or register that person is required by regulations to carry or have in his possession for the purposes of making in it any entry required by those regulations or which is required under those regulations to be carried on any vehicle of which that person is the driver;
- any book or register that person is required to preserve;
- any record sheet which that person is required by the regulation to retain or produce;
- if that person is the owner of a vehicle to which the Transport Act 1968 applies, any other document which the officer may reasonably require to inspect for the purposes of ascertaining whether the provisions of the Act or regulations have been complied with;
- any book, register or document required by the applicable Community rules which the officer may reasonably require to inspect for the purposes of ascertaining whether the requirements of the applicable Community rules have been complied with, and that record sheet, book, register or document shall, if the officer so requires by notice in writing served on that person, be produced at the office of the Traffic Commissioner specified not less than 10 days from the service of the notice;
- the officer can detain the vehicle in question during such time as is required to exercise his powers.

An officer means an examiner appointed under s 66A of the Road Traffic Act 1988 and any person authorized for the purposes of s 99(1) of the Transport Act 1968 by the Traffic Commissioner for any area. The powers conferred on such officers shall also be exercisable by a police constable, who shall not, if wearing uniform, be required to produce any authority. It is a matter for the officer to decide whether to visit the premises of the operator and require the production of documents or to give 10 days notice requiring their production at a Traffic Commissioner's office.

9.4.3 **Principal Offence**

The principal offence can be found in Article 3 of the Council Regulations 3821/85 and s 97(1)(B) of the Transport Act 1968. The Act and Regulations provide that it is an offence to use, cause, or permit to be used, a vehicle to which the tachograph provisions apply unless:

(a) there is in the vehicle recording equipment which
   i. has been installed in accordance with the regulations;
   ii. complies with the regulations; and
   iii. is being used as provided by the regulations; or
(b) In which there is recording equipment which has been repaired (whether before or after installation) otherwise than in accordance with the regulations.

A person shall not be convicted of the offence if he can prove to a court that:

(1) the vehicle in question was proceeding to a place where such equipment that would comply with the regulations was to be installed; or
(2) in a case where it is alleged the equipment is not in working order, that it had not become reasonably practicable for the equipment to be repaired by an approved fitter or workshop and the requirements to keep manual records were being complied with.

9.4.4 Other Offences

The principal offence is underpinned by numerous others relating to the improper use of tachographs and associated record keeping. These offences may be found in s 97(1)(B) and (C) of the Transport Act 1968 and Council Regulations 3821/185. In outline, the offences include:

- using damaged or dirty record sheets;
- failing to ensure the tachograph is running continuously;
- failing to operate the switch mechanism correctly;
- failing to enter correct information on record sheets;
- failing to produce record sheets;
- failing to keep records;
- failing to ensure seals remain intact (see further 9.4.5 below);
- failing to hand in record sheets after 21 days.

An employer may, in appropriate cases, be liable for using, causing or permitting an offence committed by a driver. Employers may, in their own right, commit other offences. These include:

- failing to issue sufficient record sheets to driver;
- failing to retain record sheets for 12 months;
- failing to fit tachograph to required vehicle;
- failing to allow records to be inspected.

9.4.5 Seals on Tachograph Equipment, False Entries and Alterations

When tachograph equipment is fitted to a vehicle, several seals are fitted to deter persons from tampering with the equipment. Seals generally take the form of twisted metal wire that is crimped together with a lead seal. It is rather similar in appearance to the seals placed on electricity or gas meters in ordinary dwelling houses. The seals may only be fitted by approved fitters or workshops. Section 97AA of the Transport Act 1968 makes it an offence for a person, with intent to deceive, to forge, alter or use a seal on recording equipment installed in a vehicle, or destined for installation in a vehicle to which s 97 applies.

A seal is forged if it is a 'falsely manufactured' seal. In any case, the offence is not complete unless it can be proved that the defendant 'intended to deceive'.

143

In other words, the defendant must intend (ie desire or aim) to fool others into believing the seal is genuine. Also note that the vehicle must be one to which s 97 applies (ie a PSV, vehicle constructed or adapted to carry more than 12 persons or goods vehicle). If a vehicle does not have to have a tachograph fitted but nonetheless does have one, the offence does not apply.

A defence

A person shall not be liable to be convicted of the offence above if he can prove to a court that any seal which is not intact on the recording equipment is not intact because:

(1) the breaking or removal of the seal could not have been avoided;
(2) it had not become reasonably practicable for the seal to be replaced by an approved fitter or workshop; and
(3) in all other respects the equipment was being used as provided by the regulations.

False entries and alterations

It is an offence for any person to make, or cause to be made, any record or entry on a record sheet carried for the purposes of the Community Regulations or under s 97 of the Transport Act 1968, which he knows to be false or, with intent to deceive, alters or causes to be altered, any such record or entry (s 99(5)). If an officer has reason to believe an offence under sub-s (5) has been committed, he can seize the record or document. If no person is charged with an offence in relation to that record or document within six months of its seizure, or it has not been returned, then that person or an officer can apply to a magistrates' court to make an order as to the disposal of the record or document.

Vehicle Excise Licences and Registration

The law relating to vehicle excise duty and registration of vehicles is found in the Vehicle Excise and Registration Act 1994 (VERA 1994). Generally speaking, excise licences are required by all mechanically propelled vehicles used or kept on a road maintained at public expense and recent reforms have extended the circumstances in which duty becomes payable on a vehicle.

10.1 **Vehicle Excise Licences**

It is an offence to keep or use an unlicensed vehicle. Section 29 of the VERA 1994 provides:

   (1) If a person uses, or keeps, on a public road a vehicle (not being an exempt vehicle) which is unlicensed he is guilty of an offence.

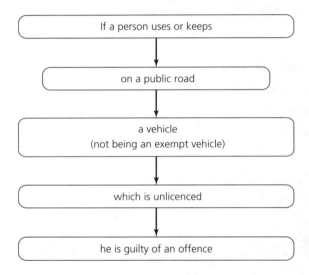

   (2) For the purposes of subsection (1) a vehicle is unlicensed if no vehicle or trade licence is in force for or in respect of the vehicle.

The penalty for this offence is a fine at level 3 *or* a penalty of five times the amount of the vehicle excise duty chargeable in respect of the vehicle, whichever is the greater, *and* to back duty.

PRACTICAL POINT

It is *not* necessary to establish ownership of the vehicle in order to show it is 'kept'. A vehicle is 'kept' on a road by anyone who causes it to be on a road, irrespective of ownership or duration (*Dudley v Holland* [1963] 3 All ER 732). If, for example, A allows B to use his (A's) vehicle and B parks it on a public road without a current

---

excise licence, then B would be liable for keeping the vehicle on the road without a current excise licence even though ownership is A's.

10.1.1 Vehicles Exempt from Duty

The VERA 1994 exempts a number of vehicles from the requirement to pay duty. The full list of exemptions can be found in sch 2 and includes:

- vehicles first constructed before 1 January 1973;
- trams;
- vehicles used for police purposes;
- fire engines;
- electrically assisted pedal cycles;
- ambulances and health service vehicles;
- veterinary ambulances;
- mine rescue vehicles;
- vehicles used for the haulage of a lifeboat;
- certain vehicles for disabled people;
- agriculture, horticulture or forestry vehicles used on public roads passing between different areas of land occupied by the same person provided the distance travelled on the public road does not exceed 1.5 kilometres;
- Vehicles that are being taken to or from a previously arranged test (eg an MOT). If the vehicle fails the test then it is still exempt from excise duty whilst it is taken, by prior arrangement, to a place where the relevant work is to be done on it. The vehicle is also exempt whilst an authorized person is conducting the test.

PRACTICAL POINT

It is a commonly held belief by owners of very old vehicles that they need not apply for a vehicle excise licence. It may well be true that they are exempt from the requirement to pay duty but this does not mean that they are exempt from the need to display a valid excise licence. A licence should still be applied for (and then displayed) but the DVLA will not charge duty. 'NIL' is written in the relevant section of the tax disc where the rate of duty normally appears (see 10.1.5).

10.1.2 Public Road

For the purposes of the VERA 1994, 'public road' has a more restrictive meaning than under the Road Traffic Act 1988 (RTA 1988). Here, it means a road repairable at public expense.

PRACTICAL POINT

Some roads display a sign which states it is 'unadopted'. Generally, these are roads that are maintained at the expense of the individual householders resident in the area and, as such, are not public roads for excise purposes. Unadopted roads tend to display certain characteristics (eg commonly having no pavements). There are also roads that display signs stating 'private road'. Roads displaying such signs are not always maintained at the expense of individual householders; residents commonly have agreements with the local authority for maintenance at public expense.

In cases of doubt, check with the local planning department. They will have details of who is responsible for the maintenance of each road within their area.

10.1.3 Registered Keepers

Section 31A of the VERA 1994 provides:

(1) If a vehicle registered under this Act is unlicensed, the person in whose name the vehicle is registered is guilty of an offence.

This section makes it an offence merely to be the registered keeper of an unlicensed vehicle. There is no requirement that the vehicle is used or kept on a public road. There are, however, a number of circumstances where the keeper registered with the DVLA does not commit this offence. The Act goes on to provide in s 31B(1) that no offence is committed if any one of a number of conditions are satisfied. The conditions are:

(2) ... that the registered keeper—
    (a) is not at the relevant time the person keeping the vehicle, and
    (b) if previously he was the person keeping the vehicle, he has by the relevant time complied with any requirements under section 22(1)(d).

(3) (a) the registered keeper is at the relevant time the person keeping the vehicle
    (b) at the relevant time the vehicle is neither kept nor used on a public road, and
    (c) the registered keeper has by the relevant time complied with any requirements under section 22(1)(d).

(4) (a) the vehicle has been stolen before the relevant time
    (b) the vehicle has not been recovered by the relevant time, and
    (c) any requirements under subsection (6)... are complied with.

(5) (a) beginning with the expiry of the last vehicle licence to be in force for the vehicle, and
    (b) of a prescribed length,
a vehicle licence for the vehicle is taken out within the grace days for a period beginning within the grace days. (14 days)

In order to avoid conviction under s 31A, the registered keeper must satisfy any one of the above conditions. The conditions place a duty on the registered keeper to show that he has informed the DVLA or other relevant authorities, within certain time limitations, that:

- the vehicle has changed ownership;
- the vehicle is not used or kept on a public road;
- the vehicle has been stolen and notification of the theft was given within 14 days to a member of the police force or person employed to assist a police force;
- they have taken out a licence within the 14 day period of grace.

10.1.4 Statutory Off Road Notification (SORN)

The Road Vehicles (Registration and Licensing) Regulations 2002, SI 2002/2742, reg 26 provides that certain particulars are to be furnished and declarations made by a person who:

(1) surrenders a vehicle licence;
(2) does not renew a vehicle licence on its expiration; or
(3) keeps an unlicensed vehicle.

The particulars that must be furnished are:

(1) the registration mark of the vehicle;
(2) the make and model of the vehicle; and
(3) the address of the premises at which the vehicle is to be kept.

The regulations provide that if the vehicle is used on a public road whenever a SORN is in force, the registered keeper shall be liable to an increased penalty (level 4 rather than level 3) if he has not first taken out a licence. It is an offence to contravene reg 26, punishable by a fine on level 3 of the standard scale.

10.1.5 Failing to Display Vehicle Excise Licence and Under Payment

Section 33 of the VERA 1994 provides:

(1) A person is guilty of an offence if—
    (a) he uses, or keeps, on a public road a vehicle in respect of which excise duty is chargeable, and
    (b) there is not fixed to and exhibited on the vehicle in the manner prescribed...a licence for, or in respect of, the vehicle which is for the time being in force.

The offence has now been extended to apply to those vehicles which require a 'nil licence'—so even though no duty may be payable because the vehicle is exempt, a licence must still be displayed (s 33(1A)). If a person has no licence (and therefore cannot display a licence) there is no legal reason why that person cannot be charged with both the offence under s 29 and the offence under s 33 (*Pilgrim v Dean* [1974] RTR 299). The only defence to the s 33 offence is where the licence has been sent to the Secretary of State with an application for a replacement. Here, a licence need not be displayed on the vehicle until the replacement is obtained (reg 6).

Each licence shall be fixed to the vehicle in a holder sufficient to protect it from the weather to which it would otherwise be exposed. The licence shall be exhibited so that all the particulars on the licence are clearly visible in daylight from the nearside of the road (reg 6). It shall be displayed:

(1) on invalid vehicles, tricycles or bicycles other than at (2) or (3) the licence shall be exhibited on the nearside of the vehicle;
(2) on a bicycle with a sidecar it shall be exhibited on the nearside of the handlebars or on the nearside of the side car;
(3) on vehicles with a glass windscreen in front of the driver it must be exhibited on or adjacent to the nearside of the windscreen;
(4) in the case of any other vehicle,
    (a) if the vehicle has a driver's cab containing a nearside window, on that window;
    (b) on the nearside of the vehicle in front of the driver's seat and not less than 760 mm and not more than 1.8 metres above the road surface.

Section 37 of the VERA 1994 makes it an offence to use a vehicle where a licence has been taken out at any rate of vehicle excise duty and, at any time while that licence is in force, the vehicle is so used that duty at a higher rate becomes chargeable and that higher rate was not paid before the vehicle was so used.

Practical Example

Although this offence arises fairly infrequently an example would be when the owner of a taxi obtains a vehicle excise licence at the rate applicable for that type of vehicle (the duty rate for taxis is less than the duty rate for a privately owned car) and then uses the taxi as a privately owned car. The duty payable for private car use is higher than the rate paid for taxi use and so constitutes an offence.

Similarly, if a vehicle has a 'nil' payment (eg certain vehicles used for disabled persons) and it is then sold to a person who would not be eligible to claim the 'nil' rate, a new excise licence at the appropriate rate of duty must be obtained before the vehicle is used on the road.

10.1.6 Trade Licences and Trade Plates

Trade licences

Trade licences give certain motor traders and vehicle testers exemption from having to have a vehicle excise licence for the multitude of vehicles that come into their possession during the course of their business. The trade licence, unlike a vehicle excise licence, is triangular in shape. It should be displayed on the front of the two 'trade plates' (see below) that are also issued to trade licence holders (reg 42 of the Road Vehicle (Registration and Licensing) Regulations 2002).

A trade licence may be issued to:

(1) a motor trader;
(2) a vehicle tester; or
(3) a person who satisfies the Secretary of State that he intends to commence business as a motor trader or vehicle tester.

A motor trader is defined in s 62 as:

(a) a manufacturer or repairer of vehicles, or dealer in vehicles;
(b) a person who modifies vehicles, whether by fitting accessories or otherwise; or
(c) a person who valets vehicles.

Section 12 of the VERA 1994 provides that the holder of a trade licence may only use that licence for one vehicle at any particular time and only for certain specified purposes connected with the business. (For offences see below.) Although the holder of a trade licence can only use the licence for one vehicle at any particular time, he can apply for two or more licences.

PRACTICAL POINT

Motor traders frequently need to move more than one vehicle at a time. If a vehicle is seen displaying only one trade plate rather than the two that should be displayed, be aware that one possible explanation is that there may be another vehicle travelling in tandem which is displaying the second trade plate. This is, of course, unlawful.

It is not generally permitted for the holder of a trade licence to carry goods other than those solely for testing the vehicle (or accessories or equipment) and provided no unloading takes place before return to the place of loading. It is also permissible when delivering or collecting a vehicle, to carry a load consisting of another vehicle to be used for travel to or from the place of delivery or collection.

Trade plates

When a trade licence is issued, the holder is also issued with a set of trade plates bearing a general registration mark. The plates take on the size and lettering of an ordinary registration plate although the numbering/lettering will be in red on a white background. As motor cycles only require one registration mark to be displayed, a motor trader who is only concerned with motor cycles will only be issued with one plate. One of the plates must have affixed to it a means of displaying the trade licence.

The trade plates, when the vehicle is being used under a trade licence, must be clearly displayed in the same manner as a normal vehicle registration mark. The plate that has the licence affixed to it must be displayed on the front of the vehicle (reg 42 of the Road Vehicle (Registration and Licensing) Regulations 2002).

Offences

The VERA 1994, s 34 provides:

> (1) A person holding a trade licence or trade licences is guilty of an offence if he—
>
> (a) uses at any one time on a public road a greater number of vehicles . . . than he is authorised to use by virtue of the trade licence or licences,
>
> (b) uses a vehicle . . . on a public road for any purpose other than a purpose which has been prescribed . . . ,
>
> (c) uses the trade licence . . . for the purposes of keeping on a public road in any circumstances other than circumstances which have been prescribed a vehicle which is not being used on that road.

10.1.7 Driver/Keeper Identity

Section 46 of the VERA 1994 contains powers very similar to those contained in s 172 of the RTA 1988 (see 3.2) obligating keepers and other persons to give such information as may be required to identify drivers and/or keepers who commit offences under ss 29, 34, 37 and 43A. The requirement to provide information as to driver identity must be made by or on behalf of a chief officer of police or the Secretary of State. Failing to provide the information required is an offence (s 46(4)). (For the general operation of driver identity provisions see 3.2.)

10.1.8 Fraudulent Use

Section 44 of the VERA 1994 makes it an offence for a person to forge, fraudulently alter, fraudulently use, lend or allow to be used, any of the following:

(1) a vehicle excise licence;

(2) a trade licence;

(3) a nil licence;
(4) a registration mark;
(5) a registration document;
(6) a trade plate.

It is not necessary for the prosecution to prove that the defendant had an intention to avoid payment of duty. The offence requires only that the defendant's aim or purpose was to dishonestly deceive an appropriate person with a duty (eg fool a police officer or traffic warden).

PRACTICAL POINT

A common method by which this offence is committed is using a vehicle excise licence that does not relate to the vehicle in which it is displayed (eg a person 'borrows' a licence from another vehicle). This situation may well give rise to suspicion that an offence of theft has been committed but irrespective of whether or not there is a theft, this offence appears to be complete. Remember also the high likelihood that other related offences may be present (eg uninsured use).

10.2 **Registration Marks**

Currently, the main provisions concerning the form and layout of registration marks (ie number plates) are to be found in the Road Vehicles (Display of Registration Marks) Regulations 2001, SI 2001/561. In order to comply with the regulations, number plates must be set out in the prescribed manner.

PRACTICAL POINT

An owner may attempt to display a version of their name (or some other word) by altering the spacing or size of the characters or font. This does not comply with the regulations and is unlawful.

Briefly, in order to comply with the regulations:

- A number plate must be displayed at the front and the rear of motor vehicles. There are exemptions, notably motor cycles and tricycles where only a rear plate has to be displayed.
- Number plates must be easy to read *and* meet the British Standard. The use of screws, bolts or other fixing devices which have the effect of changing or altering the appearance or legibility of any of the characters of the number plate is prohibited.
- The characters must be black on a white background to the front and black on a yellow background to the rear, except that vehicles constructed before

1 January 1973 can still have traditional plates (ie white, silver or grey characters on a black background).

- The background surface should be reflective but the characters must not be reflective (reflex-reflective material is prohibited).
- Lettering and spacing must be of a set size (see below).
- Number plates cannot be altered, rearranged or the letters or numbers misrepresented.
- Characters must not be moved from one group to another (eg N123 BCD cannot be rearranged to make N123B CD).

10.2.1 Size and Spacing

For vehicles registered (or plate fitted) on or after 1 September 2001

The characters, generally, must be sizes shown in the table below (except for motor cycles, agricultural machines, works trucks or road rollers).

Size and spacing on or after 1 September 2001

Character height	79 mm
Width (except the figure 1 or letter I)	50 mm
Stroke	14 mm
Space between characters	11 mm
Space between groups	33 mm
Top, bottom and side margins (minimum)	11 mm
Space between vertical lines	19 mm

For vehicles registered before 1 September 2001

Vehicles are permitted characters of a larger height if the vehicle was first registered before 1 September 2001 and it is *not* a motor cycle, agricultural machine, works truck or road roller. In these cases, the character height may be 89 mm and the size and spacing is shown at Group 1 in the table below. In the case of a motor cycle, agricultural machine, works truck or road roller, the character height may be 64 mm and in this case, the size and spacing is shown at Group 2 in the table below.

Size and spacing prior to 1 September 2001

	Group 1	Group 2
Character height	89 mm	64 mm
Width (except 1 or I)	64 mm	44 mm
Stroke	16 mm	10 mm
Space between characters	13 mm	10 mm
Space between groups	38 mm	30 mm
Side margins (minimum)	13 mm	11 mm
Space between vertical lines	19 mm	13 mm

For imported vehicles

Regulation 14A provides that if a vehicle is imported and:

(a) does not have EC Whole Vehicle Type Approval; and

(b) is constructed so that the area available for the fixing of the registration plate prevents display in conformity with the regulations;

then the spacing and size must be as shown in the table below.

Size and spacing for imported vehicles

Character height	64 mm
Character width	44 mm
Character stroke	10 mm
Space between characters	10 mm
Space between groups	5 mm
Top, bottom and side margins (minimum)	5 mm

Practical Example

A substantial number of right-hand drive Japanese vehicles (constructed under Japanese regulations) are imported into the UK as used vehicles. One of the ways in which they differ is that the space formed at the rear of the vehicle's bodywork is designed for a 'square' number plate rather than the oblong space constructed for vehicles destined for the UK market. These are lawful so long as they comply with the specifications in the table above.

10.2.2 **Construction and Specification of Plates**

In order to comply with the British Standard the registration plate must conform to certain requirements with regard to its construction (see reg 10 and sch 2). The plate must contain the following information:

- the British Standard Number (currently BS AU 145d) or equivalent EU indication of equivalence with the British Standard;
- the name, trade mark, or other means of identifying the manufacturer or supplier;
- the name and postcode of the supplying outlet.

There shall be no other markings or material contained on the number plate. However, plates fitted after 1 September 2001 may now have the symbol of the European Union (a circle of 12 stars on a blue background) with the national identification letters of a Member State included on the far left of the number plate (reg 16). It is permissible to display the Union flag, cross of St. George, the Scottish saltire or Welsh dragon in that place on the plate where other distinguishing signs are permitted. Vehicles that display such plates need not display a separate GB plate or sticker whilst driven in the EU.

10.2.3 **Registration Mark Offences**

It is an offence to contravene the Road Vehicles (Display of Registration Marks) Regulations 2001 with offences attracting a level 3 fine (s 59(2)(a) of the VERA 1994). In addition to contravening the regulations, it is also an offence if:

- a registration mark is obscured or rendered or allowed to become not easily distinguishable (s 43(1));
- a person uses or keeps on a public road an exempt vehicle requiring a nil licence and a nil licence is not in force (s 43A);
- a registration mark is not properly fixed to a vehicle as required (s 42(1)).

10.2.4 **Purchase and Supply of Plates**

All suppliers of registration marks, unless exempt, have to be registered with the DVLA (Vehicles (Crime)) Act 2001. Details of all registered suppliers can be obtained from the DVLA and also found on their website. It is an offence to carry on a business in the supply of registration marks without being properly registered.

The Act provides that when supplying a registration mark, the supplier has to take certain steps in order to verify the purchaser's identity and their relationship to the vehicle for which the registration mark is being purchased. Generally speaking, a document (such as a photo card driving licence) together with the registration document (V5), have to be produced. A full list of the relevant documents and permitted combinations can be found in Pt I of the schedule to the Regulations.

10.3 **Questions and Answers**

Q1 A vehicle without an MOT test certificate has a prearranged test at an MOT testing station. Can the vehicle be driven there even though the vehicle excise licence has expired?

A1 Yes—provided that the test is prearranged the vehicle can be driven to the test without a vehicle excise licence. If the test is failed then it can be taken, without an excise licence, to a place of repair or towed to a place where it is to be broken up.

Q2 If a vehicle excise licence is lost or stolen a driver obviously cannot display a current excise licence on the vehicle. Is it still an offence to fail to display a licence where that licence has genuinely been lost or stolen?

A2 Yes it is. A driver is obliged to display a valid excise licence at all times and it is no defence to claim the licence has been lost or stolen. In genuine cases, you may, of course, wish to exercise your discretion and not prosecute. A duplicate licence can be obtained from the DVLA for a small fee.

Q3 If a motor trader uses trade plates on his personal vehicle is this lawful?

A3 No it isn't. A motor trader can use trade plates on vehicles only for business purposes and even then, only on vehicles that are temporarily in his control.

Q4 A vehicle first registered in 1972 is not displaying an excise licence. The owner says that the vehicle is over 25 years old and is therefore tax exempt. Is this correct?

A4 No it isn't. Vehicles first constructed before 1 January 1973 are exempt from the need to pay excise duty but they are still required to display a valid excise licence. On application, together with production of a valid insurance certificate and test certificate, they will be issued with an excise licence which will show 'NIL' in that section of the disc where the amount of duty payable is normally written.

11

Fixed Penalties

The fixed penalty system is a procedure that permits a motorist who has committed a specified offence to pay a fixed sum of money and, in the case of an endorsable offence, accept a set number of penalty points to be attributed to his licence. The relevant law is now contained in ss 51–74 and ss 78–90 of the Road Traffic Offenders Act 1988 (RTOA 1988). If the procedure is correctly followed the motorist can avoid formal prosecution in court. This procedure has built-in mechanisms which allow the recipient of a fixed penalty notice to elect a court hearing should that be required. The system has a number of benefits, including the speedier resolution of minor offences and a consequent freeing up of court time. It also enables penalties imposed to be consistent for identical offences regardless of which area of the country the offence was committed in. The offences for which a notice can be issued are set out in sch 3 to the RTOA 1988. Offences can be added to (or taken away from) the list. Generally, the booklets of fixed penalty notices that are issued to police officers contain details of all offences that may be dealt with by means of the issue of a fixed penalty notice.

PRACTICAL POINT

Section 2(2) of the RTOA 1988 provides that where a fixed penalty notice is issued there is no requirement to provide a Notice of Intended Prosecution (NIP) for those offences that would normally require one. However, there is no harm in giving a verbal notice of intended prosecution and in a practical sense, it may still be helpful. For example:

(1) If a driver declines a fixed penalty notice or a notice cannot be issued for any other reason (eg too many points on licence) then the matter would have to be dealt with by summons and in these circumstances a NIP is required.

(2) It is good practice to issue a NIP anyway, even though not strictly necessary. If issuing a NIP is routine, when giving evidence in court, you can state with confidence that you always issue a NIP, irrespective of the circumstances. The defence may then find it more difficult to convince the court that a NIP was not issued.

(3) Make a note on the fixed penalty notice that a NIP was issued.

11.1 Fixed Penalty Procedure

The procedure to be followed depends upon the circumstances in which the notice was issued. Generally speaking, there are two variable circumstances:

(1) where the driver is present (for endorsable or non endorsable offences);
(2) where the driver is not present (for non endorsable offences).

11.2 **Issue of Notice—Driver Present**

Sections 54(1) and (2) of the RTOA 1988 provide that a constable in uniform who has reason to believe a fixed penalty offence is being or has been committed may give the person concerned a fixed penalty notice.

PRACTICAL POINT

Only a constable in uniform may issue a fixed penalty ticket (although there is an exception concerning the use of automatic detection devices—see Conditional Offers 11.7). Note also that the provision states that the constable *may* issue a notice. It is for the officer to decide whether or not to issue a notice. The offender does not have the right to demand a notice, although a court may (for sentencing purposes) ask the prosecution to provide reasons why a notice was not issued.

11.2.1 **Endorsable Offence**

Where the offence appears to the constable to involve obligatory endorsement, the constable may only give the driver a fixed penalty notice in respect of the offence if:

(1) the person produces a driving licence;
(2) the points to be attributed for the offence will not render the person liable to disqualification (ie will still be less than 12 in total);
(3) the person surrenders the licence and counterpart to be retained and dealt with under the procedure.

PRACTICAL POINTS

(1) The licence has to be surrendered voluntarily—there is no power to seize it. When a person has accrued 12 points (or more) he is liable to be disqualified under s 35 for a minimum period of six months, so if the alleged offence now being dealt with attracts points which would render the person liable to disqualification, a fixed penalty notice must not be issued.
(2) Both parts of the licence must be surrendered; it is not sufficient to surrender the plastic card without the paper counterpart. There are, however, many drivers who still hold 'old style' paper licences. In these cases, the paper licence alone is all that is required. It is, of course, acceptable to surrender a provisional licence, with or without counterpart as the case may be.
(3) Newly qualified drivers, within the first two years of passing their test, are liable to have full licence entitlement taken away if they amass six or more penalty points during that period. They are not, however, disqualified from driving in these circumstances so a fixed penalty notice can still be issued.

If the person is willing to receive a notice but is unable to produce the licence there and then, the constable may give him a notice stating that if, within seven days, he produces the notice together with his licence and its counterpart in person to a constable or authorized person at the police station specified in the notice (being a police station chosen by the person concerned) and certain requirements are met, then a fixed penalty notice will be issued in respect of the offence (s 54(4)).

The requirements are identical to those in s 54(2), (ie the person who subsequently produces the notice in person together with the licence and counterpart will receive a fixed penalty notice only if the constable or authorized person is satisfied, on inspecting the licence and its counterpart, that he would not be liable to disqualification under the totting-up provisions and the licence and counterpart are surrendered for retention to be dealt with under the Act).

PRACTICAL POINT

The procedure above only allows for a seven day period from issue of the relevant notice to production of that notice and the licence/counterpart at a police station. In the case of the issue of form HO/RT 1 it is common practice for the usual seven day period to be extended by the issuing officer because certain defences are available should the documents be produced within a reasonable time (which may be more than seven days). The fixed penalty system does *not* have this flexibility and no extensions beyond the seven day period are permitted.

A notice under sub-s (4) above shall give such particulars of the circumstances alleged to constitute the offence to which it relates as are necessary for giving reasonable information about the alleged offence (s 54(6)) and a licence and a counterpart surrendered in accordance with this provision must be sent to the fixed penalty clerk (s 54(7)).

PRACTICAL POINT

When a notice is presented at a police station under the above procedure then, if all the conditions have been met, the officer or authorized person to whom the licence is presented at the police station *must* issue the fixed penalty notice. Unlike the police officer at the roadside who detected the offence, there is no discretion not to issue a fixed penalty notice at this stage.

If the fixed penalty is paid before the end of the suspended enforcement period then no proceedings may be brought against the person in respect of the relevant offence (s 78(2)).

PRACTICAL POINT

There are occasions where a person is willing to accept an endorsable fixed penalty notice but is reluctant to surrender his driving licence as it is needed in the immediate future (eg the person has arranged imminent car hire). Although there may be sympathy for individual circumstances, the procedure cannot continue without licence surrender. The matter would have to proceed by way of summons. The person should be advised to include reasons on any mitigation form and a brief note to the prosecutor would also assist the court in the decision as to the appropriate penalty in the circumstances.

11.2.2 Calculating Penalty Point Validity

Penalty points endorsed onto a driving licence or the counterpart of a photo card driving licence are valid for a limited time. Generally, they are valid for a period of three years but have to remain on the licence for a further 12 months before the licence holder can apply to the DVLA for them to be removed.

On the licence or counterpart the endorsement section will show two dates. These are:

(1) the date of conviction;
(2) the date of the offence.

The date of conviction is the date on which the offence has been heard by a court, conviction imposed and penalty points ordered as part of the sentence. The three year period of penalty point validity begins on this date (eg if D is convicted on 1 December 2006, then any points imposed will remain valid until 30 November 2009).

When points are placed on a licence following completion of the fixed penalty procedure, there is no date of conviction because, obviously, no conviction has occurred. (The space on a licence or counterpart that refers to date of conviction will simply have a line drawn through it.) The date of the offence section will be completed and the three year period of penalty point validity begins from the date on which the offence was committed (eg if D has a fixed penalty notice issued on 1 October 2006 for an offence committed on that date then any points subsequently endorsed under the procedure take effect from 1 October 2006 and will remain valid until 30 September 2009).

PRACTICAL POINT

The difference between date of offence and date of conviction may not, in most cases, be of much practical significance but, on those occasions where it is necessary to determine whether or not a person has (or may have) 12 or more valid points (eg

> when deciding whether the person is eligible for a fixed penalty notice) care should
> be taken to use the correct date.

11.3 Issue of Notice—Driver Not Present

Section 62(1) of the RTOA 1988 provides that where on any occasion a constable
has reason to believe in the case of any stationary vehicle that a fixed penalty
offence is being or has on that occasion been committed in respect of it, he
may fix a fixed penalty notice in respect of the offence to the vehicle, unless the
offence appears to him to involve obligatory endorsement.

11.4 Unlawful Removal or Interference with Notice

Section 62(2) of the RTOA 1988 provides that a person is guilty of an offence if
he removes or interferes with any notice fixed to a vehicle under this section,
unless he does so by or under the authority of the driver or person in charge of
the vehicle or the person liable for the fixed penalty offence in question. Consequently, if the person removing the notice does so on behalf of the person
liable for the fixed penalty offence, then the removal would be lawful and no
offence committed.

11.5 Suspended Enforcement Period

When a fixed penalty notice has been issued, either personally to a person or
fixed to a vehicle, the procedure allows for a period of not less than 21 days
following issue of the notice, before it can be enforced. The minimum period
is 21 days but a longer period may be specified in the notice itself. This period
allows the offender to both accept the procedure and pay the penalty or to elect
to have the matter heard by a court. Generally, when a fixed penalty notice is
issued, it contains details of how to proceed and also provides a form for the person to give notice that a court hearing is preferred. If the penalty is not paid, or
no notice is given within the 21 days, then the penalty increases by 50 per cent
and can be registered and enforced as a fine at the home court of the offender.
The relevant clerk to the justices will notify the person of the fact that a fine
has now been registered against them. If, when such a notice from the justice's
clerk is received, the person wishes to contest it, then one of two courses may
be followed. If the recipient alleges they were not the person to whom the fixed
penalty notice was issued, they can make a statutory declaration to the court to
that effect. Alternatively, they may give notice requesting a court hearing.

11.6 **Choice to Issue Fixed Penalty**

As mentioned above, the officer generally has discretion as to whether or not to issue a fixed penalty notice or report for summons. In cases of exceeding a speed limit, ACPO gives guidance as to when it would not be an appropriate case to follow the fixed penalty system. The advice generally relates to high vehicle speed. It may be more appropriate to summons a driver where the penalty likely to be imposed by a court would be greater than the fixed penalty rate. Penalties available to a court for exceeding the speed limit include immediate disqualification, a range of penalty points between 3 and 6 and a higher financial penalty. If the degree of excess speed is severe (eg 60 mph in a 30 mph area) then summons would generally be the more appropriate option.

11.7 **Conditional Offers**

The above system of issuing fixed penalty notices cannot be applied when the method of detecting offences is by means of authorized automatic detection devices (GATSO etc). The nature of these devices means that issue of the fixed penalty notice at the time is impossible. Nonetheless, the procedure has now been developed so as to accommodate offences detected by automatic devices. Where a constable has reason to believe that a fixed penalty offence has been committed, and no fixed penalty notice in respect of the offence has been given under s 54 of this Act or fixed to a vehicle under s 62 of this Act, a notice under this section may be sent to the alleged offender by or on behalf of the chief officer of police (s 75(1)).

A conditional offer must:

(1) give such particulars of the circumstances alleged to constitute the offence to which it relates as are necessary for giving reasonable information about the alleged offence;
(2) state the amount of the fixed penalty for that offence; and
(3) state that proceedings against the alleged offender cannot be commenced in respect of that offence until the end of the period of 28 days following the date on which the conditional offer was issued or such longer period as may be specified in the conditional offer (s 75(7)).

If, within the time allowed, the person then opts to pay the fixed penalty and produces the licence and counterpart for inspection and retention, proceedings for the offence will be discharged. As with all fixed penalties, the person must not be liable for disqualification under the totting-up provisions, should the offence be endorsable (s 75(8)).

11.8 **Questions and Answers**

Q1 A driver is stopped having committed an endorsable offence. He is prepared to be issued with a fixed penalty notice but only has the plastic photo card part of his licence with him, not the counterpart. Is this acceptable to proceed in these circumstances?

A1 No. For a fixed penalty to be issued the driver must surrender both the photo card part of the licence and the paper counterpart. This is a common situation as most drivers only carry the photo card licence with them. In these circumstances, it should be explained to the driver that a fixed penalty notice can still be issued provided that both parts of the licence are surrendered at a nominated police station. A notice should be made out to that effect. The plastic part should not be accepted at the roadside and should be given back to the driver with notice to produce both parts at the nominated police station.

Q2 A vehicle has three defective tyres on it. Can three fixed penalty notices be issued for the three offences?

A2 Fixed penalty notices can only be issued for a sole offence. If more than one offence is disclosed then the matter should be reported for a summons to be issued for all the offences. It would be possible to issue a fixed penalty notice for one of the offences with the others being dealt with by means of verbal advice.

Q3 Can the owner of a vehicle be issued with a fixed penalty notice even though they were not the driver?

A3 In order to issue a fixed penalty notice the vehicle has to be used by the person at whom the notice is directed. An owner cannot be issued with a fixed penalty notice if he is causing or permitting the use of (rather than actually using) the vehicle. Remember though, that if the vehicle is actually carrying the owner as a passenger, he may still be deemed as using the vehicle. In this case a fixed penalty notice (eg for a defective tyre) could be issued to both the owner and the driver.

Q4 Can an endorsable fixed penalty notice be fixed to a vehicle committing an endorsable offence (eg parking on a pedestrian crossing)?

A4 Only non-endorsable fixed penalty notices can be affixed to vehicles. An endorsable fixed penalty can only be personally given at the time by police officers or traffic wardens. If an offender is traced at a later date then the matter would have to proceed by summons.

Speeding and Miscellaneous Offences

This chapter will deal with offences of speeding together with a number of miscellaneous offences that involve danger or cause annoyance to other road users and a brief summary of the regulations relevant to taxis.

12.1 **Speeding**

Offences involving excess speed will be amongst the most common that a road traffic patrol officer encounters and yet there are many common misunderstandings about them. It is common for speeding offences to be detected by automatic devices and the fixed penalty procedure is generally available for these offences (see 11.7). A Notice of Intended Prosecution is required for most offences involving speeding (but see 12.1.4 below). Both roads and individual vehicle types may be subject to speed restrictions. Temporary speed limits may be imposed in certain circumstances and there are further conditions that apply to speed restrictions on motorways. Generally speaking, before a speed limit is imposed, the approval of the Secretary of State is required, but this does not apply to speed limits of 20 mph created by local authorities as part of a traffic calming scheme. The two primary considerations for the traffic officer will usually be in relation to (a) the speed limit that applies to the road in question; and (b) the speed limit that applies to the type of vehicle that the defendant was driving at the relevant time. The primary piece of legislation that deals with speeding offences is the Road Traffic Regulation Act 1984 (RTRA 1984), but often, other legislation has a role to play.

12.1.1 **Restricted Roads**

Section 81(1) of the RTRA 1984 provides:

> (1) It shall not be lawful for a person to drive a motor vehicle on a restricted road at a speed exceeding 30 miles per hour.

What roads are restricted roads?

The answer to this can be found in s 82 of the RTRA 1984 which provides:

> (1) Subject to the provisions of this section and of section 84(3) of this Act, a road is a restricted road for the purposes of section 81 of this Act if—
>> (a) in England and Wales, there is provided on it a system of street lighting furnished by means of lamps placed not more than 200 yards apart;
>> (b) *in Scotland*, there is provided on it a system of carriageway lighting furnished by means of lamps placed not more than 185 metres apart and the road is of a classification or type specified for the purposes of this subsection in regulations made by the Secretary of State.

(2) The traffic authority for a road may direct—
   (a) that the road which is a restricted road for the purposes of section 81 of this Act shall cease to be a restricted road for those purposes, or
   (b) that the road which is not a restricted road for those purposes shall become a restricted road for those purposes.

12.1.2 **Street Lighting**

If a road has a system of street lighting with lamps not more than 200 yards apart then, in the absence of any signs stating to the contrary, it is a restricted road and subject to a 30 mph speed limit.

PRACTICAL POINT

A road equipped with street lighting not more than 200 yards apart is subject to 30 mph speed limit. No speed limit signs are required. It follows that a person will have no defence to a charge of exceeding the limit if 30 mph signs *are* provided but are not correctly placed or are obscured (see *Hood v Lewis* [1976] RTR 99).

The courts have heard several cases brought by drivers seeking to demonstrate that the road concerned was not a restricted road because the street lighting did not comply with the 200 yard provision. In one case S drove his motor car at a speed exceeding 30 mph on a road and was charged with exceeding the speed limit. The prosecution evidence was that the average distance between street lamps was 95 yards but that the distance between lamps 5 and 6 was 212 yards. The justices, being satisfied that the road had a system of street lighting by means of lamps placed not more than 200 yards apart and that the road was therefore restricted, convicted S. It was held that in a system of 24 lamps, an error of 12 yards (or 6 per cent) between two lamps was so minimal that it could be ignored (see *Spittle v Kent County Constabulary* [1986] RTR 142; [1985] Crim LR 744 (DC)). In another case, to similar effect, on a charge of exceeding the 30 mph speed limit the justices found that two of the street lamps were placed 18 inches further apart than the maximum distance of 200 yards provided by the Act, but they convicted. The Divisional Court held that the justices were right because the excess was so small that it could be ignored (see *Briere v Hailstone* (1968) 112 SJ 767).

PRACTICAL POINT

It is important that when presenting evidence of exceeding the 30 mph speed limit on a restricted road, the existence of street lighting not more than 200 yards apart is addressed. Whether or not the system of street lighting actually conforms to the 200 yard statutory requirement is a question of fact for the court to determine. Trivial

---

deviations will be ignored (as the cases above show) but more significant deviations fall to be determined by the court on the facts of each individual case.

12.1.3 Speed Limits and Traffic Signs

If there is no system of street lighting indicating a restricted road as discussed in 12.1.2 above, then a person shall not be convicted of driving a motor vehicle on the road at a speed exceeding the limit unless the limit is indicated by traffic signs (s 85(4)). The signs must conform to the requirements of the Traffic Signs Regulations and General Directions 2002, SI 2002/3113 which provide a permitted range for sizes, colour and illumination (see 8.1). The speed limit signs should also be repeated at 'regular intervals', unless it is a motorway or restricted road. The only signs which need to be illuminated are those signs at the beginning and end of the speed restricted road where there is an electrical street lamp within 50 metres. These signs should be illuminated during the hours of darkness or whilst the street lamps are lit.

> **PRACTICAL POINT**
>
> It is important that when presenting evidence of exceeding a speed limit, you are able to demonstrate that traffic signs were correctly placed and displayed and, if appropriate, that the 'beginning' and 'end' signs were illuminated. If you fail to mention these points and are then asked about them in cross-examination, and are unable to answer, the case is likely to fail.

12.1.4 Speed Restrictions and Roadworks

An order for a temporary speed restriction may, by virtue of s 14 of the RTRA 1984, be made by traffic authorities because of roadworks (or similar activities), or because of the likelihood of danger to the public or serious damage to the road. A speed restriction made under s 14 is generally limited to a maximum of 18 months duration unless approval for an extension is given by the Secretary of State. Failing to comply with a temporary speed restriction imposed by a traffic authority is an offence (s 16 of the RTRA 1984).

> **PRACTICAL POINT**
>
> An offence under s 16 of the RTRA 1984 is concerned with contravening a speed *restriction* rather than a speed *limit*. It does *not* require a NIP (see 3.1) and does *not* require corroboration (see 12.1.7) although, in practice, there will almost always be corroborative evidence from a speedometer or other form of speed checking device.

12.1.5 Speed Limits and Certain Classes of Vehicle

Certain classes of vehicle may not lawfully exceed set speeds, irrespective of any particular speed limit normally associated with the road they are using at the time. The relevant law is to be found in sch 6 and s 86 of the RTRA 1984. For convenience, a brief summary of the most commonly encountered class restrictions appears below, but the full text of sch 6 should be consulted for a definitive list.

Speed restriction by vehicle class (mph)

Class of Vehicle	M/way	Dual C/way	Other Road
Passenger vehicle, motor caravan, dual purpose vehicle, without a trailer and u/w exceeding 3.05 tonnes *or* adapted to carry more than 8 passengers:			
(a) if the overall length does not exceed 12 metres	70	60	50
(b) if the overall length does exceed 12 metres	60	60	50
Passenger vehicle, motor caravan, dual purpose vehicle:			
(a) drawing one trailer	60	60	50
(b) drawing more than one trailer	40	20	20
Goods vehicles (not articulated):			
(a) max laden weight n/e 7.5 tonnes and no trailer	70	60	50
(b) max laden weight n/e 7.5 tonnes inc 1 trailer	60	60	50
(c) with more than 1 trailer	40	20	20
(d) max laden weight exceeds 7.5 tonnes but no trailer	60	50	40
(e) max laden weight exceeds 7.5 tonnes inc 1 trailer	60	50	40
Articulated goods vehicles:			
(a) max laden weight n/e 7.5 tonnes	60	60	50
(b) max laden weight exceeds 7.5 tonnes	60	50	40

Cars, small vans and dual purpose vehicles not mentioned in sch 6 are restricted by the 70 Miles Per Hour, 60 Miles Per Hour and 50 Miles Per Hour (Temporary Speed Limits) (Continuation) Order 1978 which, despite its title, has continued in force since 1977 and has now been extended indefinitely! To put the matter more simply, cars and small vans are subject to a speed limit of 70 mph on motorways and unrestricted dual carriageways, and 60 mph on other roads unless a lower speed limit is specified.

12.1.6 **Exemptions from Speed Limits**

Section 87 of the RTRA 1984 provides an exemption from the need to conform with speed limits as follows:

> No statutory provisions imposing a speed limit on motor vehicles shall apply to any vehicle on an occasion when it is being used for fire brigade..., ambulance or police purposes, if the observance of that provision would be likely to hinder the use of the vehicle for the purpose for which it is being used on that occasion.

The provision is largely self-explanatory. It applies to *any* vehicle being used for a relevant *purpose* and not to the vehicle itself. It follows that if D uses his own private car to drive a seriously injured road accident victim to hospital, he may defend a charge of speeding by relying on s 87 because the *purpose* to which that car was being put on that occasion was an ambulance purpose. If, however, D were charged with an offence of careless or dangerous driving arising from the same circumstances, s 87 would not provide a defence.

The Road Safety Bill 2005 proposes to replace the existing s 87 with a new provision as follows:

(1) No statutory provision imposing a speed limit on motor vehicles shall apply to any vehicle on an occasion when—

    (a) it is being used for fire and rescue authority purposes or for or in connection with the exercise of any function of a relevant authority as defined in section 6 of the Fire (Scotland) Act 2005, for ambulance purposes or for police or Serious Organised Crime Agency purposes,

    (b) it is being used for other prescribed purposes in such circumstances as may be prescribed, or

    (c) it is being used for training persons to drive vehicles for use for any of the purposes mentioned in paragraph (a) or (b) above, if the observance of that provision would be likely to hinder the use of the vehicle for the purpose for which it is being used on that occasion.

(2) Subsection (1) above does not apply unless the vehicle is being driven by a person who—

    (a) has satisfactorily completed a course of training in the driving of vehicles at high speed provided in accordance with regulations under this section, or

    (b) is driving the vehicle as part of such a course.

(3) The Secretary of State may by regulations make provision about courses of training in the driving of vehicles at high speed.

12.1.7 **Speeding and Corroboration**

A person cannot be convicted of speeding solely on the evidence of one witness to the effect that, in his opinion, the defendant was exceeding the speed limit (s 89(2) of the RTRA 1984). This does not mean that two witnesses are required to give evidence that the defendant was speeding before there can be a conviction. The corroborative evidence that is needed to support a single witness's opinion of excess speed can be supplied from a number of sources but it is, of course, vital that the supporting evidence refers to the *same* period and *time* of driving that the opinion evidence also refers to. So, for example, if witness 1 testifies that the defendant was, in his opinion, speeding between points A and B on a certain road and witness 2 testifies that moments later the defendant was, in his opinion, speeding between points C and D on the same road, witnesses 1 and 2 do not corroborate each other (*Brighty v Pearson* [1938] 4 All ER 127). Note also, that the offence of exceeding the 70 mph speed limit on a motorway (s 17(4) of the RTRA 1984) is specifically excluded from the corroboration requirement.

Speedometers

One of the most common sources of corroboration comes from the speedometer reading of a police vehicle. It is well known that a police officer can support his oral testimony that the defendant was speeding with evidence of the reading from a speedometer observed at the same time (*Nicholas v Penny* [1950] 2 KB 466).

PRACTICAL POINT

When giving evidence of a speeding offence that you have observed it is important to state that you formed the opinion that the vehicle was speeding. If this point is neglected and you only give the evidence that a speed checking device provides (eg a speedometer reading or a Vascar reading) it may be argued that no corroborative evidence has been given and that there is no case to answer.

Speed checking devices

A single witness may support his opinion of excess speed by means of the reading supplied by speed checking equipment (eg a radar gun/Vascar) even if the accuracy of that equipment has not been tested against the known speed of a police vehicle with a calibrated speedometer (*Collinson v Mabbott, The Times*, 10 October 1984).

PRACTICAL POINT

Whilst it is not essential for corroboration purposes to prove the accuracy of devices such as Vascar or radar, it makes good sense to be in a position to do so. These devices are frequently used to corroborate the opinion of a police officer as to speed. Most road policing units maintain records of the testing for accuracy of these devices. It is desirable to maintain a record or note in a pocketbook to meet any

> defence suggestion that the officer's opinion is flawed and that the device was in-accurate.

12.1.8 **Prescribed Speed Checking Devices**

There has been an enormous growth in the number of roadside cameras that now detect speeding offences. The relevant legislation that permits the admissibility of evidence gathered by an approved speed checking device is s 20 of the RTOA 1988. The statute allows a documentary record produced by a prescribed device, accompanied by a certificate as to the circumstances of its production signed by a constable or by a person authorized by or on behalf of the chief officer of police of the area where the offence was committed, to be admitted into evidence. Where an offender is prosecuted for speeding based on the documentary evidence provided by a roadside camera, then the document is admissible as proof of the vehicle's speed (Road Traffic Offenders (Prescribed Devices) Order 1999, SI 1999/162). This is not evidence of opinion and so no issue of corroboration under s 89(2) arises. A device is a prescribed device if it has been approved by the Secretary of State.

PRACTICAL POINT

Defence lawyers have been known to cross-examine police witnesses on whether or not a device has been approved and whether or not there are any restrictions on the approval. For example, a GATSO device has a restricted approval and consequently cannot be used to detect speeds in an area where the speed limit is less than 30 mph. Each force area will use different types of device and it makes sense to ensure that your office has an up-to-date list of devices used in your force area that have been approved (together with any restrictions) and retain it for future reference. If such a list is not readily available then most police forces have a designated legal research officer who should be able to help with this task or a list may be held at your local CPS office.

Evidence from prescribed speed checking devices

In order to ensure the certificate and document produced by the device is admissible as evidence, a copy must be served on the defendant *at least seven days* in advance of the hearing or trial. If the defendant, *at least three days* (or within such time as the court may in special circumstances allow) before the hearing or trial, serves notice on the prosecution requiring the attendance of the person who signed the document, then the document may still be admitted as evidence of the matters shown on the record produced by the device (s 20(8) of the RTOA 1988).

PRACTICAL POINT

If you are the document signer, it follows that unless the defence specifically requires your presence at the trial or hearing, there is no need for you to attend as a witness. It is the document produced by the device that is the evidence and this can speak for itself. Even if the defence does, for some reason, require your presence at the trial or hearing, the document produced by the device is still admissible as evidence of the offence. It is perhaps in the latter situation that you should be especially prepared and able to answer any questions that may be put about the device's approval.

12.2 **Leaving Vehicles in Dangerous Position**

Section 22 of the Road Traffic Act 1988 (RTA 1988) provides:

If a person in charge of a vehicle causes or permits the vehicle or trailer drawn by it to remain at rest on a road in such a position or in such condition or in such circumstances as to involve a danger of injury to other persons using the road, he is guilty of an offence.

12.2.1 **Danger of Injury**

In order for the offence to be complete, there must be a danger of injury to some other road user caused by the position, condition or circumstances of the vehicle or trailer. The danger does not need to actually manifest itself whilst the vehicle is stationary. It is sufficient that the person in charge of the vehicle allows it to remain at rest in a condition or circumstances of danger that may not become apparent until the vehicle moves. A clear example can be seen where the driver does not set the parking brake; the danger (which is always present while the vehicle is stationary) manifests itself when the vehicle rolls away (see *Maguire v Crouch* (1940) 104 JP 445).

PRACTICAL POINT

In practice, the most commonly encountered situations are likely to involve the manner in which a driver has parked his vehicle on the highway. Clear examples would be parking in the immediate vicinity of a sharp bend in the road or in the immediate vicinity of a humpback bridge in a manner which exposes other road users to the risk of injury. The potential for injury must always be present and if it is missing then the offence is not complete.

12.2.2 **Other Elements**

The offence applies to *vehicles* not just motor vehicles and may be committed by those in charge of pedal cycles etc. The offence is not complete unless the circumstances involve danger to *another person using the road*. It is necessary, therefore, to ensure that evidence is available that illustrates how the danger (whatever form that danger took) involved danger to another and that the person or persons so affected were road users. The meaning of use, cause or permit is dealt with elsewhere (see 1.6.5).

12.3 **Driving Motor Vehicles Off-Road**

The off-road driving of vehicles on land is a problem that seems to have escalated significantly in recent times, especially with the increased use of vehicles like quad bikes and motor cycles used for scrambling. The relevant law can be found in s 34(1) of the RTA 1988 which states:

(1) ... [I]f without lawful authority a person drives a mechanically propelled vehicle—

(a) on to or upon any common land, moorland or land of any other description, not being land forming part of a road, or

(b) on any road being a footpath, bridleway or restricted byway,

he is guilty of an offence.

12.3.1 **Exceptions and Defences**

It is not an offence to drive on land within 15 yards of a road if the driver's purpose is only to park the vehicle on the land (s 34(3)). If, however, the vehicle is driven on the land for some other purpose, even if it is within 15 yards of the road, then the defence will not apply. A driver who is able to prove to the court that the off-road driving was for the purpose of saving life, extinguishing fire or other like emergency, does not commit an offence (s 34(4)).

12.3.2 **Additional Powers**

Section 59 of the Police Reform Act 2002 applies where a constable in uniform has reasonable grounds for believing that a mechanically propelled vehicle is being used or has been used in contravention of s 34 and is causing or is likely to cause alarm, distress or annoyance to the public.

12.4 **Parking Heavy Commercial Vehicles on Verges**

Section 19 of the RTA 1988 states:

(1) …a person who parks a heavy commercial vehicle (as defined in section 20 of this Act) wholly or partly—

(a) on the verge of a road, or

(b) on any land situated between two carriageways and which is not a footway, or

(c) on a footway,

is guilty of an offence.

12.4.1 **Defence**

If the person alleged to have committed the s 19 offence can prove to the satisfaction of the court that it was:

(a) parked with permission from a constable in uniform; or

(b) parked for the purpose of saving life, extinguishing fire or other like emergency; or

(c) parked for the purpose of loading/unloading which could not have been performed had it not been so parked *and* it was not left unattended during that time;

then the person shall not be convicted (s 19(2) and (3)).

PRACTICAL POINT

The law does not give a right to drivers of commercial vehicles to park where they wish in order to load or unload. It will be their task to show that they could not have unloaded or loaded satisfactorily without parking on the verge or footway *and* someone has to be in attendance with the vehicle throughout the time it is parked. As an alternative to s 19 you may wish to consider possible obstruction offences (see 12.8 below).

12.5 **Motor Vehicles and Hand-Held Phones**

After much resistance to change, the government enacted the following regulation to specifically combat the potentially lethal practice of driving while using a hand-held mobile telephone. The current law can be found in the Road Vehicles (Construction and Use) Regulations 1986, SI 1986/1078 which provides in reg 110:

(1) No person shall drive on a road if he is using—

(a) a hand-held mobile telephone; or

(b) a hand-held device of a kind specified in paragraph (4).

(2) No person shall cause or permit any other person to drive a motor vehicle on a road while that other person is using—
(a) a hand-held mobile telephone; or
(b) a hand-held device of a kind specified in paragraph (4).
(3) No person shall supervise a holder of a provisional licence if the person supervising is using—
(a) a hand-held mobile telephone; or
(b) a hand-held device of a kind specified in paragraph (4),
at a time when the provisional licence holder is driving a motor vehicle on a road.
(4) A device referred to in paragraphs (1) (b), (2) (b) and (3) (b) is a device, other than a two-way radio, which performs an interactive communication function by transmitting and receiving data.

12.5.1 Elements of the Offences

There are three offences created by the regulations which are largely self-explanatory. The first is *using* the hand-held phone while driving. The second is *causing* or *permitting* another to drive while using the hand-held phone and the third is *supervising* a provisional licence holder while the supervisor is using the hand-held phone.

12.5.2 Using Hands-Free Kits

Is it lawful to use a mobile phone with a hands-free kit and still have a conversation while driving? The answer to that lies in how the regulation defines a hands-free mobile telephone. Regulation 110(6) states:

(6) For the purposes of this regulation—
(a) a mobile telephone or other device is to be treated as hand-held if it *is*, or *must* be, *held* at some point during the course of making or receiving a call or performing any other interactive communication function.

There can be no doubt that using the phone whilst holding it in the hand when driving constitutes an offence but it will also be an offence if, at some point during the course of receiving or making a call (or sending a text message or the like), the driver of the vehicle holds the phone in his or her hand, *even if the holding is only momentary*. Accordingly, a driver with a hands-free kit who holds the phone in order to answer an incoming call commits an offence. It still constitutes an offence even if immediately after holding the phone to answer a call, it is put down and a hands-free kit is used. If, however, the phone is, for example, mounted on a dashboard holder and a call is made or answered merely by pressing a button on an earpiece or even on the phone keypad, then as the phone is not *held* at any time, even momentarily, it appears no offence is committed. The regulation makes it quite clear that the phone must be *held* at some point, even if only momentarily, in order for the offence to be complete.

PRACTICAL POINT

It is essential to have evidence that the phone is being (or has been) held by the driver. Without this evidence then a prosecution will fail. If you consider that a driver's competence is impaired because of a conversation being conducted on a mobile phone with a hands-free kit, then consider the alternative offences mentioned below.

In one sense, of course, this regulation fails to combat a large part of the mischief that it was designed to remedy. A phone that is dashboard mounted may be operated simply by pressing buttons on the keypad. It need not be held at all. Indeed, it is perfectly possible to send a text message from a dashboard mounted mobile phone without ever having to hold it. Any driver who indulges in such irresponsible behaviour does not appear to commit an offence under this regulation and yet will certainly have much reduced powers of attention and concentration, risking possibly tragic consequences. In such circumstances, where the specific regulation appears not to apply, it would be perfectly possible to consider proceedings for alternative offences such as failing to have proper control of the vehicle (see 7.3.13) or, if there is sufficient evidence, driving without due care and attention (see 2.3). When the Road Safety Bill is enacted, the offence of using a mobile telephone under the regulations will appear in s 41D of the RTA 1988 and will be endorsable and offenders may also be disqualified from driving (see further 7.3.13).

12.5.3 Defence

The regulation provides for a very limited defence arising from an emergency. If the phone is being used to call the emergency services on 112 or 999 in response to a genuine emergency *and* it is unsafe or impracticable to stop driving in order to make that call, then no offence is committed (reg 110(5)). In practice, it would be difficult to imagine this defence being successfully raised on all but the rarest of occasions.

12.6 **Seat Belts**

There are numerous requirements which relate to the fitting and maintenance of seat belts (see Road Vehicles (Construction and Use) Regulations 1986, regs 46–48) but for our purposes here, we shall consider only the principal offences relating to seat belt use that are more likely to be encountered on a regular basis.

12.6.1 **Wearing Seat Belts—Adults**

The wearing of seat belts is regulated by the Motor Vehicles (Wearing of Seat Belts) Regulations 1993 and s 14 of the RTA 1988. If an adult (ie a person aged 14 years or over) contravenes the regulations then an offence is committed by virtue of s 14(3) of the RTA 1988. Any person who is:

- driving a motor vehicle; or
- riding in the front seat of a motor vehicle; or
- riding in the rear seat of a motor car or passenger car shall wear an adult seat belt.

PRACTICAL POINT

A parent, who is the driver of a motor vehicle, and who allows his/her 14-year-old child to ride in the vehicle without wearing a seat belt does not commit an offence of aiding and abetting (s 14(3)). If the child is under the age of 14 years, then the driver does commit an offence (see 12.6.3 below).

12.6.2 **Exemptions—s 14**

Numerous exemptions are provided for in reg 6, the principal ones being as follows:

- delivering or collecting goods on a journey not exceeding 50 metres in a vehicle constructed or adapted for that purpose;
- where a vehicle is being used for fire or police purposes;
- where using a vehicle for prisoner escorts;
- taxi drivers where the vehicle is being used for that purpose;
- private hire drivers who are carrying passengers;
- while the vehicle is reversing;
- the holder of a medical certificate;
- where there is no adult seat belt available.

12.6.3 **Wearing Seat Belts—Children**

The principal legislation that regulates the wearing of seat belts by children is the RTA 1988. A child is, for these purposes, defined as being under the age of 14 years.

Front seats

Section 15(1) provides that a person must not without reasonable excuse drive a motor vehicle on a road in the front of which is a child under 14 years of age unless the child is wearing a seat belt in conformity with the regulations. The responsibility is clearly placed upon the driver of the car and not the child. A general defence of 'reasonable excuse' is provided and if the defendant wishes to plead that he had a reasonable excuse, it will be for him to prove it. What constitutes a reasonable excuse will be determined by the court on a case-by-case basis.

Rear seats

Section 15(3) provides that a person must not without reasonable excuse drive a motor vehicle on a road where a child under 14 years is in the rear of the vehicle and any seat belt is fitted in the rear unless the child is wearing a seat belt in conformity with the regulations. Further, s 15(3A) provides that where a child under 12 years and less than 150 cm in height is in the rear of a passenger car and no seat belt is fitted in the rear but there is an available seat belt in the front, a person must not without reasonable excuse drive that passenger car on a road. This latter provision is clearly aimed at compelling drivers to ensure that younger children make use of any available seat belts in the front of a car that does not have them fitted in the rear.

12.6.4 Exemptions—s 15

Should any one of the following exemptions apply, then no offence will be committed. The list below is not exhaustive and reflects only those situations that are most likely to be encountered.

Front and rear seats

- where the child is 3 years or more, a child restraint is not available in the front or back, and the child is wearing an adult seat belt;
- where the child holds a medical certificate;
- where the child is under 1 year and is in a carry cot restrained by the straps;
- where the child is disabled and is wearing a disabled person's belt.

Rear seats only

- in a licensed taxi or licensed private hire car where the rear seats are separated from the driver where the vehicle is not a motor car nor a passenger car.

Seat belts—a Summary

Child under 3 years of age	Must wear appropriate child restraint in the front or rear
Child 3 to 11 years of age and under one and a half metres in height	Must wear an appropriate child restraint in the front and rear seats if available; may wear an adult seat belt in the front or rear if child restraint unavailable
Child 12 or 13 years of age or a younger child one and a half metres in height or more	Must wear an adult seat belt in the front or rear if available
Person 14 years of age and over	Must wear adult seat belt in the front or rear if available

12.7 Motor Cycle Crash Helmets and Eye Protectors

A person driving or riding on a motor bicycle on a road must wear protective headgear (Motor Cycles (Protective Helmets) Regs 1998, reg 4). This regulation does not apply to a passenger who is riding in a sidecar.

The regulations also provide that the headgear must be securely fastened to the wearer's head by the straps so provided and the helmet must bear a mark indicating its compliance with approved quality standards. Driving or riding a motor cycle in contravention of the regulations is an offence (s 16(4) of the RTA 1988).

Motor bicycle

The regulations only apply to motor bicycles even though, confusingly, s 16 refers to motor cycles. A motor bicycle is defined as a two-wheeled motor cycle with or without a sidecar but where the distance between the centre of any two wheels of the motor cycle is less than 460 mm; it is to be treated as one wheel.

12.7.1 Exemptions

The regulations do not apply to mowing machines (reg 4(2)) or followers of the Sikh religion while wearing a turban (s 16(2)).

PRACTICAL POINT

A person will still be regarded as 'driving' or 'riding' a motor bicycle if they sit astride the vehicle and push or pedal it with their feet, even though the engine is not running. It follows that a crash helmet is required in these circumstances (see *Crank v*

Brooks [1980] RTR 441). If, however, a person is merely pushing the motor bicycle alongside himself, then he is not riding or driving it and no helmet is required.

12.7.2 **Pillion Passenger Under 16**

The driver of a motor cycle who carries a pillion passenger under the age of 16 years who contravenes the regulations is also responsible for the offence committed by the passenger. It follows that the driver can be prosecuted for aiding and abetting the offence committed by the passenger (s 16(4) of the RTA 1988). If, however, the passenger is 16 years or over, then the passenger alone has responsibility for the offence and proceedings may not be brought against the driver in respect of aiding and abetting an offence under the regulations.

12.7.3 **Eye Protectors**

There are presently no regulations that compel the riders of motor cycles to wear eye protectors though, in reality, many riders choose to do so. Riders who do opt to wear eye protectors must ensure that they comply with the Motor Cycle (Eye Protectors) Regulations 1999. The regulations impose minimum standards of quality on eye protectors that riders may wear and it is an offence to use non-prescribed eye protectors when driving or riding a motor cycle (s 18(3)) and it is also an offence to sell or offer for sale, non-prescribed protectors (s 18(4)).

PRACTICAL POINT

If the visor of a motor cycle helmet is manufactured with a mirrored finish this comes under the scope of the eye protector regulations and the visor has to conform to appropriate standards. On the visor there should be a mark to show that it conforms to those standards. Some motor cyclists adapt a quality marked clear visor by placing film over it in order to darken it or to give a mirrored effect. Adapting a visor in this way contravenes the quality standard mark so use of the visor in its adapted condition would no longer be lawful.

12.8 **Obstructing the Road or Highway**

There are three possible offences that may be considered in relation to obstruction.

12.8.1 **Offences**

- It is an offence for a person in charge of a motor vehicle or trailer to cause or permit the vehicle to stand on a road so as to cause any *unnecessary* obstruction of the road (Road Vehicles (Construction and Use) Regulations 1986, reg 103).
- It is an offence for any person in any street, to *wilfully* cause an obstruction in any public footpath or public thoroughfare to the annoyance or danger of the residents or passengers (Town Police Clauses Act 1847, s 28).
- It is an offence for any person, without lawful authority or excuse, to *wilfully* obstruct the free passage along a highway (Highways Act 1980, s 137).

Depending upon which offence is alleged it will be necessary to show the obstruction was wilful or unnecessary. Further, in respect of the Highways Act offence, the presence of lawful authority or excuse will constitute a defence.

12.8.2 **Meaning of Obstruction**

Whether or not something constitutes an obstruction is a question of fact for the court to determine. It is not confined to a simple physical obstruction but may also be an *unreasonable* use of the highway, road or footpath. The issue of what is a reasonable or unreasonable use of the highway is one of fact to be determined by the court. What is unreasonable will depend on all the circumstances of the case including the length of time the obstruction lasts, the location, the purpose and whether it causes an actual obstruction as opposed to a potential obstruction. The following are examples taken from decided cases:

- Performing a U-turn in a busy street holding up traffic for 50 seconds was an obstruction (*Wall v Williams* [1966] Crim LR 50).
- Parking a van in a busy street next to a bus stop for some 5 minutes and refusing to move it when requested was an obstruction (*Nagy v Weston* [1965] 1 WLR 280).
- Parking a van so close to another vehicle on a road and then refusing to move so as to assist the other vehicle in being able to move was an obstruction (*Mounsey v Campbell* [1983] RTR 36).
- Displays on footpaths outside shop premises were an obstruction (*Herts CC v Bolden* (1987) 151 JP 252).
- Street performers in a busy shopping street was an obstruction (*Waite v Taylor* (1985) 149 JP 551).
- Parking a van on a busy road for the purpose of selling hot dogs was an obstruction (*Pitcher v Lockett* (1966) 64 LGR 477).

PRACTICAL POINT

A driver parks a motor vehicle partly on the road and partly on the pavement. This may constitute an obstruction offence. If, for example, it can be shown that a pedestrian with a child in a pram or pushchair could not pass freely without, perhaps, stepping into the road, then that would expose the pedestrian to a potential danger and would constitute an offence under the Town Police Clauses Act. Alternatively, the driver may be prosecuted for the offence of unnecessary obstruction under the Construction and Use Regulations.

12.8.3 Wilful or Unnecessary

Depending upon which offence is alleged it will be necessary to show that the obstruction, whatever its nature, was either wilful or unnecessary.

Wilful

The offence under the Highways Act and the offence under the Town Police Clauses Act both require the obstruction to be wilful. This means the obstruction must be deliberate and so, if the driver of a broken down vehicle makes reasonable efforts to have the vehicle removed, he cannot be said to be acting wilfully with regard to any obstruction the vehicle causes during that time. A person who is requested or required to move whatever is said to be causing the obstruction and who refuses to do so is clearly acting wilfully.

Unnecessary

This element is a question of fact for the court to determine and is closely linked with the question of whether or not there is an obstruction at all.

12.9 Vehicles Used for Harassment

Section 59 of the Police Reform Act 2002 provides:

(1) Where a constable in uniform has reasonable grounds for believing that a motor vehicle is being used on any occasion in a manner which—
   (a) contravenes section 3 or 34 of the Road Traffic Act 1988 (careless or inconsiderate driving and prohibition of off-road driving), and
   (b) is causing, or is likely to cause, alarm, distress or annoyance to members of the public, he shall have the powers set out in subsection (3).
(2) A constable in uniform shall also have the powers set out in subsection (3) where he has reasonable ground for believing that a motor vehicle has been used on any occasion in a manner falling within subsection (1).

The powers available by virtue of sub-s (3) are:

- if the motor vehicle is moving, to order the person driving the vehicle to stop the vehicle;
- to seize and remove the motor vehicle;
- for the purposes of exercising these powers, to enter any premises on which the constable has reasonable grounds for believing the motor vehicle to be;
- to use reasonable force, if necessary, in the exercise of any power conferred.

PRACTICAL POINT

This power is ideal for use when complaints are received about vehicles being used on residential estates in such a manner as to cause serious annoyance (perhaps even danger) to the residents. Note that the power to enter premises does not include entry into a private dwelling house but does extend to give entry onto driveways and into garages. It should also be noted that 'motor vehicle' is defined in this Act as any mechanically propelled vehicle *whether or not intended for use on a road* and thus would include go-karts, building site vehicles, trials bikes, etc.

12.9.1 Restrictions on Power to Seize Vehicles

Section 59(5) of the Police Reform Act 2002 places some restrictions on the seizure of vehicles. A vehicle cannot be seized unless the officer:

- has warned the person appearing to the officer to be the person whose use falls within sub-s (1) that the officer will seize the vehicle if that use continues or is repeated; and
- it appears to the officer that the use has continued or been repeated after the warning has been given.

However a warning is not required if:

- the circumstances make it impracticable for the officer to give a warning;
- the officer has already on that occasion given such a warning in respect of any use of that motor vehicle or of another motor vehicle by that person or any other person;
- the officer has reasonable grounds for believing that such a warning has been given on that occasion otherwise than by him/her; or
- the officer has reasonable grounds for believing that the person whose use of that motor vehicle on that occasion would justify the seizure is a person to whom a warning under that subsection has been given (whether or not by that officer or in respect the same vehicle or the same or a similar use) on a previous occasion in the previous 12 months.

12.10 **Taxis**

There are some common misconceptions about some of the regulations that apply to taxis so the following is a brief summary of the most relevant areas.

Taxis, broadly speaking, are divided into two groups. First, there are hackney carriages (or black cabs) which may lawfully ply for hire on the street. Second, there are private hire vehicles (sometimes called mini cabs) that cannot lawfully ply for hire on the street but must be pre-booked. Local authorities are empowered to provide licences for both hackney carriages and private hire vehicles. In addition, they also provide licences for the individual drivers of taxis.

The Local Government (Miscellaneous Provisions) Act 1976 gives the local authority powers to attach conditions to licences issued to taxi drivers. Common conditions attached to licences are:

- the need to carry a first aid kit with specified contents;
- the need to carry a fire extinguisher of a particular construction;
- the need to carry a copy of the condition attached to the licence in the vehicle;
- the colour of the vehicle can be specified;
- the position of the licence plate and how it is to be fixed to the vehicle;
- the need to produce proof of insurance to the local authority;
- conditions as to appearance of vehicle;
- where and how the driver must display his licence to drive.

> **PRACTICAL POINT**
>
> The local authority will have an enforcement officer who will provide the police with a copy of the conditions attached to any licence issued by that authority. It is good practice to obtain a copy of the conditions and where necessary, conduct examinations of taxis to ascertain if conditions are being contravened.
>
> Many enforcement officers are more than willing to conduct joint operations with the police (and other agencies if necessary) to assist in enforcing the control of taxis and detecting offences.

12.11 **Questions and Answers**

Q1 A pregnant woman in a car is concerned that wearing a seat belt is dangerous to her unborn child. Is she exempt from wearing a seat belt?

A1 No she is not. There is no general exemption based on pregnancy. It is, of course, possible that a pregnant woman may obtain a medical exemption from a doctor but pregnancy alone does not afford exemption from the regulations.

Q2 Taxi drivers commonly claim exemption from wearing a seat belt. Is it true that they are always exempt?

A2 No they are not. It depends on the type of service provided and the nature of the journey. The driver of a hackney carriage (sometimes called a 'London taxi' or a 'black cab') does have a general exemption so long as the vehicle is being used as a taxi at the relevant time. A hackney carriage being used for some private purpose does not afford any exemption to the driver. A private hire vehicle (which is a vehicle that has to be pre-booked and cannot be flagged down in the street) is treated slightly differently. The driver is exempt but only while carrying a passenger in the vehicle. If there is no passenger actually in the vehicle then the regulations apply in full.

Q3 The driver's seat belt in a vehicle is broken. Can the vehicle still lawfully be used? Would it make a difference if it was a passenger seat belt that was broken?

A3 Seat belts fitted in vehicles must be properly maintained in accordance with the 1986 Regulations but if the defect or fault arose during the course of the journey in question and steps have been taken to restore the belt to working order with reasonable expedition, then the vehicle may still be used. A passenger would still have to wear a seat belt if there was another seat available with a working seat belt. If, however, all other seats are properly occupied and there is no working seat belt available, none has to be worn.

Q4 All seats are occupied by adults who are wearing their seat belts. There is a young child sitting on the lap of one of the adults. The seat belt is around both the adult and the child. Is this lawful?

A4 There is no legal obligation to give priority to a child rather than an adult as far as the wearing of seat belts is concerned. In this situation, either the adult or the child could wear the belt and the other, given that there would be no available seat belt left, would not commit an offence. However, this is certainly a dangerous situation and the adults concerned should be advised accordingly. There is also the possibility that the driver's insurance company would regard this as an uninsured use, given that there are more passengers in the vehicle than it was designed to carry. In practice, this may not be something insurance companies turn their minds to until a claim is forthcoming. You might also consider whether an offence has been committed under the Construction and Use Regulations regarding dangerous use or condition (see 7.3.8).

Appendix 1
Road Traffic Offenders Act 1988, Schedules 2 and 3

Schedule 2 Prosecution and Punishment of Offences
Part I Offences Under the Traffic Acts

(1) Provision creating offence	(2) General nature of offence	(3) Mode of prosecution	(4) Punishment	(5) Disqualification	(6) Endorsement	(7) Penalty points
Offences under the Road Traffic Regulation Act 1984						
RTRA section 5	Contravention of traffic regulation order.	Summarily.	Level 3 on the standard scale.			
RTRA section 8	Contravention of order regulating traffic in Greater London.	Summarily.	Level 3 on the standard scale.			
RTRA section 11	Contravention of experimental traffic order.	Summarily.	Level 3 on the standard scale.			
RTRA section 13	Contravention of experimental traffic scheme in Greater London.	Summarily.	Level 3 on the standard scale.			
RTRA section 16(1)	Contravention of temporary prohibition or restriction.	Summarily.	Level 3 on the standard scale.	Discretionary if committed in respect of a speed restriction.	Obligatory if committed in respect of a speed restriction.	3–6 or 3 (fixed penalty).
RTRA section 16C(1)	Contravention of prohibition or restriction relating to relevant event.	Summarily.	Level 3 on the standard scale.			
RTRA section 17(4)	Use of special road contrary to scheme or regulations.	Summarily.	Level 4 on the standard scale.	Discretionary if committed in respect of a motor vehicle otherwise than by unlawfully stopping or allowing the vehicle to remain at rest on a part of	Obligatory if committed as mentioned in the entry in column 5.	3–6 or 3 (fixed penalty) if committed in respect of a speed restriction, 3 in any other case.

(1) Provision creating offence	(2) General nature of offence	(3) Mode of prosecution	(4) Punishment	(5) Disqualification	(6) Endorsement	(7) Penalty points

Offences under the Road Traffic Regulation Act 1984—continued

			a special road on which vehicles are in certain circumstances permitted to remain at rest.			
RTRA section 18(3)	One-way traffic on trunk road.	Summarily.	Level 3 on the standard scale.			
RTRA section 20(5)	Contravention of prohibition or restriction for roads of certain classes.	Summarily.	Level 3 on the standard scale.			
RTRA section 25(5)	Contravention of pedestrian crossing regulations.	Summarily.	Level 3 on the standard scale.	Discretionary if committed in respect of a motor vehicle.	Obligatory if committed in respect of a motor vehicle.	3
RTRA section 28(3)	Not stopping at school crossing.	Summarily.	Level 3 on the standard scale.	Discretionary if committed in respect of a motor vehicle.	Obligatory if committed in respect of a motor vehicle.	3
RTRA section 29(3)	Contravention of order relating to street playground.	Summarily.	Level 3 on the standard scale.	Discretionary if committed in respect of a motor vehicle.	Obligatory if committed in respect of a motor vehicle.	2
RTRA section 35A(1)	Contravention of order as to use of parking place.	Summarily.	(a) Level 3 on the standard scale in the case of an offence committed by a person in a street parking place reserved for disabled persons' vehicles or in an off-street parking place reserved for such vehicles, where that person would not have been guilty of that offence if the motor vehicle in respect of which			

(1) Provision creating offence	(2) General nature of offence	(3) Mode of prosecution	(4) Punishment	(5) Disqualification	(6) Endorsement	(7) Penalty points
Offences under the Road Traffic Regulation Act 1984—continued						
			it was committed had been a disabled person's vehicle. (b) Level 2 on the standard scale in any other case.			
RTRA section 35A(2)	Misuse of apparatus for collecting charges or of parking device or connected apparatus.	Summarily.	Level 3 on the standard scale.			
RTRA section 35A(5)	Plying for hire in parking place.	Summarily.	Level 2 on the standard scale.			
RTRA section 43(5)	Unauthorised disclosure of information in respect of licensed parking place.	Summarily.	Level 3 on the standard scale.			
RTRA section 43(10)	Failure to comply with term or conditions of licence to operate parking place.	Summarily.	Level 3 on the standard scale.			
RTRA section 43(12)	Operation of public off-street parking place without licence.	Summarily.	Level 5 on the standard scale.			
RTRA section 47(1)	Contraventions relating to designated parking places.	Summarily.	(a) Level 3 on the standard scale in the case of an offence committed by a person in a street parking place reserved for disabled persons' vehicles where that person would not have been guilty of the offence if the motor vehicle in respect of which it was committed had been a disabled person's vehicle. (b) Level 2 in any other case.			

(1) Provision creating offence	(2) General nature of offence	(3) Mode of prosecution	(4) Punishment	(5) Disqualification	(6) Endorsement	(7) Penalty points
Offences under the Road Traffic Regulation Act 1984—continued						
RTRA section 47(3)	Tampering with parking meter.	Summarily.	Level 3 on the standard scale.			
RTRA section 52(1)	Misuse of parking device.	Summarily.	Level 2 on the standard scale.			
RTRA section 53(5)	Contravention of certain provisions of designation orders.	Summarily.	Level 3 on the standard scale.			
RTRA section 53(6)	Other contraventions of designation orders.	Summarily.	Level 2 on the standard scale.			
RTRA section 61(5)	Unauthorised use of loading area.	Summarily.	Level 3 on the standard scale.			
RTRA section 88(7)	Contravention of minimum speed limit.	Summarily.	Level 3 on the standard scale.			
RTRA section 89(1)	Exceeding speed limit.	Summarily.	Level 3 on the standard scale.	Discretionary.	Obligatory.	3–6 or 3 (fixed penalty).
RTRA section 104(5)	Interference with notice as to immobilisation device.	Summarily.	Level 2 on the standard scale.			
RTRA section 104(6)	Interference with immobilisation device.	Summarily.	Level 3 on the standard scale.			
RTRA section 105(5)	Misuse of disabled person's badge (immobilisation devices).	Summarily.	Level 3 on the standard scale.			
RTRA section 108(2) (or that subsection as modified by section 109(2) and (3)).	Non-compliance with notice (excess charge).	Summarily.	Level 3 on the standard scale.			
RTRA section 108(3) (or that subsection as modified by section 109(2) and (3)).	False response to notice (excess charge).	Summarily.	Level 5 on the standard scale.			
RTRA section 112(4)	Failure to give information as to identity of driver.	Summarily.	Level 3 on the standard scale.			
RTRA section 115(1)	Mishandling or faking parking documents.	(a) Summarily. (b) On indictment.	(a) The statutory maximum. (b) 2 years.			
RTRA section 115(2)	False statement for procuring authorisation.	Summarily.	Level 4 on the standard scale.			

194

(1) Provision creating offence	(2) General nature of offence	(3) Mode of prosecution	(4) Punishment	(5) Disqualification	(6) Endorsement	(7) Penalty points
Offences under the Road Traffic Regulation Act 1984—continued						
RTRA section 116(1)	Non-delivery of suspect document or article.	Summarily.	Level 3 on the standard scale.			
RTRA section 117	Wrongful use of disabled person's badge.	Summarily.	Level 3 on the standard scale.			
RTRA section 129(3)	Failure to give evidence at inquiry.	Summarily.	Level 3 on the standard scale.			
Offences under the Road Traffic Act 1988						
RTA section 1	Causing death by dangerous driving.	On indictment.	14 years.	Obligatory.	Obligatory.	3–11
RTA section 2	Dangerous Driving.	(a) Summarily.	(a) 6 months or the statutory maximum or both.	Obligatory.	Obligatory.	3–11
		(b) On indictment.	(b) 2 years or a fine or both.			
RTA section 3	Careless, and inconsiderate, driving.	Summarily.	Level 4 on the standard scale.	Discretionary.	Obligatory.	3–9
RTA section 3A	Causing death by careless driving when under influence of drink or drugs.	On indictment.	14 years or a fine or both.	Obligatory.	Obligatory.	3–11
RTA section 4(1)	Driving or attempting to drive when unfit to drive through drink or drugs.	Summarily.	6 months or level 5 on the standard scale or both.	Obligatory.	Obligatory.	3–11
RTA section 4(2)	Being in charge of a mechanically propelled vehicle when unfit to drive through drink or drugs.	Summarily.	3 months or level 4 on the standard scale or both.	Discretionary.	Obligatory.	10
RTA section 5(1)(a)	Driving or attempting to drive with excess alcohol in breath, blood or urine.	Summarily.	6 months or level 5 on the standard scale or both.	Obligatory.	Obligatory.	3–11
RTA section 5(1)(b)	Being in charge of a motor vehicle with excess alcohol in breath, blood or urine.	Summarily.	3 months or level 4 on the standard scale or both.	Discretionary.	Obligatory.	10
RTA section 6	Failing to co-operate with a preliminary test.	Summarily.	Level 3 on the standard scale.	Discretionary.	Obligatory.	4
RTA section 7	Failing to provide specimen for analysis or laboratory test.	Summarily.	(a) Where the specimen was required to ascertain	(a) Obligatory in case mentioned in column 4(a).	Obligatory.	(a) 3–11 in case mentioned in column 4(a).

(1) Provision creating offence	(2) General nature of offence	(3) Mode of prosecution	(4) Punishment	(5) Disqualification	(6) Endorsement	(7) Penalty points
Offences under the Road Traffic Act 1988—continued						
			ability to drive or proportion of alcohol at the time offender was driving or attempting to drive, 6 months or level 5 on the standard scale or both.			
			(b) In any other case, 3 months or level 4 on the standard scale or both.	(b) Discretionary in any other case.		(b) 10 in any other case.
RTA section 7A	Failing to allow specimen to be subjected to laboratory test.	Summarily.	(a) Where the test would be for ascertaining ability to drive or proportion of alcohol at the time offender was driving or attempting to drive, 6 months or level 5 on the standard scale or both.	(a) Obligatory in the case mentioned in column 4(a).	Obligatory	3–11, in case mentioned in column 4(a).
			(b) In any other case, 3 months or level 4 on the standard scale or both.	(b) Discretionary in any other case.	10, in any other case.	
RTA section 12	Motor racing and speed trials on public ways.	Summarily.	Level 4 on the standard scale.	Obligatory.	Obligatory.	3–11
RTA section 13	Other unauthorised or irregular competitions or trials on public ways.	Summarily.	Level 3 on the standard scale.			
RTA section 14	Driving or riding in a motor vehicle in contravention of regulations requiring wearing of seat belts.	Summarily.	Level 2 on the standard scale.			

196

(1) Provision creating offence	(2) General nature of offence	(3) Mode of prosecution	(4) Punishment	(5) Disqualification	(6) Endorsement	(7) Penalty points
Offences under the Road Traffic Act 1988—continued						
RTA section 15(2)	Driving motor vehicle with child not wearing seat belt.	Summarily.	Level 2 on the standard scale.			
RTA section 15(4)	Driving motor vehicle with child in rear not wearing a seat belt.	Summarily.	Level 1 on the standard scale.			
RTA section 15A(3) or (4)	Selling etc. in certain circumstances equipment as conducive to the safety of children in motor vehicles.	Summarily.	Level 3 on the standard scale.			
RTA section 16	Driving or riding motor cycles in contravention of regulations requiring wearing of protective headgear.	Summarily.	Level 2 on the standard scale.			
RTA section 17	Selling, etc., helmet not of the prescribed type as helmet for affording protection for motor cyclists.	Summarily.	Level 3 on the standard scale.			
RTA section 18(3)	Contravention of regulations with respect to use of head-worn appliances on motor cycles.	Summarily.	Level 2 on the standard scale.			
RTA section 18(4)	Selling, etc., appliance not of prescribed type as approved for use on motor cycles.	Summarily.	Level 3 on the standard scale.			
RTA section 19	Prohibition of parking of heavy commercial vehicles on verges, etc.	Summarily.	Level 3 on the standard scale.			
RTA section 21	Driving or parking on cycle track.	Summarily.	Level 3 on the standard scale.			
RTA section 22	Leaving vehicles in dangerous positions.	Summarily.	Level 3 on the standard scale.	Discretionary if committed in respect of a motor vehicle.	Obligatory if committed in respect of a motor vehicle.	3
RTA section 22A	Causing danger to road users.	(a) Summarily. (b) On indictment.	(a) 6 months or the statutory maximum or both. (b) 7 years or a fine or both.			
RTA section 23	Carrying passenger on motor cycle contrary to section 23.	Summarily.	Level 3 on the standard scale.	Discretionary.	Obligatory.	3

197

(1) Provision creating offence	(2) General nature of offence	(3) Mode of prosecution	(4) Punishment	(5) Disqualification	(6) Endorsement	(7) Penalty points
Offences under the Road Traffic Act 1988—continued						
RTA section 24	Carrying passenger on bicycle contrary to section 24.	Summarily.	Level 1 on the standard scale.			
RTA section 25	Tampering with motor vehicles.	Summarily.	Level 3 on the standard scale.			
RTA section 26	Holding or getting on to vehicle, etc., in order to be towed or carried.	Summarily.	Level 1 on the standard scale.			
RTA section 27	Dogs on designated roads without being held on lead.	Summarily.	Level 1 on the standard scale.			
RTA section 28	Dangerous cycling.	Summarily.	Level 4 on the standard scale.			
RTA section 29	Careless, and inconsiderate, cycling.	Summarily.	Level 3 on the standard scale.			
RTA section 30	Cycling when unfit through drink or drugs.	Summarily.	Level 3 on the standard scale.			
RTA section 31	Unauthorised or irregular cycle racing or trials of speed on public ways.	Summarily.	Level 1 on the standard scale.			
RTA section 32	Contravening prohibition on persons under 14 driving electrically assisted pedal cycles.	Summarily.	Level 2 on the standard scale.			
RTA section 33	Unauthorised motor vehicle trial on footpaths or bridleways.	Summarily.	Level 3 on the standard scale.			
RTA section 34	Driving mechanically propelled vehicles elsewhere than on roads.	Summarily.	Level 3 on the standard scale.			
RTA section 35	Failing to comply with traffic directions.	Summarily.	Level 3 on the standard scale.	Discretionary, if committed in respect of a motor vehicle by failure to comply with a direction of a constable, traffic officer or traffic warden.	Obligatory if committed as described in column 5.	3
RTA section 36	Failing to comply with traffic signs.	Summarily.	Level 3 on the standard scale.	Discretionary, if committed in respect of a	Obligatory if committed as described	3

198

(1) Provision creating offence	(2) General nature of offence	(3) Mode of prosecution	(4) Punishment	(5) Disqualification	(6) Endorsement	(7) Penalty points
Offences under the Road Traffic Act 1988—continued						
			motor vehicle by failure to comply with an indication given by a sign specified for the purposes of this paragraph in regulations under RTA section 36.	in column 5.		
RTA section 37	Pedestrian failing to stop when directed by constable regulating traffic.	Summarily.	Level 3 on the standard scale.			
RTA section 40A	Using vehicle in dangerous condition etc.	Summarily.	(a) Level 5 on the standard scale if committed in respect of a goods vehicle or a vehicle adapted to carry more than eight passengers. (b) Level 4 on the standard scale in any other case.	Discretionary.	Obligatory.	3
RTA section 41A	Breach of requirement as to brakes, steering-gear or tyres.	Summarily.	(a) Level 5 on the standard scale if committed in respect of a goods vehicle or a vehicle adapted to carry more than eight passengers. (b) Level 4 on the standard scale in any other case.	Discretionary.	Obligatory.	3
RTA section 41B	Breach of requirement as to weight: goods and passenger vehicles.	Summarily.	Level 5 on the standard scale.			
RTA section 42	Breach of other construction and use requirements.	Summarily.	(a) Level 4 on the standard scale if committed in			

199

(1) Provision creating offence	(2) General nature of offence	(3) Mode of prosecution	(4) Punishment	(5) Disqualification	(6) Endorsement	(7) Penalty points

Offences under the Road Traffic Act 1988—continued

(1) Provision creating offence	(2) General nature of offence	(3) Mode of prosecution	(4) Punishment	(5) Disqualification	(6) Endorsement	(7) Penalty points
			respect of a goods vehicle or a vehicle adapted to carry more than eight passengers. (b) Level 3 on the standard scale in any other case.			
RTA section 47	Using, etc., vehicle without required test certificate being in force.	Summarily.	(a) Level 4 on the standard scale in the case of a vehicle adapted to carry more than eight passengers. (b) Level 3 on the standard scale in any other case.			
Regulations under RTA section 49 made by virtue of section 51(2)	Contravention of requirement of regulations (which is declared by regulations to be an offence) that driver of goods vehicle being tested be present throughout test or drive, etc., vehicle as and when directed.	Summarily.	Level 3 on the standard scale.			
RTA section 53(1)	Using, etc., goods vehicle without required plating certificate being in force.	Summarily.	Level 3 on the standard scale.			
RTA section 53(2)	Using, etc., goods vehicle without required goods vehicle test certificate being in force.	Summarily.	Level 4 on the standard scale.			
RTA section 53(3)	Using, etc., goods vehicle where Secretary of State is required by	Summarily.	Level 3 on the standard scale.			

200

(1) Provision creating offence	(2) General nature of offence	(3) Mode of prosecution	(4) Punishment	(5) Disqualification	(6) Endorsement	(7) Penalty points
Offences under the Road Traffic Act 1988—continued						
	regulations under section 49 to be notified of an alteration to the vehicle or its equipment but has not been notified.					
Regulations under RTA section 61 made by virtue of subsection (4)	Contravention of requirement of regulations (which is declared by regulations to be an offence) that driver of goods vehicle being tested after notifiable alteration be present throughout test and drive, etc., vehicle as and when directed.	Summarily.	Level 3 on the standard scale.			
RTA section 63(1)	Using, etc., goods vehicle without required certificate being in force showing that it complies with type approval requirements applicable to it.	Summarily.	Level 4 on the standard scale.			
RTA section 63(2)	Using, etc., certain goods vehicles for drawing trailer when plating certificate does not specify maximum laden weight for vehicle and trailer.	Summarily.	Level 3 on the standard scale.			
RTA section 63(3)	Using, etc., goods vehicle where Secretary of State is required to be notified under section 59 of alteration to it or its equipment but has not been notified.	Summarily.	Level 3 on the standard scale.			
RTA section 64	Using goods vehicle with unauthorised weights as well as authorised weights marked on it.	Summarily.	Level 3 on the standard scale.			

(1) Provision creating offence	(2) General nature of offence	(3) Mode of prosecution	(4) Punishment	(5) Disqualification	(6) Endorsement	(7) Penalty points
Offences under the Road Traffic Act 1988—continued						
RTA section 64A	Failure to hold EC certificate of conformity for unregistered light passenger vehicle or motor cycle.	Summarily.	Level 3 on the standard scale.			
RTA section 65	Supplying vehicle or vehicle part without required certificate being in force showing that it complies with type approval requirements applicable to it.	Summarily.	Level 5 on the standard scale.			
RTA section 65A	Light passenger vehicles and motor cycles not to be sold without EC certificate of conformity.	Summarily.	Level 5 on the standard scale.			
RTA section 67	Obstructing testing of vehicle by examiner on road or failing to comply with requirements of RTA section 67 or schedule 2.	Summarily.	Level 3 on the standard scale.			
RTA section 68	Obstructing inspection, etc., of vehicle by examiner or failing to comply with requirement to take vehicle for inspection.	Summarily.	Level 3 on the standard scale.			
RTA section 71	Driving, etc., vehicle in contravention of prohibition on driving it as being unfit for service, or refusing, neglecting or otherwise failing to comply with direction to remove a vehicle found overloaded.	Summarily.	Level 5 on the standard scale.			
RTA section 74	Contravention of regulations requiring goods vehicle operator to inspect, and keep records of inspection of, goods vehicles.	Summarily.	Level 3 on the standard scale.			
RTA section 75	Selling, etc., unroadworthy vehicle	Summarily.	Level 5 on the standard scale.			

(1) Provision creating offence	(2) General nature of offence	(3) Mode of prosecution	(4) Punishment	(5) Disqualification	(6) Endorsement	(7) Penalty points
Offences under the Road Traffic Act 1988—continued						
	or trailer or altering vehicle or trailer so as to make it unroadworthy.					
RTA section 76(1)	Fitting of defective or unsuitable vehicle parts.	Summarily.	Level 5 on the standard scale.			
RTA section 76(3)	Supplying defective or unsuitable vehicle parts.	Summarily.	Level 4 on the standard scale.			
RTA section 76(8)	Obstructing examiner testing vehicles to ascertain whether defective or unsuitable part has been fitted, etc.	Summarily.	Level 3 on the standard scale.			
RTA section 77	Obstructing examiner testing condition of used vehicle at sale rooms, etc.	Summarily.	Level 3 on the standard scale.			
RTA section 78	Failing to comply with requirement about weighing motor vehicle or obstructing authorised person.	Summarily.	Level 5 on the standard scale.			
RTA section 81	Selling, etc., pedal cycle in contravention of regulations as to brakes, bells, etc.	Summarily.	Level 3 on the standard scale.			
RTA section 83	Selling, etc., wrongly made tail lamps or reflectors.	Summarily.	Level 5 on the standard scale.			
RTA section 87(1)	Driving otherwise than in accordance with a licence.	Summarily.	Level 3 on the standard scale.	Discretionary in a case where the offender's driving would not have been in accordance with any licence that could have been granted to him.	Obligatory in the case mentioned in column 5.	3–6
RTA section 87(2)	Causing or permitting a person to drive otherwise than in accordance with a licence.	Summarily.	Level 3 on the standard scale.			
RTA section 92(7C)	Failure to deliver licence revoked by virtue of section	Summarily.	Level 3 on the standard scale.			

(1) Provision creating offence	(2) General nature of offence	(3) Mode of prosecution	(4) Punishment	(5) Disqualification	(6) Endorsement	(7) Penalty points

Offences under the Road Traffic Act 1988—continued

(1) Provision creating offence	(2) General nature of offence	(3) Mode of prosecution	(4) Punishment	(5) Disqualification	(6) Endorsement	(7) Penalty points
	92(7A) and counterpart to Secretary of State.					
RTA section 92(10)	Driving after making false declaration as to physical fitness.	Summarily.	Level 4 on the standard scale.	Discretionary.	Obligatory.	3–6
RTA section 93(3)	Failure to deliver revoked licence and counterpart to Secretary of State.	Summarily.	Level 3 on the standard scale.			
RTA section 94(3) and that subsection as applied by RTA section 99D or 109C(c)	Failure to notify Secretary of State of onset of, or deterioration in, relevant or prospective disability.	Summarily.	Level 3 on the standard scale.			
RTA section 94(3A) and that subsection as applied by RTA section 99D(b) or 109C(c)	Driving after such a failure.	Summarily.	Level 3 on the standard scale.	Discretionary.	Obligatory.	3–6
RTA section 94A	Driving after refusal of licence under section 92(3), revocation under section 93 or service of a notice under section 99C.	Summarily.	6 months or level 5 on the standard scale or both.	Discretionary.	Obligatory.	3–6
RTA section 96	Driving with uncorrected defective eyesight, or refusing to submit to test of eyesight.	Summarily.	Level 3 on the standard scale.	Discretionary.	Obligatory.	3
RTA section 99(5)	Driving licence holder failing, to surrender licence and counterpart.	Summarily.	Level 3 on the standard scale.			
RTA section 99B(11) and that subsection as applied by RTA section 109A(5)	Driving after failure to comply with a requirement under section 99B(6), (7) or (10).	Summarily.	Level 3 on the standard scale.			
RTA section 99C(4)	Failure to deliver Community licence to Secretary of State when required by	Summarily.	Level 3 on the standard scale.			

(1) Provision creating offence	(2) General nature of offence	(3) Mode of prosecution	(4) Punishment	(5) Disqualification	(6) Endorsement	(7) Penalty points
Offences under the Road Traffic Act 1988—continued						
	notice under section 99C.					
RTA section 103(1)(a)	Obtaining driving licence while disqualified.	Summarily.	Level 3 on the standard scale.			
RTA section 103(1)(b)	Driving while disqualified.	(a) Summarily, in England and Wales.	(a) 6 months or level 5 on the standard scale or both.	Discretionary.	Obligatory.	6
		(b) Summarily, in Scotland.	(b) 6 months or the statutory maximum or both.			
		(c) On indictment, in Scotland.	(c) 12 months or a fine or both.			
RTA section 109	Failing to produce to court Northern Ireland driving licence and its counterpart.	Summarily.	Level 3 on the standard scale.			
RTA section 114	Failing to comply with conditions of LGV, PCV licence or LGV Community licence, or causing or permitting person under 21 to drive LGV or PCV in contravention of such conditions.	Summarily.	Level 3 on the standard scale.			
RTA section 115A(4)	Failure to deliver LGV or PCV Community licence when required by notice under section 115A.	Summarily.	Level 3 on the standard scale.			
RTA section 118	Failing to surrender revoked or suspended LGV or PCV licence and counterpart.	Summarily.	Level 3 on the standard scale.			
Regulations made by virtue of RTA section 120(5)	Contravention of provision of regulations (which is declared by regulations to be an offence) about LGV or PCV drivers' licences or LGV or PCV Community licence.	Summarily.	Level 3 on the standard scale.			

205

(1) Provision creating offence	(2) General nature of offence	(3) Mode of prosecution	(4) Punishment	(5) Disqualification	(6) Endorsement	(7) Penalty points
Offences under the Road Traffic Act 1988—continued						
RTA section 123(4)	Giving of paid driving instruction by unregistered and unlicensed persons or their employers.	Summarily.	Level 4 on the standard scale.			
RTA section 123(6)	Giving of paid instruction without there being exhibited on the motor car a certificate of registration or a licence under RTA part V.	Summarily.	Level 3 on the standard scale.			
RTA section 125A(4)	Failure, on application for registration as disabled driving instructor, to notify Registrar of onset of, or deterioration in, relevant or prospective disability.	Summarily.	Level 3 on the standard scale.			
RTA section 133C(4)	Failure by registered or licensed disabled driving instructor to notify Registrar of onset of, or deterioration in, relevant or prospective disability.	Summarily.	Level 3 on the standard scale.			
RTA section 133D	Giving of paid driving instruction by disabled persons or their employers without emergency control certificate or in unauthorised motor car.	Summarily.	Level 3 on the standard scale.			
RTA section 135	Unregistered instructor using title or displaying badge, etc., prescribed for registered instructor, or employer using such title, etc., in relation to his unregistered instructor or issuing misleading advertisement, etc.	Summarily.	Level 4 on the standard scale.			

(1) Provision creating offence	(2) General nature of offence	(3) Mode of prosecution	(4) Punishment	(5) Disqualification	(6) Endorsement	(7) Penalty points
Offences under the Road Traffic Act 1988—continued						
RTA section 136	Failure of instructor to surrender to Registrar certificate or licence.	Summarily.	Level 3 on the standard scale.			
RTA section 137	Failing to produce certificate of registration or licence as driving instructor.	Summarily.	Level 3 on the standard scale.			
RTA section 143	Using motor vehicle while uninsured or unsecured against third-party risks.	Summarily.	Level 5 on the standard scale.	Discretionary.	Obligatory.	6–8
RTA section 147	Failing to surrender certificate of insurance or security to insurer on cancellation or to make statutory declaration of loss or destruction.	Summarily.	Level 3 on the standard scale.			
RTA section 154	Failing to give information, or wilfully making a false statement, as to insurance or security when claim made.	Summarily.	Level 4 on the standard scale.			
RTA section 163	Failing to stop motor vehicle or cycle when required by constable.	Summarily.	Level 3 on the standard scale.			
RTA section 164	Failing to produce driving licence and its counterpart or to state date of birth, or failing to provide the Secretary of State with evidence of date of birth, etc.	Summarily.	Level 3 on the standard scale.			
RTA section 165	Failing to give certain names and addresses or to produce certain documents.	Summarily.	Level 3 on the standard scale.			
RTA section 168	Refusing to give, or giving false, name and address in case of reckless, careless or inconsiderate driving or cycling.	Summarily.	Level 3 on the standard scale.			
RTA section 169	Pedestrian failing to give constable his name and address after failing to stop when	Summarily.	Level 1 on the standard scale.			

(1) Provision creating offence	(2) General nature of offence	(3) Mode of prosecution	(4) Punishment	(5) Disqualification	(6) Endorsement	(7) Penalty points
Offences under the Road Traffic Act 1988—continued						
	directed by constable controlling traffic.					
RTA section 170(4)	Failing to stop after accident and give particulars or report accident.	Summarily.	Six months or level 5 on the standard scale or both.	Discretionary.	Obligatory.	5–10
RTA section 170(7)	Failure by driver, in case of accident involving injury to another, to produce evidence of insurance or security or to report accident.	Summarily.	Level 3 on the standard scale.			
RTA section 171	Failure by owner of motor vehicle to give police information for verifying compliance with requirement of compulsory insurance or security.	Summarily.	Level 4 on the standard scale.			
RTA section 172	Failure of person keeping vehicle and others to give police information as to identity of driver, etc., in the case of certain offences.	Summarily.	Level 3 on the standard scale.	Discretionary if committed otherwise than than by virtue of subsection (5) or (11).	Obligatory if committed otherwise than than by virtue of subsection (5) or (11).	3
RTA section 173	Forgery, etc., of licences, counterparts of Community licences, certificates of insurance and other documents and things.	(a) Summarily. (b) On indictment.	(a) The statutory maximum. (b) 2 years.			
RTA section 174	Making certain false statements, etc., and withholding certain material information.	(a) Summarily. (b) On indictment.	(a) 6 months or the statutory maximum or both. (b) 2 years or a fine or both.			
RTA section 175(1)	Issuing false documents.	Summarily.	Level 4 on the standard scale.			
RTA section 175(2)	Falsely amending certificate of conformity.	Summarily.	Level 4 on the standard scale.			
RTA section 177	Impersonation of, or of person employed by, authorised examiner.	Summarily.	Level 3 on the standard scale.			

(1) Provision creating offence	(2) General nature of offence	(3) Mode of prosecution	(4) Punishment	(5) Disqualification	(6) Endorsement	(7) Penalty points
Offences under the Road Traffic Act 1988—continued						
RTA section 178	[Scotland.]					
RTA section 180	Failing to attend, give evidence or produce documents to, inquiry held by Secretary of State, etc.	Summarily.	Level 3 on the standard scale.			
RTA section 181	Obstructing inspection of vehicles after accident.	Summarily.	Level 3 on the standard scale.			
RTA schedule 1 paragraph 6	Applying warranty to equipment, protective helmet, appliance or information in defending proceedings under RTA section 15A, 17 or 18(4) where no warranty given, or applying false warranty.	Summarily.	Level 3 on the standard scale.			
Offences under this Act						
Section 25 of this Act.	Failing to give information as to date of birth or sex to court or to provide Secretary of State with evidence of date of birth, etc.	Summarily.	Level 3 on the standard scale.			
Section 26 of this Act.	Failing to produce driving licence and its counterpart to court making order for interim disqualification.	Summarily.	Level 3 on the standard scale.			
Section 27 of this Act.	Failing to produce licence and counterpart to court for endorsement on conviction of offence involving obligatory endorsement or on committal for sentence, etc., for offence involving obligatory or discretionary disqualification when no interim disqualification ordered.	Summarily.	Level 3 on the standard scale.			

(1) Provision creating offence	(2) General nature of offence	(3) Mode of prosecution	(4) Punishment	(5) Disqualification	(6) Endorsement	(7) Penalty points
Offences under the Road Traffic Act 1988—continued						
Section 45 of this Act.	Applying for or obtaining licence without giving particulars of current endorsement	Summarily.	Level 3 on the standard scale.			
Section 62 of this Act.	Removing fixed penalty notice fixed to vehicle.	Summarily.	Level 2 on the standard scale.			
Section 67 of this Act.	False statement in response to notice to owner.	Summarily.	Level 5 on the standard scale.			

Part II Other Offences

(1) Offence	(2) Disqualification	(3) Endorsement	(4) Penalty points
Manslaughter or, in Scotland, culpable homicide by the driver of a motor vehicle.	Obligatory.	Obligatory.	3–11
An offence under section 12A of the Theft Act 1968 (aggravated vehicle-taking).	Obligatory.	Obligatory.	3–11
Stealing or attempting to steal a motor vehicle.	Discretionary.		
An offence or attempt to commit an offence in respect of a motor vehicle under section 12 of the Theft Act 1968 (taking conveyance without consent of owner etc. or, knowing it has been so taken, driving it or allowing oneself to be carried in it).	Discretionary.		
An offence under section 25 of the Theft Act 1968 (going equipped for stealing, etc.) committed with reference to the theft or taking of motor vehicles.	Discretionary.		

Schedule 3 Fixed Penalty Offences

(1) Provision creating offence	(2) General nature of offence
Offences under the Parks Regulation (Amendment) Act 1926	
Section 2(1).	Breach of parks regulations but only where the offence is committed in relation to regulation 4(27) (driving or riding a trade vehicle), 4(28) (exceeding speed limit) or 4(30) (unauthorised waiting by a vehicle or leaving a vehicle unattended) of the Royal and other Parks and Gardens Regulations 1977.
Offences under the Highway Act 1835 and the Roads (Scotland) Act 1984	
Section 72 of the Highway Act 1835.	Driving on the footway. Cycling on the footway.
Section 129(5) of the Roads (Scotland) Act 1984.	Driving on the footway.

(1) Provision creating offence	(2) General nature of offence
Offence under the Greater London Council (General Powers) Act 1974 (c.xxiv)	
Section 15 of the Greater London Council (General Powers) Act 1974.	Parking vehicles on footways, verges, etc.
Offence under the Highways Act 1980	
Section 137 of the Highways Act 1980.	Obstructing a highway, but only where the offence is committed in respect of a vehicle.
Offences under the Road Traffic Act 1984	
RTRA section 5(1)	Using a vehicle in contravention of a traffic regulation order outside Greater London.
RTRA section 8(1)	Breach of traffic regulation order in Greater London.
RTRA section 11	Breach of experimental traffic order.
RTRA section 13	Breach of experimental traffic scheme regulations in Greater London.
RTRA section 16(1)	Using a vehicle in contravention of temporary prohibition or restriction of traffic in case of execution of works, etc.
RTRA section 17(4)	Wrongful use of special road.
RTRA section 18(3)	Using a vehicle in contravention of provision for one-way traffic on trunk road.
RTRA section 20(5)	Driving a vehicle in contravention of order prohibiting or restricting driving vehicles on certain classes of roads.
RTRA section 25(5)	Breach of pedestrian crossing regulations, except an offence in respect of a moving motor vehicle.
RTRA section 29(3)	Using a vehicle in contravention of a street playground order.
RTRA section 35A(1)	Breach of an order regulating the use, etc., of a parking place provided by a local authority, but only where the offence is committed in relation to a parking place provided on a road.
RTRA section 47(1)	Breach of a provision of a parking place designation order and other offences committed in relation to a parking place designated by such an order, except any offence of failing to pay an excess charge within the meaning of section 46.
RTRA section 53(5)	Using vehicle in contravention of any provision of a parking place designation order having effect by virtue of section 53(1)(a) (inclusion of certain traffic regulation provisions).
RTRA section 53(6)	Breach of a provision of a parking place designation order having effect by virtue of section 53(1)(b) (use of any part of a road for parking without charge).
RTRA section 88(7)	Driving a motor vehicle in contravention of an order imposing a minimum speed limit under section 88(1)(b).
RTRA section 89(1)	Speeding offences under RTRA and other Acts.
Offences under the Road Traffic Act 1988	
RTA section 14	Breach of regulations requiring wearing of seat belts.
RTA section 15(2)	Breach of restriction on carrying children in the front of vehicles.
RTA section 15(4)	Breach of restriction on carrying children in the rear of vehicles.

211

(1) Provision creating offence	(2) General nature of offence
RTA section 16	Breach of regulations relating to protective headgear for motor cycle drivers and passengers.
RTA section 18(3)	Breach of regulations relating to head-worn appliances (eye protectors) for use on motor cycles.
RTA section 19	Parking a heavy commercial vehicle on verge or footway.
RTA section 22	Leaving vehicle in dangerous position.
RTA section 23	Unlawful carrying of passengers on motor cycles.
RTA section 24	Carrying more than one person on a pedal cycle.
RTA section 34	Driving mechanically propelled vehicle elsewhere than on a road.
RTA section 35	Failure to comply with traffic directions.
RTA section 36	Failure to comply with traffic signs.
RTA section 40A	Using vehicle in dangerous condition etc.
RTA section 41A	Breach of requirement as to brakes, steering-gear or tyres.
RTA section 41B	Breach of requirement as to weight: goods and passenger vehicles.
RTA section 42	Breach of other construction and use requirements.
RTA section 47	Using, etc., vehicle without required test certificate being in force.
RTA section 87(1)	Driving vehicle otherwise than in accordance with requisite licence.
RTA section 143	Using motor vehicle while uninsured or unsecured against third party risks.
RTA section 163	Failure to stop vehicle on being so required by constable in uniform.
RTA section 172	Failure of person keeping vehicle and others to give the police information as to identity of driver, etc., in the case of certain offences.

Offences under the Vehicle Excise and Registration Act 1994

Section 33 of the Vehicle Excise and Registration Act 1994.	Using or keeping a vehicle on a public road without licence being exhibited in manner prescribed by regulations.
Section 42 of that Act.	Driving or keeping a vehicle without required registration mark.
Section 43 of that Act.	Driving or keeping a vehicle with registration mark obscured etc.
Section 43C of that Act.	Using an incorrectly registered vehicle.
Section 59 of that Act.	Failure to fix prescribed registration mark to a vehicle in accordance with regulations made under section 23(4)(a) of that Act.

Appendix 2

Road Vehicles Lighting Regulations 1989, Regulation 27

(1) Item No.	(2) Type of lamp, hazard warning signal device or warning beacon	(3) Manner of use prohibited
1.	Headlamp	(a) Used so as to cause undue dazzle or discomfort to other persons using the road. (b) Used so as to be lit when a vehicle is parked.
2.	Front fog lamp	(a) Used so as to cause undue dazzle or discomfort to other persons using the road. (b) Used so as to be lit at any time other than in conditions of seriously reduced visibility. (c) Used so as to be lit when a vehicle is parked.
3.	Rear fog lamp	(a) Used so as to cause undue dazzle or discomfort to the driver of a following vehicle. (b) Used so as to be lit at any time other than in conditions of seriously reduced visibility. (c) Save in the case of an emergency vehicle, used so as to be lit when a vehicle is parked.
4.	Reversing lamp	Used so as to be lit except for the purpose of reversing the vehicle.
5.	Hazard warning signal device	Used other than— (i) to warn persons using the road of a temporary obstruction when the vehicle is at rest; or (ii) on a motorway or unrestricted dual-carriageway, to warn following drivers of a need to slow down due to a temporary obstruction ahead; or (iii) in the case of a bus, to summon assistance for the driver or any person acting as a conductor or inspector on the vehicle. or (iv) in the case of a bus to which prescribed signs are fitted as described in sub-paragraphs (a) and (b) of regulation 17A(1), when the vehicle is stationary and children under the age of 16 years are entering or leaving, or are about to enter or leave, or have just left the vehicle.

(*continued*)

(1) Item No.	(2) Type of lamp, hazard warning signal device or warning beacon	(3) Manner of use prohibited
6.	Warning beacon emitting blue light and special warning lamp	Used so as to be lit except— (i) at the scene of an emergency; or (ii) when it is necessary or desirable either to indicate to persons using the road the urgency of the purpose for which the vehicle is being used, or to warn persons of the presence of the vehicle or a hazard on the road.
7.	Warning beacon emitting amber light	Used so as to be lit except— (i) at the scene of an emergency; (ii) when it is necessary or desirable to warn persons of the presence of the vehicle; and (iii) in the case of a breakdown vehicle, while it is being used in connection with, and in the immediate vicinity of, an accident or breakdown, or while it is being used to draw a broken-down vehicle.
8.	Warning beacon emitting green light	Used so as to be lit except whilst occupied by a medical practitioner registered by the General Medical Council (whether with full, provisional or limited registration) and used for the purposes of an emergency.
9.	Warning beacon emitting yellow light	Used so as to be lit on a road.
10.	Work lamp	(a) Used so as to cause undue dazzle or discomfort to the driver of any vehicle. (b) Used so as to be lit except for the purpose of illuminating a working area, accident, breakdown or works in the vicinity of the vehicle.
11.	Any other lamp	Used so as to cause undue dazzle or discomfort to other persons using the road.

Appendix 3

Motor Vehicles (Driving Licences) Regulations 1999, Schedule 2 and Regulations 11 and 19

Schedule 2 Categories and Sub-Categories of Vehicles for Licensing Purposes

Part I

(1) Category or sub-category	(2) Classes of vehicle included	(3) Additional categories and sub-categories
A	Motor bicycles.	B1, K and P.
A1	A sub-category of category A comprising learner motor bicycles.	P.
B	Motor vehicles, other than vehicles included in category A, F, K or P, having a maximum authorised mass not exceeding 3.5 tonnes and not more than eight seats in addition to the driver's seat, including: (i) a combination of any such vehicle and a trailer where the trailer has a maximum authorised mass not exceeding 750 kilograms, and (ii) a combination of any such vehicle and a trailer where the maximum authorised mass of the combination does not exceed 3.5 tonnes and the maximum authorised mass of the trailer does not exceed the unladen weight of the tractor vehicle.	F, K and P.
B1	A sub-category of category B comprising motor vehicles having three or four wheels and an unladen weight not exceeding 550 kilograms.	K and P.
B + E	Combinations of a motor vehicle and trailer where the tractor vehicle is in category B but the combination does not fall within that category.	None.
C	Motor vehicles having a maximum authorised mass exceeding 3.5 tonnes, other than vehicles falling within category D, F, G or H, including such vehicle drawing a trailer having a maximum authorised mass not exceeding 750 kilograms.	None.

(continued)

(1) Category or sub-category	(2) Classes of vehicle included	(3) Additional categories and sub-categories
C1	A sub-category of category C comprising motor vehicles having a maximum authorised mass exceeding 3.5 tonnes but not exceeding 7.5 tonnes, including any such vehicle drawing a trailer having a maximum authorised mass not exceeding 750 kilograms.	None.
D	Motor vehicles constructed or adapted for the carriage of passengers having more than eight seats in addition to the driver's seat, including such vehicle drawing a trailer having a maximum authorised mass not exceeding 750 kilograms.	None.
D1	A sub-category of category D comprising motor vehicles having more than eight but not more than 16 seats in addition to the driver's seat and including such vehicle drawing a trailer with a maximum authorised mass not exceeding 750 kilograms.	None.
C + E	Combination of a motor vehicle and trailer where the tractor vehicle is in category C but the combination does not fall within that category.	B + E.
C1 + E	A sub-category of category C + E comprising combinations of a motor vehicle and trailer where: (a) the tractor vehicle is in sub-category C1, (b) the maximum authorised mass of the trailer exceeds 750 kilograms but not the unladen weight of the tractor vehicle, and (c) the maximum authorised mass of the combination does not exceed 12 tonnes.	B + E.
D + E	Combinations of a motor vehicle and trailer where the tractor vehicle is in category D but the combination does not fall within that category.	B + E.
D1 + E	A sub-category of category D + E comprising combinations of a motor vehicle and trailer where: (a) the tractor vehicle is in sub-category D1, (b) the maximum authorised mass of the trailer exceeds 750 kilograms but not the unladen weight of the tractor vehicle, (c) the maximum authorised mass of the combination does not exceed 12 tonnes, and (d) the trailer is not used for the carriage of passengers.	B + E.

(*continued*)

(1) Category or sub-category	(2) Classes of vehicle included	(3) Additional categories and sub-categories
F	Agricultural or forestry tractors including any such vehicle drawing a trailer, but excluding any motor vehicle included in category H.	K.
G	Road rollers.	None.
H	Track-laying vehicles steered by their tracks.	None.
K	Mowing machines which do not fall within category A and vehicles controlled by a pedestrian.	None.
P	Mopeds.	None.
C1 + E (8.25 tonnes)	A sub-category of category C + E comprising combinations of a motor vehicle and trailer in sub-category C1 + E, the maximum authorised mass of which does not exceed 8.25 tonnes.	None.
D1 (not for hire or reward)	A sub-category of category D comprising motor vehicles in sub-category D1 driven otherwise than for hire or reward.	None.
D1 + E (not for hire or reward)	A sub-category of category D + E comprising motor vehicles in sub-category D1 + E driven otherwise than for hire or reward.	None.
L	Motor vehicles propelled by electrical power.	None.

11 Eligibility to apply for provisional licence

(1) Subject to the following provisions of this regulation, an applicant for a provisional licence authorising the driving of motor vehicles of a class included in a category or sub-category specified in column (1) of the table at the end of this regulation must hold a relevant full licence authorising the driving of motor vehicles of a class included in the category or sub-category specified in column (2) of the table in relation to the first category.

(2) Paragraph (1) shall not apply in the case of an applicant who is a full-time member of the armed forces of the Crown.

(3) For the purposes of paragraph (1), a licence authorising the driving only of vehicles in subcategories D1 (not for hire or reward), D1 + E (not for hire or reward) and C1 + E (8.25 tonnes) shall not be treated as a licence authorising the driving of motor vehicles of a class included in sub-categories D1, D1 + E and C1 + E.

(4) In this regulation, 'relevant full licence' means a full licence granted under Part III of the Traffic Act, a full Northern Ireland licence, a full British external licence (other than a licence which is to be disregarded for the purposes of section 89(1)(d) of the Traffic Act by virtue of section 89(2)(c) of that Act), a full British Forces licence, an exchangeable licence or a Community licence.

(1) Category or sub-category of licence applied for	(2) Category/sub-category of full licence required
B + E	B
C	B
C1	B
D	B
D1	B
C1 + E	C1
C + E	C
D1 + E	D1
D + E	D
G	B
H	B

19 Full licences not carrying provisional entitlement

(1)   The application of sections 98(2) and 99A(5) of the Traffic Act is limited or excluded in accordance with the following paragraphs.

(2)   Subject to paragraphs (3), (4), (5), (6), (11) and (12), the holder of a full licence which authorises the driving of motor vehicles of a class included in a category or sub-category specified in column (1) of the table at the end of this regulation may drive motor vehicles—

   (a) of other classes included in that category or sub-category, and

   (b) of a class included in each category or sub-category specified, in relation to that category or sub-category, in column (2) of the table, as if he were authorised by a provisional licence to do so.

(3)   Section 98(2) shall not apply to a full licence if it authorises the driving only of motor vehicles adapted on account of a disability, whether pursuant to an application in that behalf made by the holder of the licence or pursuant to a notice served under section 92(5)(b) of the Traffic Act.

(4)   In the case of a full licence which authorises the driving of a class of standard motor bicycles, other than bicycles included in sub-category A1, section 98(2) shall not apply so as to authorise the driving of a large motor bicycle by a person under the age of 21 before the expiration of the standard access period.

(5)   In the case of a full licence which authorises the driving of motor bicycles of a class included in sub-category A1 section 98(2) shall not apply so as to authorise the driving of a large motor bicycle by a person under the age of 21.

(6)   In the case of a full licence which authorises the driving of a class of vehicles included in category C or C + E, paragraph (2) applies subject to the provisions of regulation 54.

(7)   Subject to paragraphs (8), (9), (10), (11) and (12), the holder of a Community licence to whom section 99A(5) of the Traffic Act applies and who is authorised to drive in Great Britain motor vehicles of a class included in a category or sub-category specified in column (1) of the Table at the end of this regulation may drive motor vehicles—

   (a) of other classes included in that category or sub-category, and

(b) of a class included in each category or sub-category specified, in relation to that category or sub-category, in column (2) of the Table, as if he were authorised by a provisional licence to do so.

(8) Section 99A(5) shall not apply to a Community licence if it authorises the driving only of motor vehicles adapted on account of a disability.

(9) In the case of a Community licence which authorises the driving of a class of standard motor bicycle other than bicycles included in sub-category A1, section 99A(5) shall not apply so as to authorise the driving of a large motor bicycle by a person under the age of 21 before the expiration of the period of two years commencing on the date when that person passed a test for a licence authorising the driving of that class of standard motor bicycle (and in calculating the expiration of that period, any period during which that person has been disqualified for holding or obtaining a licence shall be disregarded).

(10) In the case of a Community licence which authorises the driving only of motor bicycles of a class included in sub-category A1 section 98(2) shall not apply so as to authorise the driving of a large motor bicycle by a person under the age of 21.

(11) Except to the extent provided in paragraph (12), section 98(2) shall not apply to a full licence, and section 99A(5) shall not apply to a Community licence, in so far as it authorises its holder to drive motor vehicles of any class included in category B + E, C + E, D + E or K or in sub-category B1 (invalid carriages), C1 or D1 (not for hire or reward).

(12) A person—

(a) who holds a full licence authorising the driving only of those classes of vehicle included in a category or sub-category specified in paragraph (11) which have automatic transmission (and are not otherwise adapted on account of a disability), or

(b) who holds a Community licence, to whom section 99A(5) of the Traffic Act applies and who is authorised to drive in Great Britain only those classes of vehicle included in a category or sub-category specified in paragraph (11) which have automatic transmission (and are not otherwise adapted on account of a disability), may drive motor vehicles of all other classes included in that category or sub-category which have manual transmission as if he were authorised by a provisional licence to do so.

(1) Full licence held	(2) Provisional entitlement included
A1	A, B, F and K
A	B and F
B1	A, B and F
B	A, B + E, G and H
C	C1 + E, C + E
D1	D1 + E
D	D1 + E, D + E
F	B and P
G	H
H	G
P	A, B, F and K

Appendix 4
Driving Licence Information Codes

01	Eyesight correction
02	Hearing/communication aid
10	Modified transmission
15	Modified clutch
20	Modified braking systems
25	Modified accelerator systems
30	Combined braking and accelerator systems
35	Modified control layouts
40	Modified steering
42	Modified rearview mirror(s)
43	Modified driving seats
44	Modifications to motorcycles
45	Motorcycle only with sidecar
70	Exchange of licence
71	Duplicate of licence
78	Restricted to vehicles with automatic transmission
79	Restricted to vehicles in conformity with the specifications stated in brackets
101	Not for hire or reward
102	Drawbar trailers only
103	Subject to certificate of competence
105	Not more than 5.5 m long
106	Restricted to vehicles with automatic transmission
107	Not more than 8,250 kg
108	Subject to minimum age requirements
110	Limited to invalid carriages
111	Limited to 16 passenger seats
113	Limited to 16 passenger seats except for automatics
114	With any special controls required for safe driving
115	Organ donor
118	Start date is for earliest entitlement
119	Weight limit does not apply
120	Complies with health standard for category D1

Appendix 5
Driving Licence Endorsement Offence Codes

Code	Accident Offences	Penalty Points
AC10	Failing to stop after an accident	5–10
AC20	Failing to give particulars or to report an accident within 24 hours	5–10
AC30	Undefined accident offences	4–9

Code	Disqualified Driver	Penalty Points
BA10	Driving while disqualified by order of court	6
BA30	Attempting to drive while disqualified by order of court	6

Code	Careless Driving	Penalty Points
CD10	Driving without due care and attention	3–9
CD20	Driving without reasonable consideration for other road users	3–9
CD30	Driving without due care and attention or without reasonable consideration for other road users	3–9
CD40	Causing death through careless driving when unfit through drink	3–11
CD50	Causing death by careless driving when unfit through drugs	3–11
CD60	Causing death by careless driving with alcohol level above the limit	3–11
CD70	Causing death by careless driving then failing to supply a specimen for analysis	3–11

Code	Construction and Use Offences	Penalty Points
CU10	Using a vehicle with defective brakes	3
CU20	Causing or likely to cause danger by reason of use of unsuitable vehicle or using a vehicle with parts or accessories (excluding brakes, steering or tyres) in a dangerous condition	3
CU30	Using a vehicle with defective tyre(s)	3
CU40	Using a vehicle with defective steering	3
CU50	Causing or likely to cause danger by reason of load or passengers	3

Code	Reckless/Dangerous Driving	Penalty Points
DD40	Dangerous driving	3–11
DD60	Manslaughter or culpable homicide while driving a vehicle	3–11
DD80	Causing death by dangerous driving	3–11

Code	Drink or Drugs	Penalty Points
DR10	Driving or attempting to drive with alcohol level above limit	3–11
DR20	Driving or attempting to drive while unfit through drink	3–11
DR30	Driving or attempting to drive then failing to supply a specimen for analysis	3–11
DR40	In charge of a vehicle when alcohol level above limit	10
DR50	In charge of a vehicle while unfit through drink	10
DR60	Failure to provide a specimen for analysis in circumstances other than driving or attempting to drive	10
DR70	Failing to provide specimen for breath test	4
DR80	Driving or attempting to drive when unfit through drugs	3–11
DR90	In charge of a vehicle when unfit through drugs	10

Code	Insurance Offences	Penalty Points
IN10	Using a vehicle uninsured against third party risks	6–8

Code	Licence Offences	Penalty Points
LC20	Driving otherwise than in accordance with a licence	3–6
LC30	Driving after making a false declaration about fitness when applying for a licence	3–6
LC40	Driving a vehicle having failed to notify a disability	3–6
LC50	Driving after a licence has been revoked or refused on medical grounds	3–6

Code	Miscellaneous Offences	Penalty Points
MS10	Leaving a vehicle in a dangerous position	3
MS20	Unlawful pillion riding	3
MS30	Play street offences	2

Code	Miscellaneous Offences	Penalty Points
MS40	Driving with uncorrected defective eyesight or refusing to submit to a test	3
MS50	Motor racing on the highway	3–11
MS60	Offences not covered by other Codes as appropriate	
MS70	Driving with uncorrected defective eyesight	3
MS80	Refusing to submit to an eyesight test	3
MS90	Failure to give information as to identity of driver etc.	3

Code	Motorway Offences	Penalty Points
MW10	Contravention of special roads Regulations (excluding speed limits)	3

Code	Pedestrian Crossings	Penalty Points
PC10	Undefined contravention of Pedestrian Crossing Regulations	3
PC20	Contravention of Pedestrian Crossing Regulations with moving vehicle	3
PC30	Contravention of Pedestrian Crossing Regulations with stationary vehicle	3

Code	Speed Limits	Penalty Points
SP10	Exceeding goods vehicle speed limits	3–6
SP20	Exceeding speed limit for type of vehicle (excluding goods or passenger vehicles)	3–6
SP30	Exceeding statutory speed limit on a public road	3–6
SP40	Exceeding passenger vehicle speed limit	3–6
SP50	Exceeding speed limit on a motorway	3–6
SP60	Undefined speed limit offence	3–6

Code	Traffic Direction and Signs	Penalty Points
TS10	Failing to comply with traffic light signals	3
TS20	Failing to comply with double white lines	3
TS30	Failing to comply with a 'stop' sign	3
TS40	Failing to comply with direction of a constable/warden	3

Code	Traffic Direction and Signs	Penalty Points
TS50	Failing to comply with a traffic sign (excluding 'stop' signs, traffic lights or double white lines)	3
TS60	Failing to comply with a school crossing patrol sign	3
TS70	Undefined failure to comply with a traffic direction sign	3

Code	Special Code	Penalty Points
TT99	To signify a disqualification under 'totting up' procedure. If the total of penalty points reaches 12 or more within 3 years, the driver is liable to be disqualified	

Code	Theft or Unauthorised Taking	Points
UT50	Aggravated taking of a vehicle	3–11

Index